The Party is Always Right

The Party is Always Right

The Untold Story of Gerry Healy and British Trotskyism

Aidan Beatty

PLUTO PRESS

First published 2024 by Pluto Press
New Wing, Somerset House, Strand, London WC2R 1LA
and Pluto Press, Inc.
1930 Village Center Circle, 3-834, Las Vegas, NV 89134

www.plutobooks.com

British Library Cataloguing in Publication Data
A catalogue record for this book is available from the British Library

ISBN   978 0 7453 4872 8   Paperback
ISBN   978 0 7453 4874 2   PDF
ISBN   978 0 7453 4873 5   EPUB

This book is printed on paper suitable for recycling and made from fully managed and sustained forest sources. Logging, pulping and manufacturing pro-
cesses are expected to conform to the environmental standards of the country of
origin.

Typeset by Stanford DTP Services, Northampton, England

Simultaneously printed in the United Kingdom and United States of America

Do mo thuismitheoirí

The world political situation as a whole is chiefly characterized by a historical crisis of the leadership of the proletariat.

—Leon Trotsky
The Death Agony of Capitalism and the
Tasks of the Fourth International (1938)

Whoever wants to study the history of the movement closely should examine some of the party literature issued during those days. You see, it didn't cost any more to be extra-radical because nobody paid any attention anyhow.

—James P. Cannon
History of American Trotskyism (1942)

Free from loyalties to any cult, I have attempted to restore the historical balance.

—Isaac Deutscher
The Prophet Armed: Trotsky, 1879–1921 (1954)

Contents

Figures

Acknowledgements

I can't remember when I first ever heard of Gerry Healy, but by the very start of 2020 I had begun to gather material on him, not knowing whether it would lead to a piece of long-form journalism or an idiosyncratic academic article. With the onset of the COVID-19 pandemic, and lucky enough to have a job where I could work remotely, I found myself with a lot of time on my hands and began to delve further and further into the world of the Workers Revolutionary Party (WRP). Initial online research snowballed into oral history interviews and, once travel restrictions lifted, trips to archives in the UK and around the US. My immediate family – Leslie, Keir and Lena – treated this with the greatest of patience, from listening to me ramble on about anecdotes from the history of British Trotskyism to supporting me being away from home for several weeks on a research trip. My sister, Claire Bruce, kindly drove me around various parts of the UK during that trip.

My thanks to the following for sharing their knowledge about Irish and British history or the history of Trotskyism: Ciara Breathnach, John Cunningham, A.M. Gittlitz, John Kelly, Gerard Madden, Conor McNamara, Simon Pirani, Dieter Reinisch, and Evan Smith. I am especially grateful to John Bloxam for sharing his privately held material with me. Michael Ezra generously shared his own research on the WRP, particularly helping me with material on the party's hard-to-pin-down connections to Libya and Iraq. My good friend Paddy Cleary read an early draft of the manuscript and gave me great suggestions for improving it.

My research in Britain was funded by the Program on Jewish Studies and the World History Center at the University of Pittsburgh, who were generous enough to see the Jewish, Israeli–Palestinian and global connections of this project. I am grateful to my colleagues and friends at Pitt – Josh Cannon, Dave Fraser, Lesha Greene, Rachel Kranson, Ruth Mostern, Brett Say and Alexandra Straub – and all my new colleagues at Carnegie Mellon University.

The staff at Hillman Library – Megan Massanelli and Benjamin Rubin especially – gave me invaluable assistance in tracking down obscure pamphlets and newspapers. In the UK, archivists at Hull History Centre, the Modern Records Centre at the University of Warwick, and the British Film Institute were generous and patient. I am particularly grateful to Carole McCallum and her team at Glasgow Caledonian University Archives Centre, who helped me navigate the complexities of their massive, uncatalogued collection of Trotskyist literature. Thanks to Rob Marsden, whose online archive *Splits and Fusions* was a great resource for this book.

Many former members of the Socialist Labour League (SLL) and WRP, members of related groups and other figures on the left generously gave their time for interviews. They may not agree with all my conclusions but I am hugely grateful that they spoke so candidly and in a spirit of openness and I hope they appreciate that I am trying to write about their politics in good faith.

David Castle and Pluto Press have been wonderfully supportive from the very outset, helping me turn a rough manuscript into a, hopefully, more sophisticated book.

This book is dedicated to my parents. Galwegians also, that is the only thing they share with Gerry Healy.

Aidan Beatty
Pittsburgh & Galway

Note on Interviews

Across 2022 and 2023, I carried out extensive interviews with former members of the SLL and WRP, members of related groups, and activists from the broader left. Most interviews were carried out over video-conferencing software or by phone and, in some cases, in-person or by email.

I made extensive efforts to contact former members. Most of those who agreed to be interviewed were male. This partially represents the gender dynamics of this process, female comrades being less inclined to talk with a man who contacts them online asking about their involvement with a party known for its culture of sexual abuse. But this also represents the inescapable fact that the WRP was always an organisation in which men greatly outnumbered women.

Most of the interviewees were from the WRP (Workers Press) faction that emerged after the 1985 split; many members of this faction embraced a more democratic political culture and have become more willing to talk openly about their own political history.

A small number of interviewees asked to be cited anonymously; these interviewees are listed under a pseudonymous first name only. All other interviewees are cited by their full name.

Terry Brotherstone, a one-time member of the WRP in Scotland, gave me a lot of background information on the party but is not cited directly.

Attempts to contact Vanessa Redgrave via her agent received no response.

Sheila Torrance and Alex Mitchell both declined to be interviewed for this book.

David North initially expressed an interest in being interviewed until, after a weeks-long delay, he sent me a series of angry and condemnatory messages. He later denounced both me and the book in a public post on Twitter.

No current member of the Workers Revolutionary Party or Socialist Equality Party was willing to speak to me on the record.

The Healyist Genealogy

The Family Tree of Healyist Trotskyism (Up to 1985 Split)

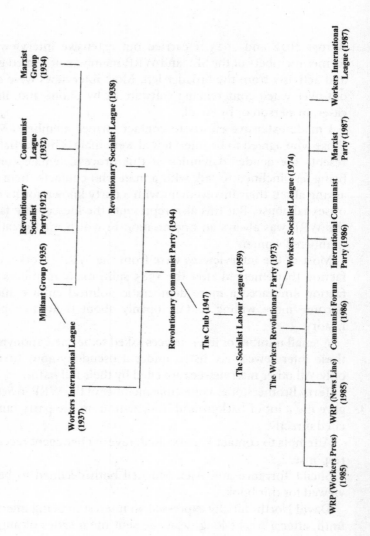

Marxist Group (1934)

Communist League (1932)

Revolutionary Socialist Party (1912)

Militant Group (1935)

Workers International League (1937)

Revolutionary Socialist League (1938)

Revolutionary Communist Party (1944)

The Club (1947)

The Socialist Labour League (1959)

The Workers Revolutionary Party (1973)

Workers Socialist League (1974)

Workers International League (1987)

Marxist Party (1987)

International Communist Party (1986)

Communist Forum (1986)

WRP (News Line) (1985)

WRP (Workers Press) (1985)

Cast of Characters

Mike Banda, Sri Lankan Trotskyist, National Secretary of WRP in 1985

Brian Behan, Irish writer, one-time CPGB member and SLL member

Dave Bruce, Scottish rank-and-file member of WRP, played key role in exposing Healy

Tony Cliff, member of the RCP, founder of the International Socialists and SWP

Clare Cowen, born in Rhodesia, full-time worker for WRP, played key role in exposing Healy

Peter Fryer, journalist for the Communist *Daily Worker*, briefly edited the SLL's *Newsletter*

Dot Gibson, rank-and-file member of the WRP, played a key role in exposing Healy

Edward 'Ted' Grant, South African Trotskyist, active in the RCP, founder of Militant Tendency

Norman Harding, rank-and-file member of the WRP

James Ritchie 'Jock' Haston, Scottish leader of early British Trotskyism, head of the RCP

Thomas Gerard 'Gerry' Healy, Irish-born Trotskyist, head of The Club, SLL and WRP

Aileen Jennings, Healy's personal secretary up to 1985, played a key role in exposing Healy

Corinna Lotz, Healy's secretary after 1985, co-author of an overly praising biography of Healy

Alex Mitchell, Australian journalist, worked on *Workers Press* and *News Line*, Healy loyalist

David North, American Trotskyist, leader of the WL from 1976, current head of the SEP

Simon Pirani, leading member of the WRP's youth-wing in 1970s, active in WRP in the 1980s

Corin Redgrave, actor, leading member of WRP, Healy loyalist

Vanessa Redgrave, Oscar-winning actor, leading WRP member, Healy loyalist

Cliff Slaughter, lecturer in sociology at Leeds University, leading intellectual of the WRP

Alan Thornett, union activist in Oxford, expelled from WRP in 1974

Sheila Torrance, Assistant National Secretary of the pre-1985 WRP

Tim Wohlforth, American Trotskyist, head of WL up to 1974, expelled by Healy

Abbreviations

CPGB	Communist Party of Great Britain
RCP	Revolutionary Communist Party
RSL	Revolutionary Socialist League
SEP	Socialist Equality Party
SLL	Socialist Labour League
SWP	Socialist Workers Party
WL	Workers League
WRP	Workers Revolutionary Party
WSL	Workers Socialist League
WSWS	World Socialist Website
YS	Young Socialists

Preface

This is a book about an authoritarian and abusive Irishman named Gerry Healy, and about the political world he helped create, focusing especially on his small Trotskyist party, the Workers Revolutionary Party, founded in 1973, which he ruled over until he was unexpectedly expelled in 1985.

It is a story of violence and scandals, sexual abuse, cults, conspiracy theories, misguided celebrities, and possibly also international espionage and murder; and at the heart of all this is one man, Healy, who has either been conveniently forgotten by those who were once his closest supporters or is openly recalled by others as a deeply ugly individual, with accounts of him often focusing unduly on his physical appearance.[1] Even one of Healy's supporters said 'The man was built like a kitchen table – flat, round and squat' and 'he appeared to have neither eyebrows nor lips'.[2]

Like a familiar Dickensian archetype, Healy's physical ugliness was often evoked as a sign of a deeper, more profound political and moral ugliness. And yet Healy could definitely be charismatic. According to Caroline Benn, wife of the left-wing Labour MP Tony Benn and who had seen him speak in person, Healy was a man with 'an electric personality'.[3] A long-standing grassroots member of two of Healy's political parties said he had a 'very simple and long-honed' style for public speeches. He would start off very softly, making the audience listen as closely as possible to be able to hear him and as his political analysis heated up, his volume would increase.[4] Another acquaintance bombastically said that 'Gerry Healy was, without question, the world's foremost radical showman' and yet also was 'a petty tyrant with global ambitions'.[5] He was physically short 'but seemed big'.[6]

As these kinds of charged memories highlight, Gerry Healy's biography is clearly a very gossipy one, and an emotional story for those who were involved. But this is also, more seriously, a story about Trotskyism, the political tradition that both birthed Healy as an activist and which he also, in turn, helped (re)create. It is a cautionary tale about the tendency that Trotskyism has always had towards schisms and personal animosity and about the inherent flaws in Leninist-style 'democratic centralist' parties that often brook no dissent and can even act as incubators for predatory men like Gerry Healy. This entire book is an argument in favour of a democratic socialism, and against any and all authoritarianisms.

Perhaps *the* standard description of Healy's Workers Revolutionary Party is that it was a 'cult', with that term becoming a shorthand for so many of the party's excesses.[7] This certainly has a lot of truth to it; the ways in which party members were expected to devote all waking hours to the organisation, the demand that they cut ties with friends and family, the expectation that comrades hand over ever-increasing sums of money to the party, the party's development of its own esoteric internal language. All this is classically cult-like. But 'cult' is also too politically easy an assessment. Dismissing the WRP as a cult means ignoring the connection between the WRP's authoritarian culture and the party's Leninist structure. The WRP can and should be understood also as an extreme manifestation of Leninist vanguardism and its anti-democratic praxis.

In his 1902 work *What is To Be Done?*, Lenin argued for a party that would value secretiveness in its work and would avoid 'broad democracy'. In theory, the membership would have the right to dissent in initial debates. In practice, it rarely worked so smoothly. It would be a *democratic centralist* party where a central committee ultimately made all major decisions and the membership *democratically* agreed to abide by these decisions. This Leninist party would strive to provide leadership and even a political consciousness to a Russian working class from whom it remained separate.[8] Bolshevism has, from the start, carried a danger within itself of elitism, even if it shared that with the more intellectually inflected socialist currents of the period (in which middle-class intellectuals sought to bring the socialist truth to the working classes).[9] Leninism was a product of a specific time and place; late Imperial Russia was a brutal environment for any kind of radical politics. Between 1895 and 1902, the average social democratic group in Moscow lasted only three months before the police exposed them; in such a situation, internal party democracy was a dangerous luxury.[10] And

Lenin himself also saw that his proposed party was the product of a specific Tsarist context: 'the national tasks of Russian Social-Democracy are such as have never confronted any other socialist party in the world'.[11] Elsewhere in his writings, Lenin did show himself to have a deep respect for democracy, presenting a future socialist society as inherently democratic.[12] It is highly doubtful if Lenin wanted to build a monolithic party where no debates could take place or where factions could not form. Indeed, scholars like Lars Lih and Paul le Blanc have shown how genuine a commitment to democracy Lenin could have.[13] But whatever the contextual cause and the countervailing strands within Leninism, the end result of this specific model of party organisation was an undemocratic politics. As Max Elbaum has said: 'Within a few years of the October Revolution, the theory and practice of the vanguard party began to harden. Greater stress was placed on discipline and centralism, less weight was given to inner-party democracy or strategic cooperation with non-party revolutionaries. Monolithic unity began to be seen as a virtue.'[14] By their moment of victory following the Russian Civil War, the Bolsheviks had ossified into a rigidly undemocratic party.

The Leninist model, as interpreted by ultra-orthodox Trotskyists like Gerry Healy, is built on the assumption that (often wrongheaded) workers can only be led to truth (and revolution) by a vanguardist intellectual leadership. That this leadership might itself be wrong is not usually considered. Nor is there usually a mechanism, in most democratic centralist parties – whether Trotskyist, Stalinist or otherwise – for lower-ranked members to correct the mistakes of the leaders.

In August 1904, a young, independent-minded theorist who had stayed aloof from both the Bolsheviks and their opposing faction, the Mensheviks, produced *Our Political Tasks*, an incisive and prophetic pamphlet analysing the dangers of Leninist democratic centralism, the form of party organisation recently adopted by the Bolsheviks and subsequently used by almost every party that claims a Leninist heritage, the Workers Revolutionary Party among them. According to the pamphlet, Leninism carried with it the inherent risk of 'substitutism' [*zamestitelstvo*]; as a vanguard party substituted itself for the working class, it would soon happen that the central committee would substitute itself for the party and then a single leader would, in turn, substitute himself for the committee. The end result would be rule by a single autocrat who cannot be questioned. The author of this pamphlet was one Lev Davidovich Bronstein, more commonly known to posterity as Leon Trotsky, spelling out the dangers of a party that would later expel him and whose subsequent leader, Joseph Stalin, would order his murder in 1940. Yet, once Trotsky switched over to the Bolsheviks in 1917, he never again explored these earlier criticisms of Leninism, and Trotskyists have generally followed his lead in that regard.[15] By 1924, Trotsky was declaring, in full-throated Leninism, 'The party in the last analysis is always right, because the party is the sole historical instrument given to the proletariat for the solution of its basic problems.'[16] Trotsky judiciously forgot his own earlier criticisms of What is To Be Done, not once mentioning Our Political Tasks in his generally excellent autobiography.[17] We can assume Gerry Healy was aware of this pamphlet and its critiques of Leninism: the WRP's New Park Publications released new editions of it in both 1979 and 1983 (suitably accompanied by a foreword dismissing Trotsky's early criticisms of Bolshevism).[18]

Trotskyists have often looked back to the moment of Stalin's victory over Trotsky, seeking to re-litigate the false charges made against the latter in the mid-1920s. In turn, Trotskyists see themselves as not just heirs of Lenin but the true defenders of a Leninism corrupted by Stalin and Stalinists. The heritage that Trotskyists sought to defend was the victorious if also authoritarian party after the Russian Civil War and after Lenin's death in 1924, rather than the earlier, relatively more democratic party from before 1917 in which factions were allowed form and some criticism of the party leadership was tolerated. Yet, in also seeking to reclaim the mantle of being the true heirs of Lenin and Leninism, Trotskyists are valorising the moment when the Bolshevik party was at a democratic nadir.

This book is a study of one of the least democratic figures to ever emerge out of the Trotskyist tradition. The chapters alternate between chronological accounts of Gerry Healy's life – his childhood in Ireland and early involvement in the Trotskyist movement in Britain, his leadership of the Socialist Labour League in the

1960s and the WRP the following decade, the shocking split in the party in 1985 – with thematic chapters exploring the central concerns of Healy's politics, accusations about state surveillance and espionage that surrounded the WRP, his dalliances with celebrities, and his attitudes to what we today call 'identity politics'. Throughout all this, I draw on archival research, the party's own publications, the various published accounts of former members – Alex Mitchell, Bob Pitt, Norman Harding, Clare Cowen, Corinna Lotz and Paul Feldman, and Bill Hunter – as well just over 40 oral history interviews.

This is a history of one strand of Trotskyism that also recognises the unusual historiographical problems that Trotskyism poses. All historians, in some way or another, are familiar with the problem of a lack of archival sources; people do not always write down their most intimate thoughts and motivations for posterity. Powerless or illiterate people, by definition, do not leave printed documents behind. Governments often suppress or censor material. Diaries, letters and other records get destroyed or lost, particularly when they contain sensitive or embarrassing material. Documents written on paper have a horrible tendency to degrade into illegibility. Trotskyism, at least in the Western countries where it has been most prevalent, poses an opposite problem; rather than there being a lack of documentary evidence, there is too much of it and it is often factually unreliable. To give one example: when Gerry Healy died in December 1989, *Workers News*, the journal of a rival Trotskyist group, began to publish a serialised obituary of him. It ultimately ran to 26 instalments and was not completed until their August/September issue of 1994, almost five years later. The serialised obituary was then published as a standalone text online. Practices like this led to an overwhelmingly large amount of material, regularly filled with invective, allegations, and rumours. For many of the major moments in Healy's life and career, there are not just rival interpretations, but drastically divergent versions of the truth. This biography wades into all this but remains cautious as to how much we can truly, definitively know about a figure who elicited intense emotions within a small Trotskyist milieu that was itself often defined by zealousness and fervent animosities.

1
Ultra-Leftism, 1913–1959

Let's start with what we do know: Gerry Healy was born in Ireland in 1913 and he became a Trotskyist in Britain just over 20 years later. Almost all the other important details that he would later recall about his childhood and early life were exaggerated, if not fabricated wholesale. According to his birth record, Thomas Gerard Healy was born on 3 December 1913 in Ballybane, now a suburb of Galway on the west coast of Ireland, then rural farmland just beyond the city.[1] One of his hagiographies even tried to tie Healy's birth year to the seminal Dublin Lockout, a major strike in 1913, as if Healy's birth was another key moment in the history of Irish socialism.[2]

Galway had a tradition of rural agitation and even militancy in the later nineteenth century but had become quieter by the early decades of the twentieth. The political violence that erupted in Ireland from 1919 onwards – posthumously called the Irish War of Independence – was mainly centred in Dublin on the east coast and in the southern province of Munster. Galway and the surrounding western province of Connacht saw less of this.[3]

Healy's father was a farmer named Michael Healy and his mother was Margaret Mary, née Rabbitte. Healy claimed, and others repeated, that he was the product of 'a poverty-stricken youth in Ireland'.[4] In fact, he grew up in relative comfort with his family owning a 109-acre farm, a sizeable amount in a country where anyone owning over 50 acres was considered a 'strong farmer'; a land-owning Catholic bourgeoisie had been crystallising in Ireland since the Famine of the 1840s and the Healys were a product of that long-term development. Most egregiously, Gerry Healy's well-repeated claim that he saw the Black and Tans shoot and kill his father during the War of Independence was an outright lie.[5] (It was a lie that he could get away with, though, because of the Brit-

1

ish's left general lack of knowledge about Ireland.) As can be heard in the few recordings ever made of him, Gerry Healy's accent – mostly cockney but with certain cadences lingering from the west of Ireland – made him seem somewhat unplaceable. He would later aver that he retained nothing 'Irish' in his identity, instead becoming a fully internationalist socialist.[6] Though this lie about his father's death at the hands of perhaps *the* greatest villains in Irish nationalism as well as an anecdote that he hated flying British Airways 'because he disliked staring at the cabin crew's Union Jack neck ties'[7] suggests something else. Other stories from his childhood have more of a ring of truth to them; that he was an altar boy or that he experienced abusive corporal punishment at school.[8]

His father was certainly still alive into the 1920s and probably even into the 1930s. Gerry was the oldest of four children. His sister, Angela, was born in July 1916 and he had two brothers, Gabriel and Brendan, born in 1919 and 1923. The family appears to have entered a financial crisis in the second half of the 1920s, possibly related to mental health problems on the part of Healy's father, Michael. By the 1930s, Healy's mother, Margaret Mary, was living in Tipperary Town, about 100 miles south of Galway, and was making a living as a dog breeder. The family's property in Tipperary was registered in the mother's name only and it is not clear what had become of his father; he may have died in a psychiatric hospital and no death record seems to exist for him. Margaret died in May 1981, by which time Gerry was estranged from her.

It is also not clear where Gerry Healy was educated. He later claimed to have attended a Christian Brothers School, but the only two such schools in Galway were St Patrick's in Tuam, in the northern part of the county, and a notorious industrial school (an Irish version of a youth petitionary) in Letterfrack in Connemara, in the remote far west of the county. Healy almost certainly did not attend the latter, since there would be court records of this and sons of the bourgeoisie were generally not consigned to such places. And indeed, some anecdotal evidence suggests he was sent to live with an uncle, a priest, in Tuam but that an attempt to force Healy to also enter the priesthood prompted him to run away from home.[9] Healy only revealed snippets about his childhood in Ireland; one Irish member of the Workers Revolutionary

Party describes him as being 'very coy about his early life'.[10] Indeed, while many WRP members may have heard Healy speak in public, most 'didn't know very much about him', especially those living outside London.[11]

In 1926 or shortly thereafter, at about age 14, Gerry Healy said he left Ireland, apparently to train and work as a radio operator in Britain, though he may also have worked as an apprentice machinist.[12] He claimed to have initially lived in Cardiff and to have received training there as a ship's telegraph operator. He also said he lived in Penarth and Barry in Wales during his apprenticeship and years later could still supposedly recall how to tap out Morse code.[13] It is not clear how true any of these claims are, but it certainly does appear that he worked on ships.[14]

He claimed that shortly after his arrival in the UK, he learned that his sister, working as a nurse in the north of England, had died of tuberculosis.[15] He may have later told party members that he scattered her ashes into the Thames (which would be a major giveaway, since cremation is exceedingly rare in Irish Catholicism).[16] In telling such stories, Healy seems to have merged a few different facts in service of a convenient fiction. His sister did actually move to Britain, but as a nun, and his two brothers also emigrated, both dying of tuberculosis in London in the late 1940s. Angela Healy, by now known as Sister Carmel and a member of the Daughters of the Cross in Torquay in the south of England, lived until 1997. Healy appears to have become estranged from his family who told extended relatives he had died at sea in 1940.[17] The most likely explanation, given the conservative mores of mid-twentieth-century Irish society, is that his family concocted that story rather than accept his far-left politics. It would not be unreasonable to interpret Healy's stories about his sister as a sign of a complicated emotional attachment to her; nuns and communists are rarely the best of friends. He seems to have never spoken to WRP members of his two brothers.

According to a chronology produced by *Marxist Monthly* as part of their obituary of Healy in 1990, he joined the Communist Party of Great Britain (CPGB) in 1928, a party that already had an outsized Irish membership. Alex Mitchell, a close ally of his in the 1970s and 1980s, gives the same date, meaning he joined the communists at age 14 and immediately upon his move to Britain (which seems just a little too neat).[18] He may not have joined the Young Communist League until 1931, when he would have been about 18 years old. The first definite record of him being a member of the Communist Party was not until 1936.[19] Both the secretiveness of the Communist movement as well as Healy's own propensity for lying about his past make it hard to reconstruct an accurate narrative. In addition, once he had embraced Trotskyism, Healy may have been reticent to discuss his decade as a Stalinist.

By 1936, aged about 23, Healy was living in London, on Belgrave Road in Pimlico, and was a member of the Westminster branch of the Communist Party. CPGB was a small party of some 2,500 members in the early 1930s but reaching 18,000 by the end of the decade, as it benefitted from anti-fascist tactics during its 'Popular Front' period.[20] As with other Communist parties around the world, the British Communists were viewed from the outside as top-down, authoritarian, allergic to internal dissent and subservient to Moscow. As elsewhere, though, the first generation of the CPGB was populated by activists who had already cut their political teeth prior to the Russian Revolution of 1917 and the founding of the British party in 1920.[21] They retained these prior political traditions and the CPGB was not as firmly anti-democratic as the caricatures suggested, though it was certainly developing into a firmly anti-Trotskyist entity.[22] As of the mid-1930s, Healy was still a party loyalist and a fervent anti-Trotskyist, a regular participant in arguments with Trotskyist speakers in Hyde Park in London, as well as some physical assaults on them.[23] It is odd then, that in 1937, at about 24 years of age, Gerry Healy himself became a Trotskyist.

Trotskyists positioned themselves as the true heirs of the Russian Revolution, which they argued Stalin and parties like the CPGB had degraded and sullied. The great genius of Trotskyism has always been that it allowed its proponents to adhere to two seemingly contradictory political viewpoints: Trotskyists could continue to uphold October 1917 – indeed could continue to believe in revolutionary socialism in general – whilst simultaneously denouncing where that Revolution had ended up by the 1930s. Condemning Stalin, they instead looked for guidance to

Leon Trotsky, the charismatic early leader and theoretician of the Revolution, one-time head of the Red Army and, by the late 1930s, an exile in Mexico. In opposition to the Stalinist position that the USSR should develop Socialism in One Country, Trotskyists advocated Permanent Revolution, in which Communism would be spread rapidly and globally. From the outset, however, Trotskyism faced the fact that, unlike Stalinism (and later Maoism), it had no socialist homeland to point to for inspiration.[24] From the perspective of official, Moscow-allied Communists, Trotskyists were, at best, irrational ultra-leftists and, at worst, devious cranks and wreckers. Trotskyists, though, never really broke with Stalinists in terms of how to organise their parties along 'democratic centralist' lines in which a central committee held an undue level of control.

Where orthodox Communists were able to gain some traction in popular politics, Trotskyists in the 1930s were generally confined to the political fringes. The first British Trotskyists, the Balham Group, had no more than 13 members at their founding in 1932.[25] This had a clear negative impact on organisational health; such closed environs bred both a tight solidarity but also a political claustrophobia, with little breathing space between the members. A larger organisation would have felt more open and allowed for greater distance between those who just personally disliked each other. Even in the 1930s, Trotskyist groups had a tendency to splinter into tiny irrelevance, a condition of many small radical groups working in adverse circumstances and failing to make a political breakthrough.[26] In the case of Trotskyism, an intellectual rigidity after Trotsky's murder in 1940 made this even more likely. And the increasing inability to influence events encouraged even more splits. Without any practical ways to settle debates, by actually putting ideas into practice, theoretical debates take precedence. Trotskyist groups often exist in a world of theory, with little in the way of practice.[27]

The Scottish Trotskyist leader Jock Haston later claimed he was the one who recruited Healy, with the conversion coming about after a violent encounter outside a public toilet:

I was selling the *Militant* [an American Trotskyist newspaper] outside the toilets in Hyde Park... and I got into an argument (we used to be beaten up, incidentally, every weekend for selling there). I got into an argument with Healy and two others who were putting the Stalinist line, and this led to a fracas. So my first contact with Healy was there, at a fracas at Hyde Park Corner... Subsequently, in discussion with Healy some months later – you know, because he came back, again and again, and argued – I won Healy over to the Trotskyist movement.[28]

Haston had been a sailor who had used his work and travels to distribute socialist literature in Nazi Germany but was expelled from the Communist Party in 1934 after questioning Soviet trade links with the Third Reich.[29] Interestingly, this mirrors just a little too closely the stories that Healy himself would later tell, about his alleged travels in fascist Europe, and that his conversion to Trotskyism happened for the most high-minded of anti-fascist reasons, allegedly in the midst of his work as a merchant marine radio operator:

> As a seaman, I [Healy] was checking the movement of ships on the Lloyds Shipping Register. Soviet cargo ships from Batum were dropping half their cargo of oil in Genoa and the other half at Barcelona. I asked Communist Party leader Harry Pollitt why it was that the Soviet Union was shipping oil to Mussolini's Italy to fuel their Carponi bombers in Spain and Abyssinia. Pollitt told me to see William Joss of the Control Commission who said: 'These are Trotskyite questions.' I replied that I had never read a word of Trotsky in my life. Joss said: 'If you persist with them you will be expelled.' I persisted and was expelled.[30]

The Communist Party did say, in an internal report on Healy during the War, that he had left in 1938, 'after discussion with Pollitt', but also later claimed he had been 'a full-time Trotskyist since the early thirties'.[31] Falsely labelling any and all party dissidents as Trotskyists was common and this often had the effect of actually turning ex-members into Trotskyists.[32] Certainly in the era of the Moscow Show Trials of the later 1930s, there were valid reasons to reject Stalinism in favour of Trotskyism, which was a path many communists did follow. Healy could certainly have been motivated by the same currents but there is also no reason to doubt that he did steal Haston's story outright. Indeed, his personal assistant in the 1970s and 1980s, Aileen Jennings, said that Healy's stories about personally witnessing the rise of fascism were falsified, plagiarised at a later date from a book he had read.[33] Healy himself was inconsistent on this score, later claiming the Communist Party expelled him in 1936 for opposing the show trials then being held in Moscow or over the question of whether the Labour Party was 'social fascist' (though the Communists had by this date abandoned the view that social democracy was implicitly pro-fascist).[34]

Whatever the actual cause, Healy became active in the Militant Group, then the largest of Britain's Trotskyist organisations and led by Haston. The most common concern for early Trotskyists was a burgeoning sense that something had gone wrong with pro-Moscow Communist parties, causing them to leave those parties; finding mainstream social democratic parties, like the Labour Party, too moderate or centrist, they instead formed Trotskyist groups, borrowing Trotsky's idea of a 'Left Opposition' that could counter Stalinism.[35] From the start, Trotskyism seemed to offer an escape from Stalinism that would not require social democracy's capitulation to capitalism. But retaining a Leninist party model, most Trotskyist groups remained vanguardist, hierarchical and non-democratic.

By August 1937 Gerry Healy had relocated to west Yorkshire to aid in the Militant Group's recruitment efforts there. And by the end of that year, Healy joined the breakaway Workers International League (WIL) alongside Haston and Ted Grant, who were employed full-time by the League.[36] A quarter century later, Healy would claim the WIL had only twelve members at its founding.[37] The WIL initially used party members' houses as offices – Millie Lee's house in Paddington was the party headquarters and Jock Haston's house nearby was used to store the party's printing press. The WIL then moved to a dedicated space at 61 Northdown Street in King's Cross.[38] Representing about a third of the membership of the Militant Group, the WIL devoted itself to 'entryism' – semi-secretive infiltration – of both the Labour Party and the more leftist Independent Labour Party and published a journal entitled *Searchlight*, of which Healy became the editor. *Searchlight* then became *Youth for Socialism* as the WIL turned its attentions more squarely on the League of Youth, the Labour Party's youth wing, hoping to find recruits there.[39] Harry Ratner, who joined the Trotskyist movement around the same time as Healy, remembers regularly going out at night with Gerry Healy to cover up fascist graffiti in London; this would have been around 1938.[40] Two other Trotskyists, Mary and John Archer, said Healy had very little knowledge of Trotsky's writings when they first encountered him in the summer of 1937; they remembered him having 'some kind of publicity job' that involved travelling around Britain and only staying for short periods in any one place.[41]

While the Communist Party in which Healy had previously been active was defined by fairly rigid orthodoxy as well as a lack of internal party democracy and remained stuck on the fringes of British politics, the Trotskyist groups in which he now operated added schisms to this mix as well as an even greater distance from the mainstream. Already in the 1930s, British Trotskyism was defined by a self-damaging 'clique atmosphere'.[42] Internationally, the Trotskyist movement was still crystallising in this period. The 'Fourth International', the umbrella group for world Trotskyism, an alternative to the reformist and social democratic Second International and Stalinist Third International, was formed on 3 September 1938, at a one-day meeting outside of Paris. Twenty-one delegates were in attendance, representing Trotskyist groups from eleven countries. The largest and most dominant was the Socialist Workers Party in America, which had perhaps two thousand members. Ominously, but stereotypically, the French Trotskyists had already gone through a schism over the question of entering the centre-left *Section française de l'Internationale ouvrière*, precursor of the current *Parti socialiste*. Though there would soon be 38 Trotskyist parties worldwide, a significant achievement, several of those countries would have competing groups.[43] Trotsky himself was living in exile in Mexico and unable to leave that country to attend the founding conference. Nonetheless, he wrote the founding document, *The Death Agony of Capitalism and the Tasks of the Fourth International* – often referred to colloquially as *The Transitional Programme* – with its bold opening line: 'The world political situation as a whole is chiefly characterized by a historical crisis of the leadership of the proletariat.'[44] Trotskyists positioned themselves as the ones who would provide that necessary leadership for the international proletariat, a big claim for so minor a movement.

Given the small numbers of people active in Trotskyism, political disagreements could easily become welded to personal hostilities (and Healy's aggressive personality was particularly primed for these schisms). Conversely, there was a serious intellectual culture within Trotskyism: Bill Hunter, a long-time rank-and-file Trotskyist who first became active in the thirties, recalls reading André Malraux's *Man's Estate* and Emile Zola's *Germinal*, having been recommended them by more veteran activists.[45] By 1938 there were five Trotskyist groups active in Britain – the Communist League, the Marxist Group, and the Scottish-based Revolutionary Socialist Party, alongside the WIL and its parent, the Militant Group – with a combined membership languishing in the hundreds. James Cannon, a thoughtful figure within American Trotskyism and leader of that country's Socialist Workers Party, encouraged the groups to merge, thus leading to the birth of the Revolutionary Socialist League (RSL).

The WIL, however, initially refused to join, claiming that the RSL had failed to clarify a position on entryism (and, as such, had not clarified if the WIL's *raison d'être* could persist). One of the RSL's first actions was to issue a resolution pointing out – quite fairly – that the WIL had emerged as a result of 'purely personal grievances' and that there was no 'justifiable political basis' for the group to maintain a separate political existence.[46] The Fourth International warned the rank-and-file of the WIL that 'they are being led on a path of unprincipled clique politics which can only land them in the mire'.[47]

By 1939, the WIL consisted of no more than 40 active members.[48] In such uncomfortably close quarters, disagreements could easily ossify into seemingly insurmountable divisions; the type of 'purely personal grievances' of which the RSL were warning. Nonetheless, the WIL could (and did) have some real political impact. With the outbreak of the Second World War, the WIL adopted a staunchly anti-war position, uncompromisingly aligning with the *Manifesto of the Fourth International*, the official statement of the international Trotskyist movement, which dismissed any differences between capitalist democracies and fascism.[49] The WIL's wartime activities would soon bring them to the government's attention (and not in a positive way).

Sometime early in the war, Gerry Healy briefly returned to Ireland; the WIL, suspecting that they would be suppressed as part of wartime censorship, were investigating the possibilities of printing their publications in Ireland.[50] Jock Haston also went with Healy, along with select other party members.[51] Healy joined the tiny Trotskyist group in Ireland though quickly clashed with their leaders. He declared that he would join the Irish Labour Party instead, leading to his expulsion from the Irish Trotskyists. Under pressure from Haston, the short-lived expulsion was rescinded.[52] The WIL could hardly afford to lose members; this was probably to Healy's benefit, since he would have found a cold reception in the notoriously right-wing Irish Labour Party. That Healy's family in Ireland said he died in 1940 is perhaps not a coincidence; he quite possibly had some contact with them during his return to Ireland but became estranged from them afterward. He returned to Britain the same year, probably having been ordered home by the WIL leaders to avoid further tensions with Irish Trotskyists.[53]

It was also at this time that he began a relationship with Betty Russell, the daughter of an estate agent and a one-time member of the Communist Party branch in Streatham in south London. Through her father they acquired a house at 77 Sternhold Avenue in Streatham, which then became a base for his political activities. Russell worked as a secretary and as a teacher, with her professional career essentially acting as a subvention of Healy's political activism. A political activist in her own right, she was an independent-minded woman and willing and able to publicly disagree with Healy when necessary.[54] They would go on to have two children, but Healy's family life would never play a major role in his politics.[55]

Perhaps seeking a more stable income as a married man, Healy attempted to enlist in the military in 1941; how this squared with his Trotskyist opposition to the war was unclear, though his political entanglements meant he was turned down for military service and thus never had to address this obvious double standard.[56]

He instead spent the war probably working (and serving as a union shop steward) in various factories in London and perhaps at Croydon airport making aircraft parts.[57] One Trotskyist, also involved in labour activism, remembers Healy working at Park Royal Coaches, which had been switched over to aircraft production for the war effort. He apparently did not stay in this position too long: 'Healy was not very good at working with his hands' but did have a clear ability to connect with other workers.[58] Wartime reports on Trotskyist activity produced within the Communist Party named Healy as an industrial organiser and an employee in the toolroom at Hoovers in Tottenham, which had switched to producing aircraft parts during the war. The reports called the WIL 'the main centre for Trotskyite activity in Britain', with a membership between 250 and 900, the latter being an over-estimation.[59]

The WIL's labour activism was both a blessing and a curse. With union militancy suppressed as a result of the war (Labour-affiliated trade unionists were already supportive of the war effort and Communist trade-unionists joined them after the USSR entered the war in 1941), the WIL was able to fill something of a vacuum, providing a forum for some worker grievances. The party saw a growth in membership, reaching a level of 300 members, and their new four-page bimonthly paper, *Socialist Appeal*, was bumped up to a print run of 12,000 copies in June 1941, espousing a policy of revolutionary defeatism – a strident opposition to the twin enemies of both fascist Germany and the capitalist Allies – as a way to simultaneously take on both Nazism and the British capitalist state.[60] Most of the new members were disaffected ex-CPGB members turned off by that party's refusal to support strikes (when the USSR entered the war, the Communists had become unashamedly patriotic and pro-Allies).[61] And indeed there was an ample amount of worker discontent that the WIL could tap into. In the spring of 1944, there were 100,000 coal miners on strike in South Wales and 80,000 more in Yorkshire. Fifty thousand munitions, aircraft and shipyard workers went on strike in April 1944, feeding into a government fear that the Normandy landings might be delayed as a result.[62] The ability to exert an influence out of all proportion to actual numerical strength would remain a feature of Trotskyism well after the war had ended.[63]

The WIL began to come under regular surveillance from Special Branch, one of the closest things to a political police force in Britain. And the party found itself targeted by a motley assortment of more mainstream opinion. The *Sunday Dispatch*, precursor of the *Sunday Express* and already a hard-right voice of a mythical middle England, printed scathing accounts of the party, often echoing Communist Party attacks on the WIL. When the Trotskyists supported the wildcat strike by Yorkshire miners in April 1944, the party's existence was discussed in Parliament and there were calls for *Socialist Appeal* to be banned.[64] The pro-Labour *Daily Herald* called the WIL a pro-Nazi party because of its undermining of the war effort. The Communist Party said Trotskyists were a 'a virus' that 'must be cleaned out of all contact with working-class organisations'. The CPGB's advice was to 'Treat the Trotskyist as you would a Nazi.'[65]

All this was taking place while the WIL maintained a separate existence from the official voice of British Trotskyism, the RSL. Attempts to merge the two had floundered throughout the war years.[66] But in March 1944, the WIL merged with the 'Trotskyist Opposition' within the RSL and all together formed the Revolutionary Communist Party (RCP). The RCP perhaps had 500 members in total, with the former WIL members tending to be younger than those from the other factions.[67] It remained a small and badly funded party; when Bill Hunter worked full-time for the RCP in 1945, he was paid 30 shillings a week (about £50 in 2024 money), though that was paid irregularly and he often had to take a day job to support himself. Hunter covered the east and west Midlands as a party organiser, often having to hitchhike since the party could not afford train fares.[68]

Healy had been one of, if not the most, vociferous of opponents to unification, a position he wholly abandoned in 1943 when he became an equally zealous proponent of unity. Advocating unification of the WIL and RSL, he had presented it as a positive end not because of the RSL itself (which he dismissed as weak and wrong-headed) but as a means to obey the strictures of the Fourth International leadership.[69] He was tasked by the WIL leadership, along with two other comrades, with unofficially approaching the RSL leadership and starting unification talks.[70] Healy had been demoted for 'indiscipline' and may have hoped to opportunistically change his status in a newly unified movement.[71] The political bureau of the RCP observed, shortly after unification with the WIL, that 'It is the fatal failing of Comrade Healy that he never likes to admit that he has been wrong; that he has changed his position.'[72] And indeed, Healy was already displaying a propensity for bad faith arguments and fractiousness. A faction orbiting Gerry Healy was also forming in 1943, despite (or because of) claims that he had a track record of 'light minded irresponsibility' and 'continued disruptive acts'. He threatened to leave the WIL on three different occasions and was 'expelled' in February 1943, but soon welcomed back.[73] Ted Grant, the South African-born political secretary of the WIL, labelled him as 'ultra left' at this time, perhaps the first ever to do so. One of Healy's faux-resignations caused him to forfeit his positions on the party's Political Bureau and Central Committee and on the editorial board of *Socialist Appeal*.[74]

By 5 April 1944, the RCP's activities were being discussed by the British Cabinet and there were police raids in the days after on the homes of RCP activists, Healy included among them, in London, Nottingham and Newcastle. The party's offices in Paddington in London were also targeted.[75] Documents were seized and various leaders of the RCP were charged under the 1927 Trade Disputes and Trade Union Act;[76] that Healy was not among those charged is suggestive of his continuing lower-tiered status within the small world of British Trotskyism. On 13 April, Herbert Morrison, Minister of Home Security in the wartime government, wrote a report for the Cabinet on *The Trotskyist Movement in Great Britain*.[77] Morrison seems to have had a mole within the RCP's Central Committee. In any case, the various sentences against RCP members were quashed on appeal.[78] Late in the war, and into the immediate post-war years, the RCP argued against anti-German prejudices; it is clear in hindsight that their goal was for British and German workers to see their shared interests and unify around those, though the wartime atmosphere meant that the subtleties of this could be easily missed and they may have come across as Nazi sympathisers.[79] At the very end of the war, the RCP contested a May 1945 by-election in Neath in South Wales. With Jock Haston as their candidate, the RCP ran on a critical line regarding Labour and 'Solidarity with the German Workers'. They won a decent 1,781 votes, 4.6 per cent, against 31,000 for Labour and 6,290 for the Welsh nationalists in Plaid Cymru.[80] It remains one of the greatest vote shares for an avowed Trotskyist in Britain's ungenerous first-past-the-post system. A Trotskyist would not contest a general election in the UK for another 30 years.

In the immediate post-war period, the RCP had somewhere in the region of 400 members, including in its ranks practically all those who would be the dominant actors in British Trotskyism in the second half of the twentieth century, such as Ted Grant (founder of the Militant Tendency) and Tony Cliff (founder of the Socialist Workers Party, who emigrated to Britain in 1946), as well as Gerry Healy. In keeping with the official pronouncements of the Fourth International, the RCP spoke of a looming revolution in post-war Britain.[81] This was not to be. As the war ended, the opportunity for growing the party via wartime strikes ended with it and there was a danger that contact with the actual organised working class could be lost; British Trotskyists turned on each other.[82]

Entering peacetime, the Labour Party won a massive landslide victory in the July 1945 general election (and worst of all for the Trotskyists, even the hated Stalinists of the CPGB won two seats). The RCP underwent a schismatic debate over the unresolved issue of entryism within the Labour Party. The International Executive Committee, the leadership of the Fourth International, recommended entryism, though the RCP itself, still led by Jock Haston, voted against the strategy, hoping to maintain their existence independent of Labour. A rump, however, led by Healy, pushed for it and after some wrangling, an 'open' RCP stayed outside of Labour and a minority of no more than 80 Trotskyists followed Healy into the Labour Party, where they acted as closeted Trotskyists and advocated for anti-imperialist policies. Healy's statements in favour of entryism were couched in the cogent view that the Labour Party represented the greatest political concentration of the British working class and 'it is our job to *participate* with the workers in their political experience, thereby demonstrating to them in practice the correctness of the programme of the Fourth International'.[83]

The American SWP probably encouraged Healy to split with Haston, believing that this would lead to successful results once the Healy faction were able to operate within Labour.[84] The Haston faction also supported this division, since they believed their actions would bear fruit *outside* of Labour.[85] Healy's secretive faction would soon become known euphemistically as 'The Club' and it is really from this post-war point onwards that Healy began to build up his status as a leader of British Trotskyism.[86] In a report just before the split from the RCP, Healy's Club said they had 60 members with a further 36 potential members identified.[87]

The secretary of the Fourth International, Michel Pablo, asserted that the goal of The Club was to win over 'whole sections of the workers in the Labour Party and in the trade unions affiliated with it to revolutionary action'.[88] But since The Club could never actually reveal itself as a real existing group, it was largely unsuccessful in this recruitment. One of the few scholarly studies of British Trotskyism suggests that The Club's critiques of the Labour Party were not much different from left-wing social democrats like Tony Benn or Eric Heffer. Moreover, The Club seemed to avoid any serious reckoning of rank-and-file Labour politics, instead viewing the membership as inherently socialist and radical but always led astray by a corrupt and right-leaning middle-class leadership.[89]

Healy became chair of the Streatham Constituency Labour Party and The Club made some connections with prominent figures on the left of the party, such as the MP Fenner Brockway. Harry Ratner, a member of The Club, points out that this non-dogmatic and non-sectarian attitude towards Labour MPs was in marked contrast to the treatment of The Club's own members, with Healy already displaying authoritarian tendencies by the late 1940s and early 1950s.[90] Healy unsuccessfully sought endorsement to be a Labour candidate for parliament, though nine members of The Club did take seats as councillors, a not insignificant achievement for a small group.[91] Healy wrote various pieces for the *Tribune*, the organ of the Labour left. A piece on the Algerian leader Messali Hadj was particularly fawning. At the height of the Suez Crisis, Healy also authored two pamphlets that merged a hostility to the Tories with undiluted pro-Nasser sentiments.[92] This willingness to reproduce propaganda from the Arab world, provided it could be tarted up as anti-imperialism, would later become one of Healy's most controversial habits. Entryism required strict internal party discipline and a strong sense of cohesion. It fuelled an authoritarian leadership style and a suspicion of those on the outside; these also were to become recurring traits of Healy's politics.[93] And yet he was capable of high-quality writing, as evidenced by critiques of the Labour Party written in the early 1950s.[94]

Confusingly, the open section of the RCP dissolved in June 1949; they had entered into a pessimistic mood since the split, their membership dropping from 500 to 200, and *Socialist Appeal* switched from fortnightly to monthly publication. Haston began to question if Trotskyism could 'do the job'.[95] He soon repudiated revolutionary politics on the road to becoming a more conventional Labour Party member (Healy had already fallen out with his one-time mentor before this – in August 1946 he had accused Haston of 'heresy' for saying that the USSR displayed 'both capitalistic and socialistic features',[96] a contentious issue in Trotskyism). Healy became Secretary of the RCP in September 1949. But since an open RCP technically no longer existed, The Club now existed only as an informal organisation within the Labour Party.[97] This informal 'Club' thus represented the British section of the Trotskyist Fourth International and, by this point, was the only Trotskyist grouping still politically active in the UK.[98] As with previous iterations of British Trotskyism, this remained a small movement and heavily prone to splits. Healy worked to expel any potential opponents, focusing in particular on former members of the RCP. By 1950, he had expelled both Tony Cliff and Ted Grant.[99]

Just shy of one hundred delegates from The Club attended the 1950 Labour Party Conference, from 53 constituencies. Already in 1948, the Labour entryists had started a newspaper, *Socialist Outlook*, edited by Healy, and were building connections on the left of Labour and in the unions. With a familiar hyperbole, one member of The Club, Robert Shaw, considered the launching of the *Socialist Outlook* newspaper in 1948 to be 'the most important event in Britain'[100] at that time. This was the era that saw the founding of the National Health Service in 1945, the British departure from the Indian subcontinent in 1947 (and its simultaneous partitioning), the British abandonment of Palestine in 1948, the declaration of the

Republic of Ireland the same year (representing the final severing of Britain's connection to most of its oldest colony), and the switch to a welfare-state economics across the five years of the Atlee government. The establishing of a relatively low circulation newspaper that lasted for only six years hardly figures among all that. The paper, though, was a professionally slick affair, not least because of the financial assistance that regularly came from American Trotskyists and kept it afloat.[101] And Healy at this time began to emulate the politics and personal style of James Cannon, the leader within the American SWP.[102] There is an oddly sycophantic tone to many of Healy's letters to the SWP from this period, as if he was in awe of them or was trying to butter them up.[103]

Socialist Outlook tended to be ecumenical in content, initially giving space to both factions within the RCP as well as to MPs from Labour's left flank. They also gave space for national liberation leaders to write articles, such as Cheddi Jagan, later to be prime minister of British Guiana, and organised public talks in Britain by these leaders. Reflecting the paper's more open, non-dogmatic nature, *Socialist Outlook* was owned by the Labour Publishing Society, with 1,200 £1 shares in the hands of approximately 600 shareholders, A good number of these were Labour Party sympathisers rather than Trotskyists. The paper had three full-time employees, working at an office near London Bridge: John Lawrence, Fred Emmet and Audrey Brown (later a Labour MP under her married name, Audrey Wise). Healy retained a seat on the paper's editorial board.

This work seemed to be bearing fruit; a *Socialist Outlook* event on the fringe of the 1949 Labour Party conference in Blackpool was attended by 160 delegates and Labour MPs Ellis Smith and Tom Braddock both gave speeches. But when *Socialist Outlook* took an anti-imperialist line on the Korean War, some (but not all) of this more mainstream support evaporated.[104] *Socialist Outlook*'s pro-North Korean stance alienated many potential recruits from the Labour Party and also occasioned an early split. Tony Cliff, already establishing himself as an incisive ideologue, advocated a policy of neutrality in the Cold War, believing that the workers' states of the Communist world had backslid into capitalism. This was the immediate cause of Cliff's expulsion from The Club, after which he went on to form the International Socialists, later becoming the Socialist Workers Party (not to be confused with the American SWP). Healy had probably been unable to answer Cliff's economistic arguments and expelled him rather than lose the debate; Cliff's biographer has aptly observed that Gerry Healy was 'an organiser of some talent' but 'he was both short on theory and very strong on authoritarian measures'.[105]

By the mid-1950s, The Club's membership numbers were stagnating. The publishing of *Socialist Outlook* had brought too much attention from the leadership of the Labour Party and the paper was suppressed in 1954, lest the members of The Club be exposed as entryists and expelled. The fact, though, that major figures on Labour's left flank, such as the future Labour leader Michael Foot, spoke out against the anti-*Socialist Outlook* actions, and that party rank-and-file also opposed this, does show that The Club had built up some support and influence.[106] That the Labour leadership were so hostile also suggests that The Club had been able to make some commensurable impact; an ineffectual operation would likely not have attracted such attentions. *Socialist Outlook* also become embroiled in a libel suit at this time, brought by the Imperial Tobacco Company; the paper had printed an article entitled 'A True Story', written by the wife of a Club supporter, which claimed that a printing factory owned by the tobacco company paid below union rates; the company had obtained witnesses who could dispute this.[107] In several accounts of this libel case written by party members, the details are only vaguely outlined, suggesting that they were suitably chastened by the experience and unwilling to risk further libel suits. In any case, the cripplingly high payment of a £2,000 fine (the equivalent of about £45,000 in 2024) brought about by this case would have done serious damage.[108] By 1956, the membership of The Club may not have been too far north of one hundred people.[109] One estimate is that, as of 1950, there was a total of 124 active Trotskyists in the UK, rising to only 475 by 1960, now split across four organisations (the SLL, Ted Grant's RSL, the Socialist Review Group led by Tony Cliff and The Week, which would later become the International Marxist Group).[110]

Help would soon come, though, from an ironically Stalinist direction. The Soviet invasion of Hungary in 1956, and, in the same year, Khrushchev's secret speech to the Twentieth Congress of the Communist Party of the Soviet Union, in which he confirmed the brutalities of Stalin's rule, caused a crisis within the global Communist movement. The CPGB lost some of its most important members in the wake of this, most famously the Communist Party Historians' Group made up of some of Britain's finest mid-century historians, such as Christopher Hill and E.P. Thompson, who left in protest of the invasion. Upwards of 9,000 members left the CPGB in the subsequent years.[111] Some two hundred exiles from the Communist Party ended up in Healy's orbits, a fraction of the exodus but a godsend for a small group.[112] Initially, The Club urged CPGB members to stay in their party and demand answers as to what had happened in Hungary, though the dissidents were defeated at the CPGB's 1957 conference and the party leadership issued a warning that all members should avoid Trotskyism.[113] After Khrushchev's speech, John Daniels, a Nottingham University lecturer, was one of the first CPGB members to move to Trotskyism. When he wrote *A Letter to a Member of the Communist Party*, The Club circulated it widely as a pamphlet. Club members also visited Communists at home, finding their addresses from letters published in the *Daily Worker* and hoping to win them over to Trotskyist ideas.[114]

Brian Pearce, an adept historian of Communism, Ken Coates, later to serve as a Labour representative to the European Parliament, and the Scottish trade unionist Lawrence Daly all joined Healy at this time.[115] As The Club slowly grew in membership, new members were listed as shareholders in the Labour Publishing Society, an enterprise which had mainly been dedicated to the printing of the now defunct *Socialist Outlook* newspaper. Club activity within the Labour Party at this point, particularly within the youth wing, the League of Youth, began to come under greater scrutiny from the Labour leadership. Undeterred, The Club continued to remain active, launching two new publications in 1957: *Labour Review*, a theory-driven Marxist magazine published bi-monthly and mainly aimed at ex-CPGB members, and a weekly news sheet given the suitably anodyne name *The Newsletter*.[116] The latter was edited by Peter Fryer who had previously been the Hungarian correspondent of the Communist Party's *Daily Worker* and had personally witnessed, and reported on, the Soviet invasion. The Irish writer Brian Behan, who had been a member of the National Executive of the CPGB, was another of the recruits.[117] Cliff Slaughter, a sociology lecturer at Leeds University who would remain loyal to Healy until the 1980s and became one of his leading ideologues, joined at this time, alongside Tom Kemp, an economic historian at Hull University, who also stayed for the long haul.[118]

The Club held its first summer camp in 1957, to train cadres in its Marxist method of political analysis, a type of event that would later become synonymous with Healy's other political operations. Members of The Club in the local branch of the Labour Party in Norwood in south London succeeded in bringing a motion to the Party's annual conference calling for the UK to pursue a total and unilateral nuclear disarmament; it was seemingly popular at the grassroots level but roundly defeated at the party's conference by the votes of 5,800,000 Labour members to 781,000. Ironically, this was one of the few times Healy managed to make a commensurable impact on mainstream British politics, and it happened when he was a member of the reformist Labour Party. Soon, though, he would realise that his future would lie outside of Labour.

By the very end of the 1950s, Healy was a recognisable presence on the British radical left. As it neared its quarter-century, British Trotskyism had made a commensurate impact both in the labour movement and on the margins of the Labour Party, though its real breakout moment would not come until the next decade. The Club's position within the machinery of the Labour Party provided an organic connection to the British working class but was also a hindrance to their independent expansion. Internationally, Healy had established a reputation as a committed activist within the Fourth International, even if he remained overshadowed by more serious thinkers like James Cannon in the US. For all his flaws, Healy did genuinely believe in socialism, however he understood that term. His flaws, though, were certainly manifold. The Club, like its successors, the WRP and the SLL, displayed a rigid dogmatism, an emphasis on the study of Marxist texts, and top-down party structures; these were all recurring features of what we might call Healyism. Whether a coherent Healyist philosophy existed is the subject of the next chapter.

2

Healyism

In Trevor Griffiths's 1973 play *The Party*, a group of smugly bourgeois leftists gather at a house party, hoping to discuss socialist
politics but later to be shocked by the incisive eloquence of 'John
Tagg', a working-class Scottish socialist based on Gerry Healy;
in the first production of *The Party*, at the National Theatre in
London on 20 December 1973, Laurence Olivier played the part
of Tagg/Gerry. In the play, one of the female socialists warns the
organiser of the leftist get-together about Tagg/Healy: 'I know
Tagg. And he's irrelevant. You can drive a coach-and-four through
his analysis. He's a brutal shite underneath with a fist where his
mind used to be.'[1] Sean Matgamna, a one-time member of the SLL
who stayed active within Trotskyism but very much moved away
from Healy, has a somewhat similar assessment today. Matgamna
denies that the SLL or WRP could even be called sectarian,
because that would be to assume they stuck to a coherent set of
principles. 'They were guided by no idea bigger than a desire to
build their organisation.' Healy and his supporters, he says, 'were
raving mad'.[2] Tariq Ali says the WRP were so sectarian, and so
given over to producing fraction and discord, that many on the left
assumed they had been infiltrated by the state security services.
And in the only direct encounter Ali remembers having with him,
Healy's sarcastic but threatening comment to him was: 'I'll see the
likes of you off before I go under.' Countering the image of him as
a genuine organic intellectual, Ali's assessment is that 'a small layer
of middle-class intellectuals were captivated by Healy. He put on
this act of being a great proletarian leader and people were taken
in by that.'[3]

Are these fair assessments? Was there an actual coherent socialist ideology that animated Gerry Healy? Or was he just a shameless
grifter? A sectarian nuisance?

Certainly, there were some recurring texts that he turned to and from which he fashioned a philosophy that could be termed 'Healyism' – Engels's *Dialectics of Nature*, Lenin's *Philosophical Notebooks* (a series of summaries of major philosophers' ideas and gathered as *Volume 38* of his Collected Works), *The Dialectics of the Abstract and Concrete in Marx's Capital* by the Soviet philosopher Evald Ilyenkov.[4] Corinna Lotz, who served as Healy's secretary in his last years, recalled that the only books in his office were the collected works of, in turn, Marx and Engels, Lenin, and Trotsky, a good indication of the orthodoxy of his outlook, as well as its narrow gauges.[5] He discovered Lenin's *Philosophical Notebooks* in 1962, when Cliff Slaughter wrote about them for the SLL's theoretical journal *Labour Review*. The *Philosophical Notebooks*, despite being 'a complex book of disjointed notes', became 'a sort of textbook for our Party', Claire Cowen recalls, and 'Gerry seemed to present *Volume 38* as a handbook of applied philosophy, a sort of blueprint for the revolution.'[6] *Volume 38* was often used for party education classes, even though it is mostly made up of Lenin's notes on Hegel and makes little sense without the requisite background knowledge on Hegel's original texts. Healy later added Lenin's *Materialism and Empirio-Criticism*, a more conventional text but certainly not an easy one, to this repertoire (and he rarely drew on texts by Trotsky himself).[7] In his formal greetings to his Spanish comrades in *Liga Obrera* in June 1989, he praised them for embodying the ideas of *Materialism and Empirio-Criticism*, taking them 'as the foundation of our consistent opposition to bourgeois ideology and all its manifestations in the everyday work of the party, its leading committees and branches'.[8]

At the end of his life, when his followers had shrunk to the lowest level, he would structure party summer schools around this bespoke materialist philosophy – 'a thorough examination of the connection of semblance with its source in the physical movement of the external world beyond thought' – with his lectures on the topic dragging on for hours. This was a well-established feature of party education long before 1985; in 1978, he gave a ten-lecture course on 'Dialectical Materialism' at the party's college, costing £24 for one week, £40 for the full fortnight.[9] The actor Kika Markham recalled the 'fierce concentration' required for the classes on *Volume 38* of Lenin's *Collected Works*, as well as the 'habitual fatigue that settled on everyone in the WRP', hinting at the soporific tone of these lectures.[10] And as early as 1957, when he was active only in 'The Club', Healy saw summer camps and summer schools as a key mechanism for propagating his eclectic mix of ontology and epistemology. The camps became a mixture of long-winded Marxist lectures by day, and social events at night.

At various summer schools, he would urge his followers to read Fichte and Hegel, though it is not clear if he had actually read either but instead just deployed their names and a basic sense of their ideas as weapons against those who questioned him – opponents would be accused of falling prey to Fichtean idealism and 'pure subjectivism'.[11] In 1980, Healy insisted that not only did all members of the Political Committee have to attend his weekly lectures on dialectics, but they also had to write a several hundred-word essay on the topic. 'It is indicative of his authority' that almost all members of the Committee 'duly completed their "homework", including Corin and Vanessa Redgrave'.[12] A piece Healy wrote in April 1988 gives a good indication of the content of his 'philosophy':

> Dialectial Logic as a science is developed in the process of cognising phenomena negated from the infinite motion of the external world. The phenomena which demand our most urgent attention are generated by the world class struggle and its continuous interaction with the property relations established by the October 1917 Socialist Revolution. This process constitutes the form and content of the political revolution now well underway in the USSR. It is achieved through the use of images which are sensations whose source is in the world of the class struggle. They are then analysed 'in themselves' through the use of dialectical thought (logic). As Lenin explains on p.225 Vol.38 [of the *Collected Works* of Lenin], 'images and thought, the development of both, nothing else'.[13]

Another representative example was *Whither Thornett?*, a theoretically inflected attack on the trade unionist Alan Thornett, published in 1975 just after his expulsion from the WRP. Written by Mike Banda, one passage stated:

Dialectical thought concepts are now entering matter through us via the self-impulse of the universal movement of matter. As this takes place we arrive at the moment of actuality, which is causality... At this dialectical moment of causality, the cause (essence) cancels itself into the effect (abstract thought already posited in us as part of a previous dialectical process). Likewise the effect cancels itself into cause.[14]

Former followers of Healy would later come to see this – quite reasonably – as an enclosed system of meaninglessness, larded with genuine philosophical concepts but ultimately devoid of any analytical utility ('incomprehensible lectures in his unique brand of pseudo-dialectical gibberish',[15] as one person present for Healy's talks called them). The American Trotskyist David North, not unfairly, labelled this 'Healy's make-believe world of Fichtean Egos, empty word forms, and Not-beings'.[16] Alex Steiner says many people joined because of the party's emphasis on philosophy but that those who were genuine intellectuals or had a grounding in philosophy were stifled and not allowed to challenge the party's line on such questions. Steiner, who had some training in academic philosophy, politely says that he does not think Healy was engaged in serious philosophy.[17] When the Scottish intellectual Alasdair MacIntyre broke with the Socialist Labour League, after a brief collaboration with them, Healy threw one of his preferred buzzwords at him: idealism. Macintyre's response was: 'You charge me with idealism. It is time to call your intellectual bluff. Frankly from your letter, I do not think you know what idealism is. I think that you are throwing a piece of vocabulary about in the hope of impressing the membership.' In the letter he then wrote in response, it is clear that Healy has no serious answer to MacIntyre's charges and engaged in word play more than anything else, as if he was trying to avoid making a response.[18] Healy seemed to have an inferiority complex in relation to actual intellectuals within the party and certainly was not a serious intellectual himself.

It is also not really clear that Healy believed in any of this. Rather, the very vagueness of his 'philosophy' provided a means to obfuscate and to retreat into a philosophical thicket as a means of evading any serious challenges. At one meeting of the International Committee of the Fourth International (ICFI) in June 1970, Healy promoted a discussion of abstract Marxist philosophy as a 'trap', so that his opponents in the international Trotskyist movement would provide 'evidence' that they were indeed guilty of 'pragmatism' and thus he could justify moving against them.[19] His use of philosophy was malleable in the extreme. On one occasion, Healy wrote to all branch secretaries to inform them that a shortfall in party funds that prevented weekly wages from being paid was 'a reflection of the inertia and idealist paralysis affecting leadership in London and provincial areas'.[20] When the SLL launched its daily paper, *Workers Press*, in 1971, the SLL declared that 'The fact that we were able to launch the Workers Press with the most modern technical facilities is itself a verification of the dialectical concept that the working class is moving towards a final conflict with the capitalist system.' 'Dialectical' here is an empty term; it means anything good that the SLL or Healy were doing. Similarly, 'Idealism' named anything that existed in opposition to Healy's own sense of himself as a gifted, if non-academic thinker and the oracle who knows best for the entire socialist movement.[21] Rank-and-file party member Robert Myers says that this use of political theory became worse and worse across the 1970s and 1980s.[22]

Tim Wohlforth, a leading figure within 1960s American Trotskyism, argued that Healy's preoccupation with intentionally obscure Marxist philosophising meant that 'the *content* of politics' was replaced by 'the *form* of dialectics'.[23] (Though obviously this could only work with those who knew little about Marxist theory – at the 1945 RCP Conference, Denzil Harber, leader of the Revolutionary Socialist League, one of the groupings that merged into the RCP, was able to use his knowledge of Marx and Engels's *The German Ideology*, only then recently rediscovered, to demolish Healy's tilting against 'empiricism'. Humiliated, Healy quickly dropped his accusations that RCP leaders were guilty of 'empiricism'.)[24] And, in any case, Healy had a remarkable tendency to fully embrace political positions he had only recently been zealously denouncing.[25]

This weaponised philosophy, in turn, was used against Healy himself. As David North began to break with Healy in the early 1980s, he produced a lengthy takedown of Healy's philosophy, *A Contribution to a Critique of G. Healy's 'Studies in Dialectical Mate-*

rialism'. In familiarly abstruse language, North accused Healy of 'idealism', by then a cardinal sin for Healyist parties.[26] After the 1985 split in the WRP, Mike Banda said of Healy and his followers that 'Their philosophy is based on the principle of "anything goes". It is positivism and pragmatism. The essence of their position is that there is no such thing as principles, that there is no such thing as objective truth and therefore no absolute within every relative',[27] though that is hardly a good definition of positivism and it is not even clear if it is pragmatism. Rather both terms function here as loaded slurs rather than three-dimensional concepts. When Banda later drifted away from Trotskyism, he condemned Trotsky, in ironically very Healyite terms, for never producing as comparably sophisticated a work as Lenin's *Materialism and Empirio-Criticism*.[28]

Intentionally or not (but probably intentionally), this internal party culture and mode of political education had the effect of breaking internal factions and reducing opposition to Healy. Indeed, in a letter that he submitted to the WRP's Seventh Congress in 1984, Healy said that party members should abandon 'idealism' as part of their mental training. A party member should learn to 'mentally and practically subordinate oneself' to the greater whole of the party and thereby acquire 'a conscious party outlook'. A party member would cease to be an *individual* member, instead becoming a *party cadre*, a distinction that Healy strongly emphasised.[29] All of this fits with the assessment of the former SLL member Sean Matgamna. Writing in *Socialist Organiser* in 1981, Matgamna said that:

> the WRP is no laughing matter. It is a pseudo-Marxist gobble-degook-sprouting cross between the Moonies, the Scientologists and the Jones Cult... It recruits and exploits mainly raw, inexperienced, politically, socially and psychologically defenceless young people. It employs psychological terror and physical violence against its own members (and occasionally against others).[30]

There does seem to have been a complicated set of dynamics within the party, in which Healy controlled party members, but in turn party members contributed to the internal regime that granted such control to Healy. Dave Bruce, a full-time employee of the WRP has a sharp understanding of this today:

Healy was almost as much a product of his colleagues as they were of him. The group dynamics, the psychology, of the WRP were not dissimilar to any group of socially isolated but intensely motivated people. Healy was a skilled and cynical manipulator of individuals but, at the same time, not without political and social insight. Many in positions of influence who should have known better were happy to support him and help to crush those who dared to defy him. They had much to answer for but never sought to try.[31]

Healy's final group, The Marxist Party, continued this process of education-as-control: all party members were told of their 'obligation' to receive 'fundamental training in the method of materialist dialectics, the history of the working class and Trotskyism, and Marxist economics'.[32] Healy and his followers had a recurring desire to depict him as a working-class autodidact who had acquired a high-cultural awareness under his own power (though one of the same followers recalled that when he attended Shakespeare plays, he would fall asleep in the audience).[33]

Another recurring feature of Healy's worldview is what might be called 'crisisism', the perennial sense that a massive crisis of capitalism is just around the corner, but never quite arrives. When The Club gave its support to a picket at a single construction site in London in 1958, Healy declared that 'We've got the bourgeoisie by the throat!', ignoring the small-scale significance of this one lone action.[34] In 1963, he claimed that a momentary economic slump and the Profumo scandal were combining to create a revolutionary situation in which the SLL could soon take charge of the country.[35] In 1966 he accused the Tories of seeking a 'British Hitler' to lead the country, though by the end of the decade he felt that the SLL were on the verge of replacing the Labour Party.[36] A March 1968 front-page article in the party's *Newsletter* was entitled 'Crisis, Panic, Crash', a good *non-sequitur* summation of this aspect of Healy's worldview.

Like a stopped clock, Healy's 'crisisism' meant he could be right a small number of times. In the WRP's attempts to intervene into the miners' strike of 1984–85, perhaps *the* sharpest moment of class conflict in Thatcherite Britain, the party issued a fairly astute statement in April 1984, warning of the Tories' determination to crush the National Union of Mineworkers, which they duly undermined with obscure talk of the 'Bonapartist regime' wishing to wage a 'civil war'.[37] (Derived from Marx's 1852 work *The Eighteenth Brumaire*, 'Bonapartist' was a favoured term – Ulster Unionism was also called 'Bonapartism in Ulster'.[38] Healy positioned Castro as a bourgeois Bonaparte as part of his attempt to portray post-1959 Cuba as a capitalist state, a lonely position on the left.[39]) In February 1985, a month before the miners' strike ended in defeat, Healy stated that a victory for Thatcher would lead to 'fascism' and a police–military dictatorship. By that summer, Healy was talking of a looming civil war in the UK.[40]

The fairly tame 1987 general election, the first after the miners' strike, and in which Labour and the Conservatives received largely the same vote-share as they had in 1983, was described in *The Marxist Review* as the 'Deaththroes [*sic*] of Parliamentary Democracy'.[41] The Poll Tax, the fight over which ultimately took down Thatcher, was instead described as 'an instrument of Tory dictatorship'.[42] Healyite crisisism, rather than providing a realistic assessment of the strengths or weaknesses of the Conservative government, provided a paradoxical image of, on the one hand, a Tory establishment inches away from imposing a full-blown dictatorship and, on the other, a soon-to-be-executed socialist revolution that always remained just out of reach. Crisisism also meant that every minor conflagration between Healy and the class enemy *du jour* became seen as the final showdown with the forces of Capital, and party members were pushed to throw their all into the fight, before the fight would rapidly shift to some other enemy or cause. Clare Cowen remembers Healy telling her 'When you have a success, go *straight in* with the next campaign. Never let the enthusiasm die down.' As Cowen recounts, 'We were in perpetual campaigning mode.'[43] Another party member said the SLL and WRP were both adept at convincing members, particularly young members, that a revolution was imminent.[44]

Party members constantly shifted from one final showdown with capitalism to another, fatiguing them and contributing to the high rate of membership turnover.[45] That also meant that the party cadres remained perennially new and inexperienced and thus more controllable by the party leadership. And the sheer pace of work left little time for serious self-reflection or political education.[46] Mike Richardson, a WRP member in Bristol, says the continual pressure to sell party newspapers represented a 'day-to-day drudgery', and there was no political discussion as a result. Richardson's feeling is that the WRP leadership wanted raw, naïve people who could be indoctrinated and all this came down from Healy as a kind of dictatorial leader.[47]

Bob Pitt, a one-time supporter turned harsh critic, pointed out that this 'catastrophism', as he calls it, was a recurring feature of Healy's politics throughout his career, a combination of 'subjective fantasy' and 'ultra-left bombast'.[48] Healy rarely showed much of an investment in the questions that usually animate Trotskyists, such as the debate over whether the USSR was a deformed workers' state or had backslid into state capitalism or the need to develop a clear, consistent position on 'The National Question'. The party was agnostic about Irish nationalism, producing adept if very Republican histories of Ireland's place within global capitalism and sending delegates to the 1986 Sinn Féin *Ard Fhéis*.[49] Working with the Prisoners Aid Committee, itself allied to the Provisional IRA, the WRP made the 1978 documentary, *Prisoners of War*. The IRA accepted the support of British Trotskyists, organised through the Troops Out Movement, but also remained wary of their internal politics and their tendency to split.[50] Healy himself, though, remained 'very suspicious' of potential Irish members, believing the IRA and Sinn Féin were full of MI5 agents.[51] The strands of conservative Catholicism that ran through the Provisional IRA remained a major stumbling block for the WRP.[52] The party also dismissed Black nationalism as reactionary and petit bourgeois.[53] Yet, infamously the WRP became overly receptive to Arab nationalism. The SLL had alienated many others on the left in the late 1960s when it refused to support anti-Vietnam War protests, but the WRP enthusiastically hailed the victory of the Viet Cong and the American retreat from Vietnam in 1975.[54] There was a lack of ideological consistency here.

Healyism was also defined by a clear hostility toward all other iterations of Trotskyism. Alex Mitchell said he once asked Healy whether it would be worthwhile holding a reunification conference to bring the various strands of Trotskyism together. 'He gave me a pained look and said, "We don't need to have a meeting with them, Alex – we need to destroy them. They are an obstacle to the revolution."'[55] In 1962, Healy justified the SLL's sectarian attitude to all other Trotskyists by dismissing them as 'revisionists', 'nothing more than shock troops of capitalism which are being employed at this stage to weaken the revolutionary movement'.[56] Healy may have, on one occasion, dispatched a spy to infiltrate the rival Trotskyists in the International Marxist Group; the spy was allegedly Adam Westoby, a lecturer and well-known political campaigner.[57]

There is a specific kind of irony in the fact that in one of Healy's final long-form articles – a piece entitled 'The Political Revolution in the USSR, a Process of Contradiction', written in the summer of 1988 – he stressed that: 'We start from the reality of today, in which is contained the historical content, and not from the past turned into historical dogma.' Ironic because his was always an acutely dogmatic philosophy. One perceptive post-mortem of the Healy era WRP said that the 'barbarism' of the party was defined by sectarianism, 'slander towards others in the workers [sic] movement', opportunism, and anti-internationalism. The collective result of all this is that Healyite parties espoused a proletarian ideology but were simultaneously incapable of good faith cooperation with other working-class activists.[58] When Healy called his final party 'The Marxist Party', the barely concealed claim was that no other party was truly Marxist. This was the ultimate distillation of Healyism – dogmatic orthodoxy, a disdain for anyone that dissented, and nominative sloganeering.

3
I Specialise in Clique Busting,
1959–1972

By the end of the 1950s, Healy had certainly made headway within the Labour Party. Whatever the moment of The Club–Labour co-operation represented, though, it was short-lived. Hugh Gaitskell became leader of the Labour Party in 1955. In the context of a booming economy in the late 1950s, Gaitskell began to move the party away from the left, seeking a more pro-business and less socialist orientation. The existence of a small but vocal Trotskyist faction within Labour obviously did not sit easily with that. And so, in late 1958, members of The Club began to be expelled from the Labour Party.[1] Fearing that these Trotskyist activists would fade away from politics – since The Club had no official existence, there was no actual formal way to organise them outside of Labour – Healy and his core supporters decided to come out of the shadows and declare themselves an open political organisation. Thus, adding to the Trotskyist alphabet soup, the Socialist Labour League (SLL) was born.[2] This was to be Healy's political vehicle through to the start of the 1970s. In a unanimous decision, the new group was almost instantly put on the proscribed list of organisations banned from acting within the Labour Party.[3] One of the first publications released by the SLL was a thoroughgoing denunciation of Labour's right-wing turn under Hugh Gaitskell; written by Healy himself, it provided a well-researched and well-argued critique of Labour.[4] One Club-cum-SLL member, Norman Harding, said that the switch to the SLL 'was a deliberate attempt to transform ourselves from the small circle... that we had been'.[5] Bill Hunter's appraisal was that it was a 'league' and 'not a party in a real sense. Nor had we given up our orientation to the Labour Party.'[6] Healy may have established the SLL without actually consulting any other members of The Club and the question of the SLL's actual attitude to or relationship with the Labour Party remained unresolved.[7] In 1961, the SLL's annual conference reaffirmed 'the perspective that its main orientation is towards work inside the trade unions and the Labour Party'.[8]

The ethos of the SLL was summed up on the League's membership card: 'The aim of the Socialist Labour League, which is based on the theory of Marxism, is to prepare the working class for the replacement of capitalism by a socialist society.'[9] The same cartesian separation that regularly defines Leninism was at work here, as is the paradox inherent in this; the working classes are the sole agent of the Communist future but they apparently need to be trained and prepared by a vanguardist League that always exists at a remove from them. The proletarian body is to be guided by the vanguardist brain.[10]

At the time of the founding of the SLL in 1959, Healy was predicting a major economic crisis on the horizon, a 'crisisism' that would come to define his worldview. SLL predictions of a massive crisis grew stronger and stronger across the party's history. A British government intelligence report from 23 March 1971 describes the League as follows:

> A classical Trotskyist party devoted to the overthrow of the capitalist system in accordance with the Transitional Programme prescribed by Trotsky. It believes that international capitalism is facing unprecedented crises which will precipitate a revolutionary situation which the SLL must be prepared to exploit.[11]

By the end of the SLL's life-cycle in early 1973, Healy was claiming concentration camps were being built to intern trade unionists. One overview of British Trotskyism suggests Healy had already developed his taste for apocalyptic predictions during the first Atlee government after 1945, when the construction of the welfare state undercut Trotskyist visions of socialism and crisisism emerged as a means to distract from the dismal conditions and prospects facing Trotskyists.[12] Alan Thornett, one of the few opponents of Healy to emerge within the SLL, would later observe: 'the leadership group gradually lost touch with reality'. This poses the question of why a leadership clearly unmoored from reality was not removed? The historian John Callaghan explains this in terms of the high rate of turnover of party members within the SLL, which both prevented an opposition faction from forming but also meant party members had no institutional memory of what the party had been saying in previous years.[13] Another Trotskyist said that 'the constant wearing away of active and leading members' had been a perennial feature of Trotskyism from the very start and 'made it extremely difficult to carry forward experience from one generation to another'.[14]

The question of how the SLL would interact with the two major divisions of the international Trotskyist movement immediately came to the fore. Trotskyism had been growing ever more sectarian in the post-war years. In 1951 an exasperated Natalia Sedova, Trotsky's widow, resigned from the Fourth International, writing to the Executive Committee that 'I do not see his ideas in your politics.'[15] By the early 1950s, the Fourth International was dividing into two camps, the Pabloites and the non-Pabloites. Very broadly speaking, the Pabloite camp, followers of an Egyptian-born Greek Trotskyist named Michalis N. Raptis (pseudonym: Michel Pablo) advocated some kind of rapprochement, via entryism, with both Communism and reformist social democracy as well as building links with Third World anti-colonial movements; all of this was presented as an escape from the irrelevancy Trotskyism had collapsed into since 1945. The non-Pabloites resisted any kind of bridge-building with mainline Communism, seeing this as a slippery slope to Stalinism. The anti-Pablo International Committee for the Fourth International (ICFI) split from the Pablo-dominated Fourth International in 1953. Healy sided strongly with the ICFI, brooking no compromise and writing voluminously on the matter to various other international Trotskyists, often signing his letters with various code-names such as 'Comrade Burns' or 'Preston'.[16] The refusal to compromise, the willingness to split with former comrades, and the cloak-and-dagger tactics were all becoming hallmarks of Healy's politics. Moreover, that the Pabloites within the Fourth International leadership were seeking to make common cause with a faction within the SLL almost certainly added to the break between Pablo and Healy.[17] And yet, for all such posturing, in Pierre Frank's history of the Fourth International, originally published in French in 1969 and which takes the story up to the end of the 1960s, Gerry Healy is mentioned only once and only in the context of his sectarian opposition to a unification of the world Trotskyist movement, testament to both his relative obscurity by that time and, for those who did know him, the contempt with which he was often held.[18]

The American Socialist Workers Party (not to be confused with the Tony Cliff's SWP in Britain) were soon advocating a rapprochement with the Pabloites and urged other Trotskyist groups to do the same. Healy travelled in this period to Canada to discuss all this with the SWP (as a known communist, he was barred from entering the United States). The talks led nowhere.[19] A similar SLL fraternal gathering with Italian Trotskyists in June 1958 was even frostier; the two sides could not even agree on a co-signed document of their shared principles. Joseph Hansen, a journalist and activist within the American SWP encouraged the SLL to ditch Healy as leader, seeing him (not at all inaccurately) as a barrier to unification of the diverging strands of Trotskyism. The SWP left the ICFI in 1963, as they made amends with the Pabloites. And in time Healy's SLL and the French *Parti Communiste Internationaliste* (PCI) would come to dominate the ICFI. Hansen had problems with Healy, however, that went beyond party organisation and complicated questions of Trotskyist political praxis.

Physical assaults of Healy's opponents within the SLL were not uncommon and he had a propensity for authoritarian control of the organisation; even in the period of The Club, Healy had a violent temper and a tendency to verbally attack party members.[20] Granville Williams, who had joined the SLL as a student at Leeds University before organising for the party in mining areas of Yorkshire, says Healy engaged in a performative 'simulated rage' in which he would 'savagely' attack SLL members for not having the right attitude. This kind of 'thuggish' behaviour and a lack of political consistency soon alienated Williams from the SLL.[21] Joseph Hansen was certainly aware of Gerry Healy's penchant for violence and the ugly rumours that were already spreading in the British labour movement. In November 1966, SLL members violently attacked a rival Trotskyist, Ernie Tate, when Tate had been selling publications criticising Healy outside an SLL event. According to one account:

> Six young toughs jumped Tate, smashing his glasses and bringing him down to the pavement. In commando fashion they continued to kick him, aiming at his genitals, kidneys and head, until pulled off by horrified spectators. Tate had to be hospitalized. Witnesses stated that they recognized the assailants as members of the Socialist Labour League. Thomas Gerard Healy, the general secretary of the organization, appeared to be supervising the action personally.[22]

Healy was called before Isaac Deutscher, Trotsky's biographer and a figure esteemed by all the differing branches of Trotskyism, and forced to apologise. This incident was well known among the left, though Healy threatened libel action against both *Peace News* and *The Socialist Leader*, which published articles about the assault; rather than fight this out in the courts, both papers printed apologies and each paid 10 guineas (10 pounds 10 shillings) to Healy.[23] There were also serious allegations of violence against SLL opponents within the Labour Party's youth wing.[24] That Healy terrorised the membership of the SLL was practically an open secret. Bob Pennington, an SLL member who later joined the International Marxist Group, 'walked out of the SLL on the eve of the 1960 conference, spreading a trail of gossip and unsubstantiated allegations of violence against himself and others by leaders of the SLL'.[25] Foreshadowing what would later cause his downfall, in 1964, a 'control commission' had to be convened within the League because of Healy's inappropriate relationship with a female leader of the SLL's youth wing; it is not clear how consensual, if at all, the relationship was.[26] This would only be publicly revealed in 1985, suggesting that information about this incident was kept under very tight seal. On the other hand, Healy was probably quite happy to have rumours of his violence circulate. One former WRP member says Healy propagated an aura of total ruthlessness but then could benefit from that aura, since potential followers believed he was totally ruthless, in a kind of feedback loop.[27]

Healy's violence was bound up with the excessive control he had over the SLL: he was general secretary, party treasurer, manager of the print shop, and the official owner of the party's assets. An Irish Trotskyist who visited the SLL's offices in April 1960 took a dim view of Healy's domineering tendencies: 'I don't think much about Healy. He seems like a dictator. He treats everyone at the centre and the printshop like children and they seem scared of him.'[28] When Brian Behan questioned Healy's monopolising of party assets, he was duly expelled from the new organisation. Behan had suggested that the party should practise what it preached and 'nationalise' all SLL assets, for which Healy both violently denounced him and arranged to have one of his 'henchmen' assault him. Behan's wife, Celia, had also tabled an unsuccessful motion within her branch, expressing concern over how much responsibility and control was held in Healy's hands.[29] The prominent Scottish philosopher Alasdair MacIntyre, briefly an SLL fellow-traveller who wrote a pamphlet for the League, had reached the conclusion that those with dissenting opinions 'cannot exist in your organisation'.[30] MacIntyre shared Behan's concerns about internal democracy in the party (or the lack thereof) as well as the ownership of party assets.[31]

Peter Fryer also did not last long in the SLL. One of Fryer's last actions within the SLL was to write *The Battle for Socialism*, a solid mix of history and theory, published under the League's imprimatur.[32] But shortly after this, Fryer had 'explosive disagreements with Gerry'[33] and in an 'Open Letter to Members of the Socialist Labour League and other Marxists', he described the League as being ruled by 'the general secretary's personal clique, which will not allow the members to practise the democratic rights accorded to them on paper, and which pursues sectarian aims with scant regard for the real possibilities of the real world'.[34] It very much seems, from the tone and content of his open letter, that Fryer was on the verge of some kind of emotional breakdown.[35] When Fryer left the SLL in 1959, Healy essentially stalked him, probably not wanting to lose so prominent a journalist. Fryer eventually had to hire a lawyer and threatened Healy with legal action if he did not cease.[36] Freed from the orthodoxies of the CPGB and SLL, Fryer would go on to be an early pioneer in the writing of Black British history.[37] Harry Ratner says Healy initially welcomed ex-CPGB members and was willing to push the party to be non-dogmatic so as to give these new recruits space in which they could choose to embrace Trotskyism. But, Ratner says, by 1959 Healy was actively pushing them out, not tolerating any challenges to his leadership.[38] Ratner points out that Healy was able to do this, because he had enabling supporters within the SLL, naming Cliff Slaughter, Bob Shaw, Bill Hunter, and Mike and Tony Banda as culprits, as well as naming himself.[39]

Healy had a massive presence within the SLL, deeply involved in all aspects of the party and working with a tremendous level of energy and dedication. But this was a blessing as well as consciously constructed curse:

> the party, and each and every member in it, became dependent on Gerry Healy the individual. His strength was also his weakness: He built an impressive movement, yet that movement was the creature of his personality, suffering from the idiosyncrasies that any strong person has. When Healy was wrong there was no way internally to correct him, to even check him – and Healy could be very wrong![40]

What Andy Blunden, an Australian Trotskyist, said of the WRP was almost certainly equally true of the SLL: it is impossible to talk about the party other than through Gerry Healy's personality, since his personality saturated the organisation.[41]

Those who did stay with the League came under intense pressure to devote their entire lives to the SLL; they were often expected to quit their jobs at a moment's notice if the SLL needed them as full-time activists. Bridget Fowler, a sociology student at Leeds University, joined the SLL in early 1962, recruited by her lecturer, Cliff Slaughter. She joined because of a disillusionment with Fabian socialism, which she began to see as too gradualist. The SLL seemed to offer a more fundamental social transformation. She felt her time in the SLL was intellectually important and gave her a valuable introduction to Marxism even as she also began to find herself 'repelled' by the party. She began to see how easy it was to 'get in the bad books' with Gerry Healy and that hidden within a seemingly voluntaristic organisation that gave a place to intellectuals was a culture of sanctions and very strict discipline. Fowler sees this internal regime as stemming from the fact the SLL leaders, were, at root, Stalinists who had learned their politics in the CPGB. Already in this period, the group was perceived by some outsiders as a cult; Fowler says it was hard to be taken seriously as an emerging sociologist if you were a known member of the SLL. Having read Karl Popper's *The Open Society and its Enemies*, she went through a period of doubt about Marxism and requested a leave of absence from the SLL in 1964 but then never went back. She would go on to become a left-leaning sociologist at the University of Glasgow and still identifies with Marxism.[42]

In one case, Healy drove a wedge between a female party member and her husband, forcing the latter to leave both his wife and the SLL.[43] This kind of thing was not an irregular occurrence. Tariq Ali remembers an SLL student couple he knew at Oxford in the early 1960s who ended their relationship because of a decision of the party leadership.[44] It may have been an intentional act to break up couples within the organisation, as a form of control over them. Couples went along with this as a function of their ideological commitment and a belief that the revolution came first.[45] Ali also remembered the SLL as 'an ultra-orthodox sect... run like a one-party statelet by the supreme leader, Gerry Healey [*sic*]'. Ali found its politics and practices decidedly off-putting.[46] Notwithstanding his later involvement with Trotskyism, Ali said the SLL turned him off from Trotskyism. If the SLL had been the only Trotskyist group, he would have 'run a million miles' from Trotskyism: 'I had absolutely no respect for them on any level.'[47] And yet, for all its undeniably ugly sides, some members of the SLL also remember it fondly. Dave Bruce, who joined the SLL in 1967, is open about the flaws of the organisation but also recalls the excitement of working within the League, feeling connected to international political developments, from Paris in 1968 to the Palestinian national struggle, and running the party's newspapers. Most of the grassroots members of the SLL and later of the WRP were, Bruce says, 'likeable, hard-working people who sacrificed much in pursuit of a goal they fervently believed in, however unachievable it eventually proved to be'.[48]

Healy's high-ranking supporters, such as Cliff Slaughter, not only defended Healy and his violence, but also denied all such accusations and labelled them as misinformation. Slaughter argued that the prevalence of these accusations was in fact proof that Healy's leadership was worrying the elite so much that these accusations were being propagated to undermine him. Of course, this line of defence massively overstated Healy's political importance; in reality, the SLL remained a fringe organisation that struggled to make a continuous political impact. One exception to this was in the Labour Party's youth wing, where SLL still maintained some influence and was apparently finding some successes with recruiting new members there.[49] Harold Wilson, who became leader of Labour in 1963 and apparently was unable to clear out the SLL, replaced the party's youth wing with a new structure (Sean Matgamna, a member of the SLL at this time, alleges that Wilson was not initially hostile to the group, but that the SLL leadership deliberately sought a confrontation with him[50]). Labour youth members associated with their in-house newspaper, *Keep Left*, defected to the SLL and became the youth wing of the latter. *Keep Left* had a circulation of perhaps as high as 10,500 but was proscribed by the Labour Party in May 1962 and three SLL supporters were removed from the National Committee of the Labour Party's Young Socialists towards the end of that year.[51] 'Judith', a youth member who served on the editorial board of *Keep Left*, does say that her time in the SLL were her most formative years and feels they were important in her political and intellectual development. She says she gained a certain resilience, but this mainly came from the constant and excessive demands made on her as a member. And she agrees it was an abusive organisation. (When 'Judith' left what had then become the WRP in 1975, party members would come and wait outside her workplace all day to try unsuccessfully to get her to rejoin. She says this went on for months.)[52]

Trotskyists regularly displayed an adept ability to critique Communist parties but, not willing to break with top-down Leninist-style party structures, they also had no ability to turn ex-Stalinists into committed long-term Trotskyists; those who had been dismayed with Communist Party organisations often found Trotskyist parties just as bad.[53] By 1960, the SLL had squandered whatever bump it had received in the aftermath of the Communist Party crises of 1956. One study of the British far left suggests that these Communist recruits were never converted to Trotskyism and so most of them soon fell away, after which Healy turned his attentions to recruiting from the Labour Party's youth wing.[54] And that avenue too was now gone.

The SLL, though, did make some inroads into industrial organising. When Garth Frankland, later a Labour councillor in Leeds, joined in 1967 as a chemistry student in Bradford, he was impressed that they had working-class members – coal miners – with a serious command of Marxist ideas.[55] Most famously, in the British Leyland car plant at Cowley, on the outskirts of Oxford, the SLL recruited at least 40 new members, with Alan Thornett, a young shop steward, at their nucleus. Thornett and his SLL comrades in the factory gained a reputation for militancy and even violence; some of this was tabloid sensationalism, some of it allegedly well-founded.[56] In the early 1960s, the SLL had, at most, one thousand members, if even that.[57] Healy remained frustrated with the quality of the members:

> New members are not being assimilated through the educational and practical work, but are rather allowed to hang on the periphery. Some of these periphery elements are, of course, of petit-bourgeois origin and are, in fact, politically highly undesirable. They bring all kinds of personal problems with them and occupy the time of branch leaders with the most trivial questions.[58]

From 1964, the SLL began to work to establish its own daily newspaper for adult members (a long recurring concern of Healy's). Over a five-year period, funds were raised from party members as well as trade unionists and students. The SLL paper, *Workers Press*, was finally launched in September 1969, the first ever daily Trotskyist newspaper in the world and described, with due lack of humility, as 'the greatest achievement of the world Trotskyist movement. It is a living testimony to our political preparation for the leap in the development of the revolutionary vanguard.'[59] The American Trotskyist Tim Wohlforth remembers talking to Healy shortly after this and observed that Healy had not really figured out how to nationally distribute a daily paper nor how to sustain it financially. Harry Wicks, an early pioneer of British Trotskyism, was impressed by the creation of a daily paper but had fears about the publishing devouring all the party's time and energy.[60] Indeed, the paper required immense work by rank-and-file members, with sales of the paper often becoming an end in itself rather than a means for promoting socialism. Moreover, having something as unique as a daily Trotskyist newspaper became a key part of Healy's self-created mythology and his claims that he was building a mass revolutionary party; it probably sold six thousand copies a day, perhaps ten thousand at weekends (poor by the standards of mainstream tabloids, nonetheless impressive for a fringe political group).[61] Liz Leicester worked on *Workers Press* and says there was a close-knit community among the staff. She was paid £7 (approximately £100 adjusted to 2023) a week, with much of this often handed back to the party to cover unsold papers.[62]

The paper and the League maintained offices at 186a Clapham High Street in London, at a location that is now a Caffè Nero, and also later rented eight flats nearby at 155a Clapham High Street, where full-time party workers lived.[63] Party members also lived on Orlando Road a half mile away; in some cases, full-time security guards shared beds, with those working nights taking the bed during the day, and vice versa.[64] The party headquarters were unmarked and had no public signs.[65] As the SLL took a dominant role within the International Committee for a Fourth International, it made some connections to the Spartacist League, an especially doctrinaire American Trotskyist group, the Workers League, another American Trotskyist group with roots in both the SWP and the 1960s New Left, and briefly flirted with Lyndon LaRouche, an especially angry American Trotskyist who later went down a rabbit hole of extreme far-right conspiracy theories and antisemitism.[66] The Workers League would become the unofficial section of the ICFI in the US and 'a lighter version of the WRP' in terms of its internal regime, according to one former member.[67] When the French Trotskyists left to form their own international, the ICFI 'was now the personal possession of Gerry Healy'.[68] The SLL also developed an Irish branch at this time. Initially, the SLL's Irish presence was confined to a small number of almost exclusively working-class Protestants in Belfast. A small group in Dublin, the League for a Workers Republic, had attempted to start a dialogue with the SLL at the very end of the 1960s. Rather than engage with them in good faith, Healy and Slaughter convinced a handful of members to break away and form a rival (and presumably more controllable) group, the League for a Workers Vanguard.[69] This Irish League did not seem to develop a separate, non-British identity and generally showed up at international meetings, the American Trotskyist Tim Wohlforth recalls, 'to explain why, once again, everything had gone so poorly in their little group'.[70] Dermot Whelan, a member of the League for a Workers Republic, said the SLL only allowed an Irish section to emerge so as to generate an extra vote within the ICFI: more broadly, he said that the SLL always saw Irish politics as just existing in a minor role alongside British political interests, because of a refusal to see Ireland as a colonial space.[71] Conversely, the Australian section, also called the Socialist Labour League, had relatively better successes, practising entryism within the Labour Party and building a presence in suburban Brisbane as well a noticeable presence in Perth. John Troy, Labour MP for Fremantle, the port area of Perth, was an SLL member. They also had a serious youth movement. The Australians very much adopted Healy's stylings and had a similar reputation for violence.[72]

In theory, the SLL should have seen a bump in membership numbers during the social upheavals of the later 1960s. It started the decade as a recognised force on the British radical left. Even if Labour had a hegemonic status, with the Communists remaining small but noticeable, the SLL remained one of the few alternatives to reformism or Stalinism. As the sixties progressed, anti-Vietnam War protests became stronger and stronger, but the SLL refused to take part. A sympathetic interpretation is that they refused to offer uncritical support to the Stalinism of the Viet Cong. A blunter view is that they balked at a popular movement they could not control. This opposition to anti-war protests, which even led to SLL members handing out flyers encouraging people not to join marches, confused and alienated potential allies on the left.[73] Other Trotskyist organisations, whether Tony Cliff's International Socialists (later to become the Socialist Workers Party) or the

International Marxist Group in which Tariq Ali was active, more plugged into student movements, came to the fore instead and the SLL slipped in relative prominence.

A different development did aid the SLL, though. By the late 1960s, Healy started to attract a small but noticeable number of recruits from the film and entertainment industries. Alex Mitchell, an Australian-born journalist working at the *Times* and soon to switch to working for Healy's newspapers, began to attend a chain of debating parties held in private homes around London, and where Healy was making a strong impression on at least some of the attendees, who were too radical for Labour but disillusioned with Stalinism. The film directors Roy Battersby and Ken Loach, the film producer Kenith Trodd, Clive Goodwin, a film and literary agent, playwrights like Roger Smith, Tom Kempinski, Jim Allen and David Mercer, and the actor Corin Redgrave were all attendees at these private events.[74] According to Mitchell, Healy's hard-nosed Marxism always saw him win out at these debates. The feminist historian Sheila Rowbotham remembers these events very differently, recalling Healy's inability to deal with criticism or new ideas, particularly ideas drawing on feminism, anti-racism or psychoanalysis.[75] (An Australian Trotskyist who attended a private talk given by Healy in a suburban home in Canberra in the mid-1970s, said Healy seemed unable to answer basic questions about Trotskyism and 'I honestly thought he was a fucking idiot'.[76]) Attendees' own personal politics played an obvious role here: those less amenable to Healy's version of Marxism came away unimpressed, and those receptive to his clear-eyed (or simplistic, depending on one's view) politics were captivated. Stuart Hood, a well-regarded Scottish novelist and a bigwig at the BBC who also moved in these social circles, was simultaneously attracted by the clarity of the SLL's political analysis but turned off by their authoritarianism.[77]

In any case, these parties would become favoured events for Healy, not least because of the funds they brought in via donations from affluent attendees.[78] Moreover, they were a rich source of high-profile new recruits. One of these was Corin Redgrave, son of one of Britain's most prominent acting families. Redgrave had been recruited by his then lover – later his wife – the actor Kika

Markham, who had been an SLL member since the late 1960s.[79] Markham had also attempted to recruit the French *nouvelle vague* director François Truffaut, or at the least to secure a 'huge donation' from him; they instead had a brief affair, and it is unclear what Truffaut thought of Healy or the SLL.[80] Corin Redgrave had already been moving in leftist currents in London, but was apparently turned off by the 'soft-centred and flimsy' politics of hippies. He found the 'structure and discipline' of the SLL's ultra-orthodox Marxism far more attractive.[81] When Corin Redgrave joined the party, Healy allegedly told party members that he still needed to recruit Vanessa, Corin's sister and the wealthier of the two: 'It's the big one I'm interested in, the one with the money.'[82] Like Corin, Vanessa Redgrave was already a well-known sympathiser of left-wing causes, from Black Power to Irish Republicanism to opposition to the Vietnam War. Healy and Corin both began pressuring her to join.

By the early 1970s, all the dominant elements of Gerry Healy's politics were now in place and would intensify and worsen in the coming years:[83] an authoritarian leadership style; a doctrinaire belief that his group always held the correct Marxist line coupled with an opportunistic willingness to change their mind at a moment's notice; apocalyptic prophecies about a capitalist collapse that was always just around the corner; an oversized sense of his own importance; violence against his opponents as was meted out to Ernie Tate and Brian Behan; a desire to recruit celebrities and, if at all possible, grift them for money; and uncritical admiration for Third World leaders like Nasser in Egypt and Messali Hadj in Algeria (in the subsequent decade Healy would pursue actual connections with Muammar Gaddafi in Libya). And with the SLL now again relatively growing in numbers, Healy rebranded the party in July 1973 as the Workers Revolutionary Party. His ambitions were growing and the change in name was intended to denote a change in tactics; no longer an agitational grouping, it was now a true vanguard party in the Leninist mould, one that would supposedly lead the British working classes to victory in the looming terminal crisis of capitalism (and names clearly mattered – some other proposed names for the rebranded SLL were: Revolutionary Socialist Party, Socialist International Party, Marxist Workers

Party, Workers Unite Party, Workers' Rights Party and International Workers Party (UK)[84]). The WRP would be the apotheosis of Healy's political career even if, aside from a few celebrity members, it remained a small force, with no more than three thousand members scattered across the United Kingdom. The next chapter is a brief study of one of their most famous members.

4

The One with the Money

Vanessa Redgrave seems to have first met Gerry Healy at the end of the 1960s, when he was still operating via the Socialist Labour League. By this time, Redgrave was already not only a renowned actor and the daughter of a theatre legend but also a well-known leftist.[1] She may initially have had negative views of Healy's small group. In a temporarily effective injunction, the Trinidadian Marxist C.L.R. James had apparently warned her: 'Don't go near that outfit. It is run by Gerry Healy; he's a Stalinist.'[2] Redgrave's brother, Corin, an actor but one who never achieved his sister's renown, pressured her to join. Problems in her relationship with the actor Timothy Dalton may have contributed to a sense of vulnerability that she allayed by joining Healy.[3] Tim Wohlforth recalls her joining as follows:

> One day early in 1973 Vanessa Redgrave walked into the offices of the Socialist Labour League in Clapham, accompanied by her brother, Corin. She sat down in Healy's office and Healy launched into a long explanation of his plans to transform the SLL into a new party, the Workers Revolutionary Party (WRP). At the end of the talk Vanessa asked to join the group. Healy turned to Corin and said: 'So now Mary, Queen of Scots, has joined us.'[4]

The involvement of the Redgraves, and the growing presence of theatre people within the group, led to the joke that the WRP stood for West End Revolutionary Party.[5] Vanessa Redgrave's critical, but not unsympathetic biographer, Dan Callahan, argues that Healy was drawn in by the star appeal of having her join his party.[6] When Corin was first recruited, Healy was alleged to have exclaimed 'It's the big one I'm interested in, the one with the money,'[7] in reference to Vanessa. She would become Healy's 'most prized recruit' and an indefatigable 'raiser of funds', her presence serving to boost attendance at party meetings.[8] One member of the WRP says both Vanessa and Corin were used by the party as props; 'in a sense, they were victims of Healy'.[9]

Healy certainly had a recurring interest in recruiting celebrities to his party; at various points, the directors Derek Jarman and Ken Loach, Chris Hughton, a left-back for Tottenham Hotspur FC, and Rynagh O'Grady, an Irish actor who later had a recurring role as one half of a violent shopkeeper couple in the *Father Ted* sitcom, all moved in SLL/WRP/Marxist Party orbits.[10] The legendary comedian Spike Milligan once appeared at a concert organised by the SLL in December 1972.[11] In the sixties, Healy had courted the playwright David Mercer, who had written the script for Karel Reisz's film *Morgan: A Suitable Case for Treatment*, the film that launched Vanessa Redgrave's career.[12] The actor Frances de la Tour, best known for her role as Miss Jones in the BBC's *Rising Damp* was a regular at WRP events.[13] Melvyn Bragg, then an up-and-coming broadcaster, later a major presenter at the BBC, contributed to a 1973 WRP 'Anti-Tory Rally and Pageant of History'.[14] The film director Roy Battersby was a deeply committed member; his step-daughter, Kate Beckinsale, sold copies of *News Line* as a child.[15] Celebrity members were generally assigned to the Outer London branch of the WRP and were not always expected to carry out the same kinds of activities as regular members.[16]

Healy may have been interested in such celebrities because, with no background in the labour movement, these actors and sport stars were won over by him personally and thus would be more likely to remain loyal and uncritical of his leadership. Tim Wohlforth also suggests that such recruits – generally of a privileged *haute-bourgeoisie* background – could be made to pay up a 'guilt gelt' and enjoyed the feeling of being part of a radical bohemian set. Celebrity members, especially those who came from wealthy backgrounds, had a tendency to throw themselves fully into party work 'because none of us wanted to face the accusation that we were shirkers, dilettantes, wankers or "subjective idealists"'.[17] Healy used their middle-class guilt against them. He may also have welcomed these new celebrity recruits as compensation for the more genuinely proletarian members who had left with Alan Thornett in

1974.[18] (The WRP's American sister party, the Workers League, attempted to replicate all this but their only brief celebrity catch was the folk singer Dave Van Ronk.[19]) Various accusations soon swirled around Vanessa Redgrave, that this was just another acting role for her or that she was searching for a strong male figure to replace her own father; these, it must be said, are unfounded speculations and fairly sexist to boot (such accusations generally not being made about her brother).

Celebrity members received special treatment and were generally flattered; Deirdre Redgrave recalled her husband, Corin, being made to feel that he had a crucial role to play in the development of Britain's socialist future.[20] Vanessa Redgrave received hours of personalised training in Marxist philosophy from Healy.[21] Both Redgraves as well as the journalist Alex Mitchell were fast-tracked into leadership positions in the party's Central and Political Committees, despite their lack of prior political experience.[22] As Mitchell himself openly admitted: 'My path was made easier than almost everyone else's because I was one of Healy's favourites.'[23] Rank-and-file members never received such careful and attentive support. After a party meeting when Vanessa Redgrave had been upstaged by the editor of *Keep Left*, who seemed better equipped to answer questions, Healy ordered the editor to take a back seat rather than offend Redgrave's ego.[24] Celebrity recruits were generally also spared Healy's violent tempers. Redgrave never directly saw Healy's negative qualities. She would later call him 'the best political orator I have ever heard' and assessed his skills as follows:

> If it is said that Marxism is the conscious expression of the unconscious historical process, such a union could be observed for sure on those occasions when Gerry spoke to an audience of workers. Without rhetorical tricks or flourishes, he would use the full range of his political vocabulary, expressing complex ideas in a way that everyone understood. I never saw an audience who did not respond.

Her 1994 autobiography describes Healy in overly rosy terms, focusing on his supposed abilities to preternaturally understand workers.[25] For Redgrave, Healy was the 'foremost Trotskyist of his time'.[26]

Figure 1   Vanessa Redgrave standing as a WRP candidate in the general election demands total nationalisation and workers control during a campaign speech in Newham, North East London, 24 February 1974. (Photo by Bill Rowntree/Mirrorpix/Getty Images)

When the WRP was formed in 1973, Redgrave dutifully joined and soon become highly active. She often voluntarily involved herself in the selling of their newspaper in central London, which party members did every morning outside Rathbone Post Office, as well as at colleges, pubs and hospitals.[27] Healy probably preferred that his celebrity recruits do this kind of work – over which he had a strong control – rather than allowing them to produce agitprop socialist theatre, where he would be out of his depth.[28]

In one anecdote that she later recounted, Redgrave described an incident where, sitting on the side of the bed of her daughter, Natasha Richardson, she 'appealed to me to spend more time with her. I tried to explain that our political struggle was for her future, and that of all the children of her generation. She looked at me with a serious, sweet smile. "But I need you *now*. I won't need you so much then."'[29] In general, Vanessa Redgrave gave all the signs of being a loyal and hard-working party member, adopting a kind of tough-nosed Bolshevik persona that also allowed her to excuse the party's violent internal culture as part of that communist toughness.[30]

Redgrave gave paid lectures on Marxism during visits to Los Angeles, donating her fees to the WRP's college in Derbyshire. When that school opened, she would spend at least two weeks studying there every year, until 1985. She also periodically taught her own classes there.[31] Most prominently, she ran for parliament on a WRP ticket in the solidly working-class Newham North East constituency in east London in two elections in February and October 1974; her campaign team mainly used the election to warn of a looming military dictatorship in Britain and to call for a workers' militia that would replace the police and army. She received only 760 votes in February, dropping to 572 later in the year. Running as a candidate in Manchester at the end of the decade, she got an even more dismal 394 votes.[32] Several party members who worked on her campaigns remember her painful inability to connect with voters or to understand the actual concerns of real-life working-class people.[33]

Redgrave also actively worked to raise funds from celebrities for the party; at one point, an elderly Groucho Marx promised to send funds but seemed to later think better of this and no money was forthcoming. When she pressured Andy Warhol in 1976, he insultingly offered her 20 cents.[34] In the early years, Redgrave's entanglement with the WRP did little to help her public status but was probably little more than a minor embarrassment. That changed in 1975 with the police raid on the party's Derbyshire college. Redgrave immediately requested that other members of the acting community come to the defence of the WRP. One prominent voice, Laurence Olivier (who had played a version of Healy two years earlier in *The Party*), wrote to the *Times* calling for the defeat of 'the extremists'[35] of the WRP. Nonetheless, the WRP was able to bring out 6,000 supporters at a rally in London that December, denouncing the raid. With the WRP already given over to paranoia and a culture of distrusting anyone outside of the party, the belief took hold that a mole within the party had tipped off the police. This paranoia soon fixated on Irene Gorst, a minor actress and Corin Redgrave's mistress. In an article published in the *Observer* on the eve of the raid, Gorst claimed that she was held against her will for six hours at the college and interrogated violently by the Redgrave siblings, the sort of incident that one-time

Healyite Tim Wohlforth would later call 'a typical kind of thing'[36] in the WRP. Ill-advisedly, Vanessa Redgrave proceeded to sue the *Observer* for libel.

The trial was eventually held in 1978. Six WRP members – Gerry Healy, Corin and Vanessa Redgrave, Roy Battersby, Roger Smith and the actor Michael Harrigan – were named as the plaintiffs. The party, incongruously, had elite legal representation, including Michael Rubinstein of Rubinstein Callingham Nash, copyright, contract and defamation specialists who had previously represented Penguin Books during the *Lady Chatterley* obscenity trial.[37] Witnesses called by Redgrave's legal team vainly sought to downplay any radicalism whatsoever on the part of the WRP, in an attempt to prove that the party was a respectable and non-subversive organisation.[38] The *Observer*'s legal team punctured this by aggressively going on the attack against the WRP and its politics. According to one eye-witness account, when Healy heard of the thickness of the *Observer*'s lawyers' file on him, he hurriedly arranged for his doctor to give him a medical clearance to say he was not fit to take the stand.[39]

The libel case lasted 14 days and ended with the jury determining, almost sarcastically, that while the *Observer* article was libellous, the WRP had no fit reputation to protect. The judge imposed the full costs of the proceedings – about £70,000 (just shy of £325,000 if adjusted to inflation for 2024) – on the plaintiffs.[40] Both Vanessa and Corin Redgrave presented this as a victory, since the jury had found that the original article was partially defamatory and untrue, but that claim did little to convince anyone.[41] The bill for all this appears to have been paid with a Libel Fund raised from willing party members.[42]

Where this incident should, perhaps, have prompted introspection and even self-criticism, Redgrave instead continued her commitment to the WRP. When she went to north-western Canada in late 1978 to film *Bear Island*, an Arctic-themed spy thriller with Donald Sutherland and Lloyd Bridges, Healy accompanied her as part of her entourage.[43] By 1979, Redgrave was attempting to sell the WRP's newspaper on the set of John Schlesinger's war movie *Yanks*. Redgrave certainly had the strength of her convictions; nominated for an Oscar in 1978 for her role in the Holocaust period drama, *Julia*, her past history of pro-Palestinian activism was seized on by Meir Kahane and his far-right Jewish Defense League, who staged protests against her (Alex Mitchell has claimed Redgrave was actually in Tripoli selling the broadcast rights for *The Palestinian* to Libyan TV when she heard she had been nominated[44]). In her acceptance speech, Redgrave commended those who refused to be cowed by 'a bunch of Zionist hoodlums', a reasonable and quite accurate description of Kahane and the JDL which nonetheless was jeered by the Hollywood crowd. Kahane's irritation at the tenor of her response was the direct catalyst for his writing of *Listen World, Listen Jew*, the most developed statement of his ideology but also his most anti-democratic.[45]

But Redgrave's doggedness could also slip into dogmatism. When credible accusations of sexual violence finally surfaced against Healy in 1985, she denied their seriousness. At a particularly explosive meeting of the WRP's Political Committee on 1 July 1985, when a letter from Aileen Jennings that painfully recounted Healy's acts of sexual assault was read out, Redgrave was, allegedly, 'screeching at the top of her voice' that this was an act analogous to the Black Hundreds, the hired thugs of Tsarist Russia.[46] As she bluntly claims in her own autobiography: 'The technique of the frame-up is by now all too familiar. The FBI, for instance, bugged Martin Luther King, Jr., in their efforts to build up a dossier of scandal and "immorality" against him.'[47] Redgrave did not directly compare Healy and MLK, but that was the obvious inference.

Both Redgraves became charter members of Healy's new grouping, the Marxist Party, in 1987; Corin at one point served as General Secretary of this tiny party.[48] As Tim Wohlforth commented on Vanessa's unwavering loyalty:

> she was still like an acolyte... She would bring fish over and cook it for him. You know, this world-class star cooking this smelly fish for this ugly guy. He had the kind of charisma that a really good guru or cult leader has. He would make it very personal. He knew how to flatter and he knew how to manipulate people and how to control their emotions, their psyche, and their thinking. Vanessa was searching for something, and he provided it for her. They had this very simple way of explaining

everything. Anything that came up, they would just say it was all a matter of the CIA.[49]

Toward the end of his life, Healy gave Redgrave power of attorney over his possessions and named the two Redgrave siblings as the executors of his will. Healy in turn was one of the directors of 'Vanessa Redgrave Enterprises Ltd', along with Redgrave herself and the actor and producer Thelma Holt, also a WRP fellow traveller.[50] In November 1987, on the seventieth anniversary of the Russian Revolution, Vanessa Redgrave Enterprises Ltd produced a play in collaboration with the Marxist Party 'October 1917 – the world socialist revolution – then and now'. The play garnered a sarcastic commentary from the Workers International League, one of the groups that emerged out of the post-1985 schism in the WRP: 'May we suggest that in future the Marxist Party stages a production of *King Lear* – the story of a demented old man cast out of his kingdom by his once sycophantic admirers and deserted by all except a blind man, a fool and the ever-faithful Cordelia.'[51]

When Healy died on 14 December 1989, Redgrave wrote his obituary for *The Guardian*. Her posthumous view, even with the opprobrium that engulfed him, remained positive, even adulatory: 'The main point was that Gerry never said or did anything for personal advantage. His life was a single piece of steel, and that was why he was feared and hated by the state and by political opportunists.'[52] (The 'single piece of steel' line was taken from Lenin; this was his label for Marxist philosophy in *Materialism and Empirio-Criticism*.)

In a long interview with Lynn Barber in 2006, in the *Observer* of all places, Barber asked Redgrave about Healy; she said she regretted nothing about her involvement with the WRP and then refused to discuss the issue any further.[53] As Redgrave's biographer has commented, 'Healy was obviously a touchy subject. Even at this late date, she could still never admit to herself or anyone else just how bad he had been.'[54] Into the 2010s, Redgrave remained unrepentant about her time in the WRP:

The period of time in which I was in that political party, which had followed being in the Labour party, which I had done a lot of campaigning for in the sixties, what interested me in this particular party, the Workers Revolutionary Party, was the enormous amount of study... Study of history and philosophy. Although I've never asked enough questions, I've had to learn to ask questions. It began to feed questions that were teeming in my brain, and I'd never found anybody who could answer them.[55]

There was clearly something intellectual that attracted Redgrave to Healy; her sister-in-law Deirdre Redgrave claimed Vanessa had once told her: 'I have always loved fanatics... the only truly genuine people in the world.' Deirdre Redgrave claims Corin was attracted to the WRP's 'puritan and disciplined structure'.[56] And it is quite possible that his sister gravitated to the same.

5

I am the Party, 1973–1984

Shortly before his murder, Leon Trotsky had predicted that the end of the Second World War would lead to a revolutionary upsurge just like the end of the previous world war. When that failed to come to pass, the more orthodox Trotskyists, rather than reassessing the old man's predictions, simply assumed the revolution was postponed but still on the near horizon. By the end of the 1960s, the revolution looked to have finally arrived. In 1968, students took to the streets in Paris and soon made alliances with workers, the Prague Spring sought 'Socialism with a Human Face', and anti-war protestors outside the Democratic National Convention in Chicago met a violent police reaction. After the disaster of the Six Day War, Palestinians stopped looking to various Arab regimes for assistance and instead turned to their own leadership in the Palestine Liberation Organisation (PLO), which espoused an assertive and revolutionary nationalism. In the United Kingdom, there were large-scale anti-Vietnam War protests and in August 1969 British troops entered Northern Ireland, creating a sense that the same international ferment had arrived. The number of strikes in Britain had been rising since the mid-1960s, which would only increase into the next decade. 1972 was 'a glorious summer' for labour militancy: 23.9 million days were lost to strike action, up from five million in 1968.[1] What Max Elbaum observed as he looked back at the American New Left is also true of the British radical left: 'shocking as it seems today – winning power seemed like it might just be possible'.[2] All the major British Trotskyist groups benefitted from this unrest and saw their membership numbers increase accordingly; the historian of Trotskyism John Kelly rightly sees the 20 or so years after 1968 as the Golden Age of British Trotskyism, with total membership numbers rising from 2,000 to perhaps as high as 20,000 at the most generous estimate, eclipsing the size of the CPGB (though with members divided across multiple parties rather than unified in a single, disciplined organisation).[3] Healy's decision to recast the SLL as the Workers Revolutionary Party in 1973 was an attempt to ride this wave, even if the SLL had been talking of building a mass party as early as 1965.[4]

In hindsight, if not at the time, it is easy to see how quickly the revolutionary upsurge of 1968 was soon defeated in counter-revolution; the May '68 protests in Paris fizzled out and by June, Charles de Gaulle had handily won a snap re-election. The Prague Spring was crushed by a Soviet invasion. By January 1969, Richard Nixon was inaugurated; when he ran for re-election in 1972, he cruised 49 states and 520 of 537 electoral college votes. By 1973, rather than being checked by global protests, the Vietnam War had expanded to round-the-clock bombardment of Laos and Cambodia. Palestinian revolutionaries clashed with the Jordanian government and were massacred in the thousands during 'Black September' 1970; the rest of the decade in the Middle East was defined more by the morass of the Lebanese Civil War and the seemingly inexorable rise of a reactionary political Islam, than by radical left insurgency. British troops in Northern Ireland were sucked into the ethno-religious complexities of the Troubles, possibly up to and including collusion with Protestant paramilitary forces.[5]

Those politicised by '68 did not disappear in the 1970s, but the undeniable lurch away from what, in Trotskyism, is called a 'pre-revolutionary scenario' prompted debate and soul-searching. Some of the '68 generation moved to the right. Groups like the Red Army Faction (*Rote Armee Fraktion*) in Germany and the Weatherman Underground in the US turned to terrorism, at best hoping that violence would reawaken the masses, at worst lashing out in inchoate anger at those same popular masses who were failing to push the Revolution forward.[6] Those with academic or political ambitions burrowed into existing institutions from where they could hopefully ride out the counter-revolution while also promoting more radical politics. Others embraced 'new' movements like gay liberation, women's rights or environmentalism. The WRP offered another choice: rather than capitulating to the right, working within the status quo or pivoting to identity politics, they offered a model of rigid orthodoxy. Rather than self-defeating terrorism, they offered a different kind of stiff-necked militancy.[7] As party member Mike Richardson recalls, the WRP was a party that 'appeared utterly convinced they had the answer to how to bring down the capitalist state'.[8] And like British Trotskyists more generally, even with the downturn after 1968, they retained their belief that revolutionary change was only a matter of time.[9] As the WRP declared, one year into its existence: 'Actuality of revolution is here and now'.[10] This dogmatism – and the constant insistence that the revolution was just over the horizon – was never going to appeal to everyone, but it would appeal to a specific set of people still searching for the certainties and lost revolution of '68.[11] With the sense that there was a revolution brewing, party members were not too invested in internal party democracy because of an assumption that a centralised Leninist party was the necessary tool; they were a rigidly hierarchical vanguard party based on the assumption that that was what the Bolsheviks had been and that is what it took to win. This would have clear implications for the internal regime of the WRP.

While there was always going to be a rough continuity from the SLL, the WRP's dogmatism was also the product of something new: a dissipating revolutionary sentiment. They formed as revolution was still in the air, even as they were too late to help secure it. A hope for victory and a background hum of despair would always characterise the WRP. For broader sections of British society, their rhetoric did more harm than good. As one prominent member would later recognise, during the oil crisis of 1973, 'Healy was predicting imminent collapse of the capitalist system' and talking of a looming military coup or a Tory dictatorship: 'Two months later we had a Labour government'.[12] The mismatch between WRP rhetoric and British political realities was a clear liability. Moreover, whatever lingered of the post-1968 ferment, the election of a new Labour government in October 1974 created a 'problem solved' mood among politicised workers and WRP membership ranks shrank after a more successful expansion in their first year.[13]

Two of Gerry Healy's most loyal supporters said that the Workers Revolutionary Party was 'Britain's biggest Marxist organization'.[14] In the most obvious sense, this was an absurd claim; it was a small grouping, always smaller than the Communists and soon eclipsed by the Socialist Workers Party and the Militant Tendency within the Labour Party. The claim was 'true', though, in the sense that Healy's adherents saw themselves as the only 'real' Marxists, everyone else being milquetoast reformists, opportunists or class traitors. The WRP was the *biggest* Marxist party (and the *smallest*) because it was *the only* Marxist party. At the WRP's founding in July 1973, the party's 'Perspectives' described how the Socialist Labour League had become inadequate and must now be converted into a vanguard force that could provide workers and youth with a suitable training in Marxism. The hope was that as the SLL became the WRP, 'hundreds of new members' would join and transform the old SLL into 'a real party', a tacit admission that the SLL had never been such a thing. Healy said that WRP members needed to stop 'arguing among ourselves',[15] which he presumably felt was a defining trait in the defunct SLL notwithstanding the organisation's relative lack of internal debate. How it would achieve all this was never really publicly explained.[16] The goals of the WRP were neatly summarised on the party membership card:

> The aim of the Party is to prepare and mobilize the working class for the overthrow of capitalism, the establishment of working class power and the building of a socialist society. This Party bases its policy on the theory of Marxism as developed by Lenin and Trotsky, the decisions of the first four Congresses of the Communist International and the Founding Programme of the Fourth International (1938). This Party is the British Section of the Fourth International affiliated to the International Committee and fighting to build the Fourth International.[17]

In November 1973, the WRP held its first conference. Healy delivered the main report at the conference, reiterating the need for revolutionary, correctly Marxist leadership. Healy's conception had a certain Cartesian ring to it; the party was the brain of the working class, leading it but always separate from it. Inevitably, schisms soon started. The rigidly hierarchical structure of the WRP, harsh even by the usual standards of Leninist 'democratic centralism', was a recurring problem for many members. Mike Banda and

Geoff Pilling, two leading personalities within the WRP, dismissed the concerns of 'these middle-class Philistines'. Healy's partisans dismissed the criticisms of the party's non-democratic culture as 'a middle-class obsession with "individual rights"', naming Mark Jenkins and Robin Blick, 'disgruntled ex-members of the SLL' who were now moving in the orbits of the Labour Party, as leading culprits. Blick had been a member of the SLL for a decade, from 1961 to 1971 and worked on the party paper as well as writing a 440-page denunciation of the CPGB – hardly a light commitment.[18] When the WRP eventually imploded after 1985, Blick had little good to say about 'the Gerry-built internal regime' that he likened to 'a religious cult rather than a secular political movement', or perhaps it was a prison or insane asylum, since he spoke of 'former WRP inmates' rather than ex-members.[19] Blick (like Jenkins) had been physically assaulted by Healy and his supporters, so his anger was understandable.[20] Two Healy supporters later claimed Jenkins and Blick had been 'recruited as British agents' of the *Organisation Communiste Internationaliste* (OCI), the French Trotskyist group that had split from the Healy-allied International Committee for a Fourth International. The language here ('recruited... agents'), reminiscent of spy novels and shadowy espionage, gestures towards a paranoia that soon defined the WRP.[21]

When party member Tony Richardson questioned Healy, he was first forced to admit, on threat of expulsion, that he had been wrong to do so. He was then assaulted by Healy at the WRP's offices in Clapham in London.[22] Healy is credibly alleged to have once broken a chair over the back of his secretary, Aileen Jennings, an action that was hushed up at the time. Tim Wohlforth recalled that violence and intimidation were common features at both WRP summer camps in the UK and their international meetings in Montreal: 'Late at night, when everybody was bleary-eyed, Healy would have people taken into his tent and, in at least two cases I know of, he would hold these people and have them beaten up.'[23] Once Deirdre Redgrave made it clear that she would not follow her husband, Corin, into the ranks of the party, she faced a 'constant verbal onslaught' from 'openly aggressive'[24] members. Their marriage broke down soon after this, an event she evocatively calls 'Fleeing the Cage'.[25] Andy Blunden's accurate assessment is that the WRP's tough image and reputation for violence belies the fact that violence was far more commonly used internally, against party members, than externally against perceived enemies.[26] And as with the SLL, violence against party members existed in an intimate relationship with the expectation that party members should go to extreme lengths in their work for the WRP. Both were forms of abuse. When Cliff Slaughter took time away from party work to devote to his sick wife, he was reprimanded (and had to make a contrite apology) for both his 'petty bourgeois character' as well as for not leaving his wife for the party.[27] Mike Banda regularly worked all night at the party's printing works, falling asleep on the rubber conveyor belt at the end of the printing press.[28] When Andy Blunden joined the WRP, the party became his life. He says he worked 364 days a year (taking only Christmas Day off). 'I hardly slept for a decade', though he retained a regular day job rather than working full-time. Becoming a full-timer 'was a terrible thing to happen to you' because of the unfulfillable demands made of staff members and the shame they were treated with for not fulfilling those demands.[29] The party remained small and membership turnover was high, partly because of the intense volunteering work that was expected of recruits. Potential members often had to go through a probationary period before being accepted into party ranks.[30] Other members were accepted almost without a second thought.

A good example of the latter is Philip Edwards, an unemployed recent university graduate who joined at the very end of the 1970s, having already become hostile to Thatcher but sceptical of Labour and attracted to revolutionary politics. Edwards had been at a reggae night at the All Nations Club in Hackney in east London; he and his then partner were the only two white people there until two WRP members came in selling papers. They recruited him then and there. Within two weeks he was a branch secretary in Hackney, delivering copies of the party paper for about three hours every day, at picket lines, in pubs, at street corners. The fundraising quotas given to branches were impossible to meet. If a party member didn't meet the quota, they would be accused of being infected by bourgeois ideology. A music fan, Edwards sold his guitar, his only major possession, to provide funds to the party. He would donate portions of his unemployment benefits 'and then I donated my rent'. After being kicked out of his flat, he ended up sleeping on the floor of a party sympathiser's house. The pace of work exhausted him, he had a breakdown after this and left the WRP: 'That party destroyed so many people'.[31]

Norman Harding, who also worked in the party's printing operations, said that a clear 'class division' soon emerged within the party, with rank-and-file members expected to devote themselves fully to tedious but necessary work while the growing number of celebrity members were treated far more respectfully.[32] From early on, the WRP had about 80 full-time party employees, a hugely inflated staff for so small a group (though the existence of a vast nationwide network of dedicated activists was key to how the WRP presented itself to the world). Their wages, not extravagant to begin with, regularly went unpaid. London-based party employees lived at the eight apartments rented in Clapham in London. While Healy and Betty Russell were never formally divorced, their marriage did break down in the early 1970s as he devoted more and more time to the WRP.[33] Healy began to live permanently in the party's flats in or around 1974, though his living quarters were more spacious and with a greater privacy than that afforded to others.[34] There is also some evidence that party workers lacked freedom of movement, being required to register their whereabouts regularly with party leadership (with Healy most especially).[35] And in a 'daily ritual', Healy opened all letters delivered to the party's London offices.[36] The party was also centrally and vertically organised; rather than regional branches being able to freely communicate with each other, interactions were mostly routed (and controlled) through London. This had the effect of preventing local innovations in the party.[37] The WRP was, in theory, overseen by its central committee, but that body could have anywhere between 20 and 50 members at a time; the smaller political committee, six to ten members, was far more decisive.[38]

Alex Mitchell observed quite frankly that part of the training of WRP members led them to be 'unusually hard on defectors from the struggle',[39] though of course it remained Healy's prerogative to define who was or was not a 'defector'. Some 200 party members – a massive amount relative to the party's size – were purged in the early years of the WRP. A hundred members alone were lost when Alan Thornett, a well-known trade unionist in Oxford's British Leyland car factories, publicly disagreed with party leadership: 'the whole party machinery was mobilised to counter his views'.[40] Garth Frankland, a supporter of Thornett's, says that Healy had developed a tendency to switch back and forth from moderate, populist politics to ultra-leftism and in the course of 1974, he had become convinced there was a looming right-wing coup and began to push party members towards an ultra-leftist politics. Because of his status as a trade unionist, Thornett was able to resist this, angering Healy.[41] In effect, Thornett was trying to redirect the WRP away from its dogmatic insistence that a revolution was imminent. One rank-and-file member present for the expulsion of Thornett said that party members were coached as to how they should act when Thornett and his supporters contested their expulsion. Supporters were effectively instructed not to listen to any of Thornett's arguments since they already 'knew' Thornett had become an enemy of the party. Healy knew how to use party loyalty to discredit his opponents.[42]

The purges of people like Thornett functioned as a blunt instrument for uniting those who stayed behind: at one WRP meeting, a vote was taken on expelling disruptive members. All those who voted, voted to expel, but a handful abstained. Healy then demanded a second vote and insisted that *all* must vote and vote to expel. 'Later at a party rally Healy electrified the audience when he declared war on anti-party cliques, delivering the memorable line, "We will split, split and split again!", with his tiny fists waving in the air.'[43]

The WRP's American sister party, the Worker's League, expelled its own leader, Tim Wohlforth, in 1974 when it was discovered that his partner, Nancy Fields, had an estranged uncle who worked for the CIA. Wohlforth's account of this is genuinely disturbing (and is confirmed by Workers League member Alex Steiner, who was also present): Healy's accusations were produced during a stage-managed move against Wohlforth at an international party meeting in Montreal. Allowing tension to build over several days, Healy finally dropped his bombshell during a marathon all-night meeting, when attendees were bleary-eyed and exhausted and more liable to go along with Healy's actions.[44] The CIA connection, though, was a ruse; Wohlforth had observed at an international meeting a few months earlier, in April 1974, that Healy's purging of Thornett had cut off devoted and skilled party members and thus hurt the WRP at a critical point of early development.[45] Healy did not tolerate such criticism. His willingness to use violence against his erstwhile comrades, already a well-established trait, came more to the surface within the WRP.[46]

Vincent Doherty, who joined the SLL in September 1973 and then stayed active in the early years of the WRP, says the 'internal regime' of the new party 'was frightening', and violence was a widespread phenomenon across much of the leadership (he names Mike Banda, among others, in this regard). Doherty also says there was a casual acceptance of extreme verbal abuse within the party. Prior to joining the WRP, Doherty had been active in Official Sinn Féin in Northern Ireland: 'I came from the Republican movement, so I knew what political discipline involved. I'm not a shrinking violet', but this violence was something of a different degree.[47] Garth Frankland, active in the Leeds branch of the party, was always 'a bit frightened' of Healy, but that Healy could also be 'extremely kind' to new members, the inference being that these were intentional choices.[48]

Alex Steiner, a member of the Workers League, recalls attending WRP Central Committee meetings regularly while visiting from the US and witnessing the targeted abuse of members. The abuse was called 'taking someone up' and involved all those present directly denouncing the person. Cliff Slaughter was a regular target. The denunciation would continue until the targeted person admitted that they had become infected by bourgeois ideology and promised to rectify their actions in the future. Steiner says all members willingly took part.[49] Geoff Barr, a member of the WRP in Exeter, says Healy would intentionally divide the party by using intellectuals to criticise workers for being ignorant and would use workers to criticise academics for being too distantly intellectual.[50]

WRP paranoia about infiltration by state security services simultaneously reflected a genuine concern within all far-left parties in the Cold War era as well as being a useful cudgel for suppressing dissent and purging internal critics. The Australian SLL adopted the tactic of accusing any enemies of being CIA or FBI agents.[51] When the American SWP praised Wohlforth for his break with the Healyites, the ICFI staged an 'investigation' that concluded that the SWP had shadowy connections to the FBI and that their leaders had been complicit in the murder of Trotsky.[52] Truthfully, the SWP *was* monitored and infiltrated by the FBI, as were almost all large leftist groups in the US. Notwithstanding that, the absurdity of the bigger accusation – practically an allegation of deicide in Trotsky-ism – was such that it prompted a rare moment of Trotskyist unity, with various factions coming together to a large joint meeting in London on 14 January 1977 to publicly defend Healy's targets, Joseph Hansen and George Novack, two of the smartest leaders in American Trotskyism.[53] The WRP were 'unanimously con-demned' by the left for their allegations about Trotsky's murder.[54] The condemners included Vsevolod Volkov, Trotsky's grandson, and Marguerite Bonnet, the executor of his estate; in turn, Healy and his supporters also accused them of being part of the conspir-acy.[55] These accusations also seemed to have hurt the standing of the Workers League in the United States.[56] Wohlforth later named the tactics at work here:

> We are not dealing here simply with a matter of paranoia or 'crazies'. There is a method to the madness of Healy, for surely it is madness. Healy has developed a method of political functioning consistent with his idealist philosophical method and sectarian policies, whose aim is to perpetuate himself and a small group of cult followers at the expense of the interests of the working class and of the principles and traditions of Trotskyism.[57]

There was a 'war footing' in the WRP from the very start, and the party acted as if it would soon be made an illegal organisa-tion.[58] Claims that shadowy global security forces were working against the WRP provided a convenient explanation for the party's failures as well as creating a sense of internal cohesion that cut off WRP members from the outside world in general and from more critical leftist voices in particular.[59] A paranoid atmosphere was often intentionally created at party summer camps, creating an odd sense of 'us versus them' in these temporary spaces.[60] At an ICFI summer camp in Montreal in 1973, there was an evening screening of *Night of the Living Dead*, wilfully adding to the febrile atmosphere. The next day two listening devices were discovered, allegedly placed there by Canadian intelligence.[61]

On the other hand, Healy did seem to believe in these conspiracies and had a fear of officialdom. Clare Cowen says that 'Even traffic wardens terrified him, apparently'.[62] The party acquired expensive assets as a result of this paranoia: the car Healy travelled in had its own two-way radio (a luxury in a time before mobile phones) and a telescopic aerial was built on the roof of the WRP's offices for this radio; a German party member was brought in as 'head of security' to operate these various pieces of security tech.[63] In one incident, Healy had become convinced that an extractor fan in his apartment contained a 'directional microphone for spying on him' and discussed this with the head of security, who of course found nothing.[64] Tariq Ali recalls a rumour that Healy had once held a party political committee meeting under a table to avoid being spied on.[65]

In 1975, the WRP acquired its own 'College of Marxist Education', in an incongruously repurposed country home on two acres of land near Parwich, a small village in the Peak District in Derbyshire; this was a prime piece of real estate that would be enviously eyed up during the WRP's split a decade later. The party would later insist that all new members attend a one-week course in Marxist theory at the college, though it is doubtful if all did.[66] One comrade remembered the college negatively: 'Something about the place gave me the creeps'.[67] Mike Richardson, active in the WRP's Bristol branch, likewise remembers it as a 'foreboding' place. The college was also inhabited by 'a small resident colony of bats', which added to the uncomfortable 'sense of remoteness'.[68] As with the summer camps, a paranoid atmosphere pervaded the college. Those attending the college would have their luggage checked for weapons, recording devices or cameras or for phone numbers that spies might be using to call their higher-ups.[69] There was a telephone to make outside calls but students had to get permission to use it. Comrades attending the college were not allowed leave without permission and if they had contact with neighbours, they were expected to report this. There were patrols every 15 minutes between midnight and 7 a.m. to enforce this security. Those at the college were to only use first names, not last names, to avoid anyone being identifiable.[70] Andy Blunden describes the college as miserable and even scary; it had a repressive and paranoid atmosphere. People attending various philosophy classes there were afraid of saying the wrong thing and being that day's target for attack.[71] Another WRP member says if someone like Geoff Pilling, an academic economist, was the lecturer, it could be useful, but the atmosphere would change for the worse when Healy would show up.[72] Unsurprisingly, take up of classes was slow; to cover costs, the college needed 35 students a week to attend and seems to have not secured that.

Figure 2   White Meadow House, Derbyshire, acquired by the WRP in 1975

The disused house was purchased for £23,000 in 1975, to be used by both the WRP and the ICFI, even if its ownership officially stayed in Corin Redgrave's name.[73] Locals were told it was being used as a drama centre, in keeping with Redgrave's background.[74] Extensive refurbishments to the cost of £38,000 (the equivalent of about £280,000 in 2024) were carried out, with WRP members – carpenters, plasterers, plumbers, electricians and painters – providing free labour. Funds were raised from British and American sympathisers to pay for all this. When it was finished in the summer of 1975, it could accommodate 60 students at a time, in gender-segregated dormitories. There was also 'a main lecture room, study room, kitchen and dining room, an upstairs apartment for the college director and his family, and a flat for Healy'.[75]

The college even featured a custom-built playroom for children.[76] The first director of the college was the film producer Roy Battersby, who lived at the house from 1975 to 1978, along with his partner Liz Leicester and their two children. Battersby was the Central Committee's point person there, initially in charge of renovations and then in charge of day-to-day running of the college and of events held there.[77]

Then, on the night of Saturday 27 September 1975, just over a month after the refurbishments were completed, the British police raided the college, supposedly acting on a tip-off that arms were being stockpiled there. An ICFI school was taking place that night, so there was a large contingent of international Trotskyists present.[78] The evening of the raid, party member Norman Harding was in London when he saw an article in the next day's edition of the *Observer*, published late on Saturday in the city. The article focused on Irene Gorst, an actor recruited via the Redgraves who was also having an affair with Corin Redgrave, and recounted both the WRP's coerciveness as well as an interrogation Gorst had allegedly suffered at the hands of the Redgraves, having been accused of being a police spy.[79] The interpretation that would soon come to predominate within the WRP was that the *Observer* was collaborating with the police and had received prior notice about the raid.[80] Harding promptly called the college, to inform party members of the article and within minutes the police had arrived.[81]

The raid was led by Chief Superintendent Horobin from Matlock police; Alex Mitchell remembers him not producing a proper search warrant.[82] Somewhere in the region of 70 officers searched the college for six hours, leading to the 'discovery' of some bullets but no guns, though Alex Mitchell claims that these bullets were themselves planted there by the police. The police may also have taken away various documents, notebooks and other written materials. That all charges against the WRP related to the raid were dropped within a few months suggests Mitchell's accusation about faulty, planted evidence was correct. Mitchell also suggests the raid was then the pretext for Parliament's passing of the Prevention of Terrorism Act; this is plainly absurd, since that Act was in direct response to developments in Northern Ireland. Likewise, Mitchell's claim that this was 'The first political raid in Britain since World

War II' ignores state crackdowns on Northern Irish groups as well as Black activists.[83] The raid on the college signposted an emerging theme: a genuine state interference coupled with paranoid and overblown claims about that interference. The raid on the college played a positive role in party recruitment, fuelling the feeling, as a recruit in Bristol said, 'that rebellion was once again in the air, and perhaps I should put aside my reticence and join the WRP in the fight for socialism.'[84] Security at the college became even more intense from this point on.[85] The fallout of the raid would also lead to the embarrassing libel case against the *Observer*, discussed in the previous chapter.

The college continued to receive unwanted attention into the following year: in August 1976, Shelley Rohde, a journalist for the right-wing and perpetually aggrieved *Daily Mail*, went undercover under her married name and enrolled on a course at the college. She said she was strip-searched by a female party member on her arrival. Her article was written with a certain kind of spy-novel tone, but as is often the cause with these kinds of things, there did not actually seem to be much to report; she discusses how very few of the women present wore makeup, there was a screening of a film on the General Strike, some visiting Germans were sleeping in tents outside, and attendees had to do the washing up. Security procedures at the college were ratcheted up after Rohde's infiltration.[86] Another storm in a tabloid teacup came out when the *Mail* found out the WRP had convinced two local authorities, Inner London Education Authority and Hackney Borough Council, to send 50 teenagers to weekend courses at the college (the *Mail* called it 'the notorious Red House') at a rate of five pounds per student. The *Mail* obviously deplored this, but the WRP's *chutzpah* was undeniable.[87]

In 1976, Healy expanded the party's capital assets even further by acquiring a high-tech printing works in Runcorn in Merseyside. Writing in 1994, Vanessa Redgrave estimated its plant and equipment at £750,000.[88] Healy had supposedly developed an active interest in printing technology in the years prior to this and was attending trade fairs and reading specialist publications for the printing industry. Cutting-edge printing equipment was imported secretively from Germany and a dedicated phone line was established between the offices in Clapham and the printing shop in Runcorn, over which copy, pictures and layouts could be transmitted, a previously unused system in British newspaper publishing.[89] The Runcorn printing works also had contracts to produce *Labour Herald*, a paper connected to Ted Knight and Ken Livingstone, prominent left-wing figures in the local government in Greater London Council, and the *Dundee Standard*, a newspaper ran by George Galloway.[90] Galloway was, at this time, an emerging figure on the left flank of Labour. He has since dramatically broken with the Labour Party.

Healy's obsession with party newspapers chimes with an observation that the historian and journalist Theodore Draper made many years ago about Communism more broadly: 'To no other movements have publications, no matter how small or obscure, meant so much as to radical movements. It is sometimes hard to determine whether a radical movement exists for the sake of its organ or vice versa.'[91] The *Workers Press*, a hangover from the SLL, was wound up as part of this project and on May Day 1976 a new party paper appeared, with the more anodyne and less visibly Marxist title of *News Line*. While a variety of more avowedly Marxist names had been considered – *Socialist Tribune, Workers World, Marxist Daily, Spark (Iskra), Daily 4th International, Workers News, Unite, The Struggle, Vanguard of the Masses* – *News Line* was chosen as a neutral name so as to attract non-political readers while still suggesting that this was a paper espousing a party line. *Workers Press* was probably ended because of the high costs of producing it; *News Line*, of course, would be produced by party members working for free or for low pay. The new paper – which sold for 15 pence a copy – had very little advertising and thus no ad revenues.[92] The ability to maintain a daily paper acted as a recruitment tool, giving the party an attractive aura of seriousness.[93]

Utilising the cutting-edge technology at Runcorn, *News Line* was the first full-colour daily paper in the United Kingdom, 'a remarkable achievement for such a small group'.[94] For a time, *News Line* and *Labour Herald* were two of the only colour papers in Britain, and many on the left were able to join the dots and realise that the two publications had a connection (Ken Livingstone did attend some public *News Line* events).[95] Vanessa Redgrave claimed the

Runcorn works could produce a quarter-million copies of *News Line* every day,[96] though its actual distribution was far lower than that. It looked, from a distance, like a familiar red-top tabloid, albeit one that devoted excessive space to sectarian-inflected news from the international Trotskyist movement. *News Line* also had a fairly well-written and apolitical sports section, *Sports Line*, whose columnists included Chris Hughton, Tony Grealish and Gary Waddock (three Irish footballers), as well as the English players Paul Davis and Brian Stein and, from Wales, Kevin Ratcliffe.[97] The art critic Kenneth Tynan also briefly had a column.[98] *News Line*'s racing pages were also said to be of a strong quality, such that bookies became an unlikely market for the paper.[99] In the main, it probably remained a mostly loss-making enterprise for the party.[100] By September 1980, Healy admitted to party members that the paper was losing £10,000 a month.[101]

As with the *Workers Press*, the sales of this paper required herculean efforts on the part of rank-and-file members, who either sold the papers in the early mornings outside factories or in pubs at the weekend. The sales were overseen by Sheila Torrance, the Assistant National Secretary, who used form letters to not only inform branches how many papers they were expected to sell, but also regularly raised those quotas.[102] Peter Money, active in the WRP in both Newport in South Wales in the 1970s and then in Manchester in the next decade, sees the creation of a daily paper as the central cause of the party's degeneration, because of the manner in which it became an end in itself and prevented any other kind of work within the WRP (though Money does recognise how good an idea a Trotskyist daily paper seemed at the time).[103]

Party branches were given impossible sales targets to fill; when they inevitably failed to meet these, they were either lambasted as "'social democrats" who did not understand the need for a revolutionary party' or they used their own personal money to buy unsold copies.[104] At some point in the late 1970s or early 1980s, the party purchased a fleet of mopeds, 'which Gerry had bought in one go'. Branches often requested them to assist with paper deliveries, but they seemed to have just gathered dust in a warehouse.[105] Norman Harding, the de facto national distribution manager for the paper, recalls the plight of 'Eric', a comrade in Tottenham in north London, who piled up reams of unsold copies of *News Line* at his family home:

> The pile of unsold papers was creating a problem between him and his Mum. I arranged to meet Eric at his home with a transit van. The papers were in one of the downstairs rooms. Eric opened the door as far as he could and slipped in. It was wall-to-wall, floor-to-ceiling parcels of *News Line*. It took two or three trips to a dump before the room was clear.[106]

Nonetheless, Sheila Torrance, a full-time party worker who rose to higher levels of importance coming into the 1980s, always claimed that the sales of *News Line* was perennially increasing, never falling: 'The pressure to sell more papers, raise more money, recruit more members was relentless', Clare Cowen recalls.[107] Like the college, the nationwide printing operation was a target in the 1985 party split.

The paper was professionally edited by Alex Mitchell, an Australian journalist who had previously made a strong name for himself at the *Times*. WRP members worked as drivers to ensure the paper had a nationwide distribution. At this time, the WRP also had a weekly youth paper, *Keep Left*.[108] The printing works also brought out new editions of works by Trotsky and gained contracts to print the journal of the Association of Scientific, Technical and Managerial Staffs, a trade union that later merged into Unite, today one of the largest unions in the UK. They also had a commercial contract to print a paper from an Irish Republican prisoners' group.[109] The free labour of party members was key to fulfilling these contracts. Ironically, by locating the printing facility in Runcorn, a rundown industrial town outside Liverpool, the WRP received a grant from the British government for businesses creating jobs in areas of high unemployment. A red-baiting and often unsubstantiated BBC exposé of the WRP in 1983 estimated that they had received a £59,000 regional development grant for this.[110] In keeping with the party's paranoia, the facility at Runcorn had hi-tech security cameras.

The WRP also opened up bookshops in the West End of London[111] and then two more in London – in Brixton and Upton

Park – as well as shops in Norwich, Liverpool and Glasgow.[112] Dave Bruce remembers the Glasgow shop as being one of the best booksellers in the city; they sold leftist literature as well as books for a general readership. They acted as important social centres, were well run and, Bruce believes, *News Line* would have folded much earlier without the profits from the bookshops.[113] In time, the party also established a small film unit 'and a theatre company capable of staging production to the highest professional standards'.[114] The various properties owned by the party all had 24-hour security, provided by male party members.[115]

Paper sales were one of, if not *the*, central tasks of party members, ostensibly to bring the Marxist truth to the masses, in actuality to fund the party. Critics of Healy would later observe that 'a fetish was made of the party's material assets, and finding the cash to keep the show on the road became more important than political tasks'.[116] In one of the WRP's most ostentatious purchases, when Trotsky's death mask was auctioned by Jean-Claude Binoche, a high-end auctioneer in Paris, the party spent FR38,500 (about £4,400) to buy it. It was then displayed at a 2,000-strong Trotsky centenary rally in Wembley Conference Centre in London on 4 November 1979.[117] Andy Blunden remembers this as a humiliatingly weird event, in which attendees were asked to stand for a minute's silence before the quasi-religious 'relic'.[118] Mike Richardson says the displaying of the death mask struck a lot of people as having an oddly religious vibe. He remembers being personally shocked at the high price tag (about £20,000 when adjusted for inflation in 2024).[119]

The WRP forged a number of international links, partly within global Trotskyist networks, but more infamously outside them. The party certainly made efforts to cultivate links with the Palestine Liberation Organisation; party members Roy Battersby and Vanessa Redgrave directed and produced a pro-PLO documentary in 1977, *The Palestinian*. The high quality of the film was a source of pride within the party and indeed the WRP were pioneers in the developing of pro-Palestinian sentiments on the British radical left.[120] Moreover, the party was able to make some connections with the PLO, a broad movement at this time and open to discussions and cooperation across the left spectrum. Corinna Lotz and

Paul Feldman claim that Healy met with Palestinian leaders Abu Jihad, Abu Iyad and Yasser Arafat at this time and lectured PLO cadres in Marxist theory.[121] This probably happened in the mid-1970s. The lecture seems to have been a one-off event, attended by younger members of the PLO and not repeated again. The PLO was internationally isolated in its early years than would later be the case and that the WRP had a daily paper and could muster celebrities like Vanessa Redgrave to the Palestinian cause smoothed their reception. Yet, for all of the overtures from Redgrave, the PLO leadership probably knew to keep a certain distance from the

Figure 3   *News Line* special report

WRP. As the Palestinian historian Yezid Sayigh, has shown, by this period the mainstream of the PLO was becoming more interested in building high-level connections and gaining formal diplomatic recognition at an international level.[122]

Less astutely, Muammar Gaddafi, installed as 'Chairman of the Revolutionary Command Council of Libya' after a 1969 coup, seemed to have an open willingness to forge connections with the WRP. Healy's party and the General People's Congress of Libya, Gaddafi's parliament, signed a joint declaration in July 1977, pledging each to a struggle against imperialism, Zionism, fascism and colonialism, drafted following a meeting in London.[123] WRP delegates allegedly visited Libya in April 1976, and Healy himself is said to have gone there on a fundraising expedition in August 1977.[124] Healy is alleged to have met with Gaddafi on a small number of occasions, and indelicately spoke of how he had flown on the colonel's private jet. According to one legend, Healy once caused a minor incident when he landed at Heathrow in Gaddafi's jet; this sounds implausible though it is confirmed by Norman Harding, who not only broke with Healy in the 1980s but also developed a strong antipathy toward him and so presumably had no desire to spread affirming tales of Healy's high-level political connections.[125] The WRP also developed an affinity for the newly enthroned Iraqi president, Saddam Hussein. *News Line* published a series of adulatory accounts of life under Ba'athism in 1980, to mark the first dozen years of that party's rule. These articles were then published as a standalone pamphlet. In April 1979, Healy and Vanessa Redgrave travelled to Kuwait for a screening of *The Palestinian*; they were met by the crown prince, Sheikh Sabah al Sabah, a leading figure in the country's feudal-style family dictatorship, who donated £25,000 for a proposed second film on life under Israeli occupation in Gaza and the West Bank.[126] These connections with dubious regimes in the Middle East would come to fuel a whole slew of recurring rumours about the party (discussed more in depth in Chapter 8).

Closer to home, the WRP refused to develop a clear position on Northern Ireland, an obviously contentious question in 1970s and 1980s Britain. In this they diverged drastically from other, more prominent Trotskyist parties, such as the Socialist Workers Party and the Militant Tendency, for whom Northern Ireland was both a live contemporary issue as well as a proxy for theoretical debates about 'the national question'. This probably came directly from Healy, who seems to have systematically sabotaged work to build the Irish section of the ICFI, believing it was impossible, because of police interference there, to build an Irish Trotskyist party. He instead may have urged Irish members of the WRP to take out British citizenship, a policy almost tailor-made to alienate Irish people.[127]

The WRP also actively threw itself into electoral work, running nine candidates in the February 1974 general election and a high of 60 candidates in Thatcher's watershed year of 1979. The Runcorn printing works turned out 'literally millions'[128] of leaflets and election literature and the WRP's 60 candidates earned the right to a televised Party Political Broadcast in 1979.[129] In that 1979 broadcast, Corin Redgrave wrote and delivered a brief but astute analysis of British capitalist crisis at the end of stagflation; Alex Mitchell tried to warn him about how bleak it was and wrote an alternative script, which he ignored.[130] And certainly the party's call for nationalising all land, without compensation, probably jarred the vast majority of voters in the aftermath of the labour disputes of the 'Winter of Discontent' of 1978-79. There was similar grimness to the election campaign of Mike Banda in October 1974, with Banda describing how the WRP's warnings about the nature of the capitalist crisis having been fulfilled and claiming a Tory dictatorship was in the works.[131] Amid the full-time party workers and the celebrity candidate in October 1974, there was an admirable number of working candidates, but only two were women.[132]

The party's election results were generally poor; the journalist Stephen Johns, for example, received only 52 votes from the 50,000 voters of Dunbartonshire East in 1974 (0.1%).[133] Roy Battersby received a total of 95 votes in 1979 in Dundee. Of the 31 million votes cast across all of the United Kingdom in the 1979 election, the WRP received a total of 12,631, a cost of about £8 per vote in terms of the party's General Election Fund.[134] WRP candidates generally lost their deposits, a classic sign in British politics of a poor electoral performance. This was the standard pattern for Trotskyist politicos: when Tariq Ali ran in Sheffield Attercliffe in

1974, he received only 424 votes (0.89%) even with his undeniable public prominence. Despite Trotskyist candidates running in every British general election since 1974, they have rarely broken a ceiling of 1 per cent.[135] It is easy to sneer at these poor results, and certainly they did not do much to improve the mainstream perception of Trotskyism. Yet it is also worth remembering that groups like the WRP saw no parliamentary road to socialism; elections were understood as a single element in a much larger revolutionary project. For example, Liz Leicester, active in the WRP in London before relocating to the college in Derbyshire, says that the party ran candidates to publicise their politics and to promote a socialist debate; actually winning seats seems to have been of secondary importance.[136]

While the WRP saw itself as the rightful leaders of the proletariat, the same working class mostly remained loyally committed to the middle-of-the-road social democracy of the Labour Party, an inconvenient reality that Healy generally ignored in place of his steadfast view that a switch to the WRP was imminent.[137] Even celebrity glamour did not help this; when Vanessa Redgrave ran for the party in October 1974 in Newham North East in London, she received 572 votes versus Labour's Reg Prentice, who won with 22,205. Redgrave was openly mocked at the official announcement of the results.[138] In July 1978, shortly after winning an Oscar for Best Supporting Actress, she received only 394 votes in a by-election in Manchester, just over half what the neo-fascists of the National Front got (623 votes) and a tiny fraction of the winning Labour candidate, at 12,556 votes. In the 1983 general election, Corin Redgrave received a meagre 72 votes (out of 45,000) in the Tooting constituency in south London. Gerry Healy himself never stood for election, maybe as a reflection of his vanguardist/Cartesian desire to remain the Marxist brain divided from the body of the proletariat or perhaps because of a cultish need for the leader to avoid the embarrassment of being trounced by a Labour or Tory incumbent.[139] Possibly channelling their embarrassing electoral results, the party switched focus from parliament to Community Training Centres in 1980, arguing that such community Soviets would be the basis for Britain's imminent switch to socialism. With lofty plans to eventually set up 25 in total, the WRP established six such Community Centres, with an emphasis on youth training for 16–25-year-olds, leading to some negative attention from the mainstream and right-wing press as well as legal responses from the litigious Vanessa Redgrave; she sued Coventry Newspapers LTD, owners of *Coventry Evening Telegraph*, for their articles on the training centres.[140] While properties were purchased, it does not seem any of these youth training centres ever got off the ground.[141] The centre in Calton, a strongly Irish Republican part of Glasgow's East End, did have some success, but Peter Money, active in Manchester, says 'absolutely nothing' was ever done at the WRP youth training centre in that city.[142] Likewise in Nottingham, the WRP purchased an eight-storey derelict wool factory but it was never used for its stated youth training purpose. Instead, Scotty Clark, a teenage WRP member, lived in it for 'the best part of a year'.

Clark's story is fascinating and exemplifies some of what was genuinely good about the WRP, as well as some of their worst tendencies. From a Glasgow-Irish Republican background and having left school at age 16, he already had a left-wing worldview which the WRP helped him shape up. When other boys his age would have been taking a skilled apprenticeship, he talks of this as an apprenticeship as a revolutionary. And looking from the other side of the miners' strike, he does think the WRP was correct in their predictions about the aims of the British capitalist state. Notwithstanding his age, Clark became a leading activist for the party in Nottingham. He walked six miles daily, delivering copies of *News Line*, before selling them on the street. One day, not wanting to do this any longer, he told higher-ups in the party that he had been abducted by 'state agents', as a way to explain why he had not shown up. This 'unleashed' a situation that led to Clark being personally grilled by Healy and Mike Banda about what happened. Rather than coming clean, he doubled down on the story. The WRP leaders filed a police complaint about the abduction; it was only when the police went to Clark's father's house and were told Scotty had been home at the time of the 'abduction' that the truth came out. He fled the party after this. Since he lived at the Youth Training Centre, he had to move in with a friend. Despite having left the party, he and the friend continued to collect money in mining towns around Nottingham saying it was for the WRP, collecting up to £30 in a night, but keeping it for themselves. 'I then got a visit by two WRP people... and they gave me a hiding... they gave me a right fucking beating, in fact.'[143]

When a genuinely socialist struggle did emerge in Britain, during the miners' strike of 1984–85, the WRP played a negligible role. Their claims that Britain was on the verge of 'Bonapartism' had a certain truth to it – Thatcher did have an undeniable authoritarian streak – but this was presented in obscure Marxist terms and with an always hysterical edge to it. Healy seems to have discouraged any involvement in rank-and-file union activities during the miners' strike, instead exclusively pursuing connections with the leadership of the National Union of Mineworkers. WRP members who were involved in the strike were understandably aggrieved by this.[144] The party's failures to make any positive contribution during the miners' strike fuelled an emergent discontent. During the strike, the WRP deterred party members from becoming involved in any of the support groups that emerged around the miners, instead encouraging local members to concentrate their energies on selling copies of *News Line* to picketing miners. The general view in mining areas was that the WRP leadership was out of touch with realities on the ground.[145]

By the mid-1980s, Healy was beginning to be sidelined within the party; he had suffered a heart attack in September 1983 whilst giving lectures on philosophy at the Derbyshire college. This was kept secret from all except the party leadership,[146] though for those who did know, it exposed his vulnerability.[147] Healy was somewhat aware that factions were organising against him, understanding the looming split within the party via his preferred language of 'idealists' and 'individualists', as opposed to those who loyally follow the party line. A slump in *News Line* sales following the defeat of the miners' strike had hurt the party's finances, though Healy continued spending money on expensive equipment. And the WRP maintained 90 salaried employees, a bloated full-time staff for a party that rarely exceeded 3,000 active members. Healy was also alleged to be retaining £20,000 in cash and a BMW, to be used to flee the country if and when a fascist coup took place.[148] The WRP suffered from 'excessive and uncontrolled expenditure': by mid-1985 the organisation owned its own printing press (purchased for an estimated £686,802, at historic prices), an educational college, seven youth training centres (£207,762), five trucks (£55,399) and a fleet of motorbikes (£32,000).[149] Party finances would soon cause the first cracks in Healy's control. But the biggest crack would come from Healy's appalling treatment of women. The gender and racial politics of the WRP are the subject of the next chapter.

6

Identity Politics

In 1945, when Healy was emerging as a leader within British Trot-skyism, he advocated entry into the Labour Party as the only conceivable means of connecting to the organised working class. In his better moments, he pragmatically recognised the strength and power of Labour in British politics. Paul Dixon, one of his anti-entryist critics within the Revolutionary Communist Party, though, argued that there were other avenues to explore outside of Labour, suggesting that women and youth could also be worthy allies for Trotskyists:

> Entirely new strata of the oppressed will be drawn into the strug-gles. The women who today, play a subordinate role, will be drawn into the front rank of battle both inside and outside of industry. Above all, the youth, aroused as a result of the imperial-ist war, will be drawn into politics. The youth do not suffer from bitterness, cynicism and disillusionment of the older workers, betrayed so many times by the 'Socialists' and Stalinists.

This was clearly a view made in good faith and could have been the start of a meaningful conversation about worthwhile forms of polit-ical activism outside of the Labour Party and outside of narrowly defined concepts of 'the working class'. But alongside a supporter, John Goffe, Healy took a highly disdainful view that they should concentrate their energies on 'the backward strata in preference to work amongst the politically advanced elements inside the Labour Party'. Women, for Healy, were part of the 'backward' elements of society, as opposed to politically conscious workers implicitly assumed to be male. Dixon pointed out the selectiveness of this bad-faith argument, arguing for a kind of feminist Trotskyism that was expansive enough to include recruiting of both male workers and of women. Dixon saw this as an essential part of Trotskyism and suggested Healy and his co-writer would 'be all the better' if they read 'The Road to the Woman Worker – The Road to the Youth', a feminist section in Trotsky's *Transitional Programme*, the founding document of international Trotskyism.[1] Healy had a long reputation for the kind of sectarianism briefly on display here, but the inability to properly include gender inequality in his politics was also there from practically the start. Healy was a misogynist and the groups he led had a set of profound gender biases. The WRP was a very good example of a trend that the Communist philosopher Søren Mau recently identified: 'the tendency among (certain kinds of) Marxists to de-prioritise struggles around gender because of a narrow-minded, masculinist ideal of revolutionary class struggle'.[2]

Clare Cowen, who played a key role in taking down Healy, has said that the WRP lacked a language to discuss Healy's sexual abuse, partly because British society in general did not have such a language at the time, partly because the WRP didn't seek to develop a feminist language.[3] This was indeed a pervasive problem, in a party that steadfastly refused to directly engage with gender politics or to reflect on the biases underpinning their own worldview. The authoritarian culture of the WRP effected a further chilling of internal discussion and open communication.

Representative of the party's general approach, the WRP's 1974 election manifesto made no mention whatsoever of issues related to race or gender. In an early 1970s SLL leaflet, *A Message to all Housewives*, the language makes it clear that the Healyites uncritically accepted a gendered division of labour, with women as housewives and 'wage-earner' being tacitly coded as male: 'Many housewives by now will have woken up to the Tory con-trick on prices. They do the shopping and they have seen prices going up and up while *their husband's wage packet* is kept down by law.' The leaflet reviewed the various increases in prices happening under the Conservative government, arguing that they are part of a general assault on the working class before stating: 'Perhaps the most serious thing of all, however, is the attack the Tories make on *your husbands' right* to earn a decent wage and fight for *his* basic rights.' And the answer to this was that 'all housewives and tenants should unite with trade unionists and shop stewards' in an anti-Conservative campaign. That women are themselves wage labourers, tenants or members of unions, or might even aspire to be shop stewards, is ignored here.[4] An even more blatant expression of this kind of blind spot was featured in two duelling essays in a March 1970 issue of *Workers Press*. In the initial article, Janet Williams, Hazel Twort and Ann Bahcheli, members of the Peckham Rye branch of the Women's Liberation Workshop, took the SLL to task for its 'barren' conception of women's liberation; the SLL recognised the oppressed status of women under capitalism while also expecting women to postpone their own liberation until after the revolution. The three feminists had an opposing view:

> The road to a workers' revolution goes via women fighting for their liberation. The idea of a workers' revolution made by men workers, who would presumably 'give' the women 'their freedom', is mere idealist fantasy. It has its origins in self-deluding male chauvinism, and must be exposed as such.

The response to this was written by SLL member Mark Ruskin, who dismissed the arguments without ever really engaging with them. Ruskin said that capitalism wants more female workers to exploit and said that marriage was thus a 'liberation from this work'.[5] This was not just a highly patronising comment, it was also a position guaranteed to alienate feminists. Unsurprisingly, the Women's Liberation Movement generally ignored the WRP, recognising them as barren soil for feminist politics.[6] Like many of the other dominant parties in the post-'68 radical left, the WRP focused only on the shortcomings of feminism, 'in particular its domination by white, middle class women'.[7] These were not false claims, and the class blind spots of *some* feminists were real. But this also ignored the genuine achievements of feminism, as well as its vitality and the important political insights it generated. Alongside the valid critique, outright sexism was also undeniably at work.

As well as perceiving labour in British society along gendered lines, the WRP also saw work within the party in gendered terms. Cowen says women were seen as 'less important than men' within the WRP. Even if some women were also pushed into leadership roles, control within the party remained always male. Women were not seen as serious. Sheila Torrance, for example, was allowed a leadership role as Assistant General Secretary, but never an intellectual role. Women were generally given the backroom tasks and worked so hard that they did not have time to read or write articles.[8] A good example of this is the Summer Fair organised in 1974 by Margaret Beeks, where handmade crafts and household goods were sold as part of a fundraising campaign for the WRP. This was the kind of 'feminine' work that female cadre were assigned.[9] Liz Leicester, another long-standing member of the SLL and WRP, describes the party's conceptions of work in similar terms: women were often (but not exclusively) given the administrative and fundraising tasks and were more likely to be the typesetters for *News Line* rather than writing as intellectuals for the paper.[10] As with the Communist Party, the WRP required a level of intense devotion to party work that only the 'devoted' could maintain alongside their actual paid employment. This also served to distil the party, removing anyone not amenable to this level of work; only those who tolerated this party-form would and could stay in this party, completing party work on top of their paid employment. But in addition, this was a work culture that was even less conducive to women, who on top of their jobs also had housework foisted on them.[11]

Going back to Trotsky himself, John Kelly has identified a 'great man' model of leadership at the heart of Trotskyism; 'women rarely appeared in these discussions'.[12] The SLL and WRP reflected this broader trend, where leadership positions are almost always taken by men. For all the schisms of Trotskyism, their male leadership remained remarkably stable. In the 1950s, the three main Trotskyist groups in Britain were the International Socialists, led by Tony Cliff, the Revolutionary Socialist League, led by Ted Grant, and Gerry Healy's SLL; 35 years later all three men still led their organisations, even if the groups had evolved or the names had changed.[13]

Gerry Healy was described as 'a very hard and aggressive man' by those who knew him and reports of physical violence meted out on Healy's instructions are legion. Robin Blick, Stuart Carter, Dot Gibson, Aileen Jennings, Mark Jenkins, Tony Richardson and Ernie Tate (a member of the International Marxist Group) all suffered violent, physical assaults for challenging Healy. John Kelly argues that this aggressiveness was a function of the hierarchical and authoritarian leadership style in the organisation.[14] But the violence against party members within the SLL and WRP was practically unique in British radical left-wing politics; no other group had this problem, even if they did have similarly hierarchical structures.[15] Healy's influence was the cause of much of this.

A result of the SLL and WRP being less student-oriented than other Trotskyist groups was that their high-ranking members tended to be older and this in turn buttressed the hierarchical age dynamics of the WRP, where an older leadership led (or controlled) a generally younger rank-and-file. Viewed differently, older male comrades acted as mentors to younger, also male, comrades. The fact that this hierarchical world was also a gendered one is an important point. This was not a wholly negative phenomenon; there was a strong level of social cohesion within the WRP. But the obvious problem is also that this easily slipped into something exclusionary, misogynistic and overly hierarchical.[16] The lack of female leaders meant younger female rank-and-file members were denied the same kind of mentors, thus perpetuating the skewed gender dynamics of the party.

A good sign of the party's cynical approach to women's rights is how willing they were to defend the gender record of both Ba'athist Iraq and the post-1979 Islamic Republic of Iran; for convoluted reasons the WRP was, at different times, sympathetic to both and published incredulous articles trumpeting the regimes' records on women's rights or downplaying repression.[17] They defended the enforced wearing of chadors in post-1979 Iran, claiming that this was a customary practice akin to saris in India, which greatly understates how many women did not veil in pre-1979 Iran. The WRP also alleged that the source of this feminist criticism was the Revolutionary Workers Party of Iran, 'fake Trotskyists', that they accused of being a front for both the CIA and American State Department as well as the American SWP.[18]

The party's record on race was not much better. After the notorious Smethwick by-election in 1964, the SLL produced a pamphlet entitled *Racialism: A Danger to Labour*. While it was obviously a step in the right direction for the SLL to target racial bigotry, the piece started with an uncharacteristically non-theoretical statement that racism was being stirred up by 'psychopaths and criminals', rather than understanding this sociologically or in terms of how capitalism produces racism (though the pamphlet did go on to say British capitalism *is* responsible for racism).[19] From time to time, the party would focus on racism but generally as a contingent thing, never incorporated into their central theories of capitalism.[20]

Anti-racism never came into the mainline of the party and they never incorporated anti-racism into their theoretical understandings of capitalism. At their 1967 annual conference, for example, the SLL produced 34 pages of resolutions. Twenty-two were taken up with 'economic' perspectives on contemporary Britain, and in the remaining twelve pages there is the same focus on a thing called the 'economy'. But there is never a three-dimensional understanding of how the economy is embedded in, and in turn reproduces, things like gender, race or culture. At best, this is operating at a high level of abstraction; at worst, it is economistic and simplistic and is offering a theory that operates at too much of a remove from the lives of ordinary people. And this was generally true of the SLL and WRP's crude way of conceptualising politics as always being a product of the economic base, rather than identifying the economic base as producing the ideological and cultural superstructure, including race and gender, which in turn reproduces the economic base (which, of course, would be the truly dialectical way of understanding how the thesis relates to the antithesis).[21]

It was only a short step from this refusal to engage critically with the problem of racial capitalism to the party's later dismissal of the Anti-Nazi League as 'a revisionist fraud got up by political opportunists and muddleheads',[22] their crowing about the British SWP's embrace of anti-racism as an attempt to appease 'anti-Soviet trendies',[23] or the accusatory statement made to Gary Younge – a young Black British member of the party in the early 1980s and today a well-known journalist – who had expressed an interest in Fidel Castro: 'I was told that I only liked him because he was black.'[24] Castro, of course, was white. Put simply, the WRP had a sloppy and unsophisticated understanding of race and gender.

There was also a general homophobia within the party or, at best, an apathy to gay issues. Clare Cowen today admits that 'We were very much trapped in all the prejudices of the era. We certainly weren't in the forefront of challenging them. Not at all.' When two women asked to join the party and revealed to Healy that they were lesbians, he not only rejected them but then also mocked them to other party members. Likewise, when former comrade Peter Fryer wrote a book in 1964 about British sexual prudery, Healy accused him of engaging in pornography, being generally dismissive of such issues.[25] Robert Myers, today still active in a group called 'Angry Workers', a far more democratic operation that the WRP, says of his old party: 'You've got to remember we were incredibly reactionary on the question of the rights of women, the rights of gays.' Gay people were not even allowed to join because of an assumption that they could be blackmailed by the state.[26]

Again, this was common across the international left in the late 1960s and afterwards: 'most Marxist-Leninists shared the homophobia prevalent in society as a whole, and on the issue of gay rights they surrendered to prejudice instead of analysing and opposing it'.[27] One of the first ever Healyist discussions of homosexuality, printed in *Newsletter* when Peter Fryer was still editor, displayed a telling mix of progressivism and ingrained homophobia, recognising the liberalisation of British laws as a positive step, while still calling same-sex attraction 'an integral, if unfortunate part of the individual', comparable to having an ingrowing toenail.[28]

The general disdain that the WRP had for feminism and the gay liberation movement were more than just surface-level phenomena; there was a deeply masculinist ethos at work here.[29] Trotskyism promoted a selfless devotion to the cause – not necessarily a bad thing – alongside a political seriousness slipping into humourlessness and a suppression of personal emotions and intimate relationships. Gay and Women's Liberation were dismissed as too emotional and intimate, too bound up in one's own selfhood, not revolutionary enough.[30] David North, for all his harsh attacks on Healy, was still impressed that Healy was 'undoubtedly, a "hard man"';[31] this veneration of hard-bodied and tough masculinity led easily to a misogynist environment. Healy was the only leader of any of the major British Trotskyist groups who did not claim to be an intellectual, standing in stark contrast to people like Tony Cliff or Tariq Ali. While he did surround himself with obedient intellectuals, he instead sought to project an image of toughness and determination.[32] At party events, Vanessa Redgrave regularly appeared in military-style khaki clothing, 'to look unfeminine and proletarian', while Corin Redgrave supposedly once said humour was 'the last bastion of the bourgeoisie', preferring a mirthless seriousness.[33] Clare Cowen remembers him as projecting a 'chilly and chilling' personal demeanour (though she also says he was 'a very unconcrete person').[34] This kind of posturing – a 'masculine militant culture'[35] existing across much of the Trotskyist left – was taken as revolutionary gravitas by many of those on the inside but probably came across as po-faced and off-putting to outsiders. When Granville Williams, an SLL member in Yorkshire, later moved to the International Socialists, he was intrigued to now be in a group where members would laugh and tell jokes; humour was not welcomed by the leaders of the SLL, who tended to project an austere tone.[36]

In the post-Healy WRP (Workers Press), there were attempts to break with this legacy. Already in December 1985, Stephen Wey, secretary of the Huddersfield branch of the WRP, wrote a piece entitled *The Liberation of Women and the W.R.P.* Wey made the amenable point that Lenin and Trotsky viewed the struggle against the oppression of women as part of the struggle for Communism, to make it clear that a welding of Trotskyism and feminism was not just possible but politically desirable also. With his orthodox bona fides confirmed, he could then proceed to the meat of his critique. He pointed to the refusal of the party leadership to take a stand on abortion, gay liberation, contraception or equal pay. He alleged that internal discussions of feminism had been systematically avoided; classic Marxist-Feminist texts by Rosa Luxemburg and Alexandra Kollontoi were ignored and a piece that veteran party member Mickie Shaw (Aileen Jennings's mother) had written on 'The Woman Question' was suppressed. Wey's astute argument was that the WRP had, for too long, advocated a fake universalism, in which women's rights or racial discrimination could be sidestepped because they would supposedly be dealt with after the revolution.[37] A year later, Clare Cowen collaborated with Liz Leicester on an article for *Workers Press* entitled 'Healy's Sexual Abuse: Towards a Theoretical Understanding', which began to break ground on an analysis of what had gone wrong within the party. A Women's Commission was established within the party and this group asserted that Healy's sexual abuse 'was not so much rape but is more accurately described as "incest": sexual abuse by someone in a position of power and trust'.[38] Deepening this, the WRP (Workers Press) conference of 1987 passed a 'Resolution on Women', which stated quite bluntly that 'Before the expulsion of Healy and his supporters there was systematic repression of women in the WRP'. The authors of the resolution – which included Cowen and Leicester – urged Trotskyists to take their role in the broader feminist movement. With well-deployed statistical evidence, the resolution recognised the complicated ways that gender discrimination was bound up with class privileges.[39] The party around this time began to provide childcare facilities at meetings, in an effort to be more inclusive.[40] A Midlands branch of the party moved a motion in the late 1980s that strongly urged party members to be mindful of still using sexist language.[41] The party became more open to discussions of intimate sexuality, recognising sex's inherently political nature.[42] Nonetheless, for all these positive notes and the warm reception of feminist commentary, the post-1985 WRP made the right noises but was still unwilling to bend Trotskyism too much to incorporate feminism. The intellectual and political focus of the party remained largely as it had been before.[43]

In many communist and socialist parties, it was, and is, standard for all members, whether leaders or cadre, to address each other with the egalitarian title of 'comrade' partly because of the idea that they should rehearse the kind of society they want to achieve in the future. Surely that should also extend to practising racial and gender equality. Gender politics are a positive thing in and of themselves and a good socialist party should invest time and energy into the difficult – but not impossible – project of merging class politics with gender and sexual politics. The WRP failed to even try this. A party that displayed such open contempt for feminism and actively avoided developing a language to talk about the politics of emotions and intimacy, that venerated toughness and the ability to endure privation and pain, was a party in which abuse of women could easily go unchecked. The failure to figure out how to reconcile socialism and feminism was bound up with an explosion about to erupt within the party ranks.

7

The Split, 1985

In the spring and summer of 1985, and into that autumn, the Workers Revolutionary Party tore itself apart and Gerry Healy ended up being expelled from the party that he had so tightly controlled for its entire existence.[1] One of those centrally involved says it was an uprising of the membership against the leaders.[2]

The story of what took place is sometimes murky and hard to pin down, with all the various factions producing drastically differing accounts of what took place and why. This is all made more difficult by the fact that several factions continued to operate under the name 'Workers Revolutionary Party', to claim allegiance to different 'International Committees of the Fourth International', or to publish rival papers called *News Line*.

Tensions had been building well before this. Between October and December 1982, David North, the leader of the Workers League, the WRP's sister-party in the United States, had begun to tentatively criticise Healy's pseudo-philosophical posturing, always a taboo move within the ICFI. When his criticisms were 'unanimously condemned and rejected', he quickly retracted them.[3] Mike Banda, though, a Healy loyalist up to this point, privately told North that he shared these criticisms of Healy. North then moved on to making various criticisms of Healy's closeness to Arab dictators and to Ken Livingstone, the reformist social democratic head of the Greater London Council. By the time of the 10th Congress of the ICFI in January 1985, David North was publicly pronouncing his critiques of Healy; Healy was not a delegate to this conference, perhaps an ominous sign of his declining prestige, perhaps also just the result of his poor health. Adding to the general air of unease, Alex Mitchell, 'Gerry's right-hand man', suddenly disappeared just before Christmas 1984 and rumours were soon on the fly about what had happened to him.[4] In reality, he had become burnt out on

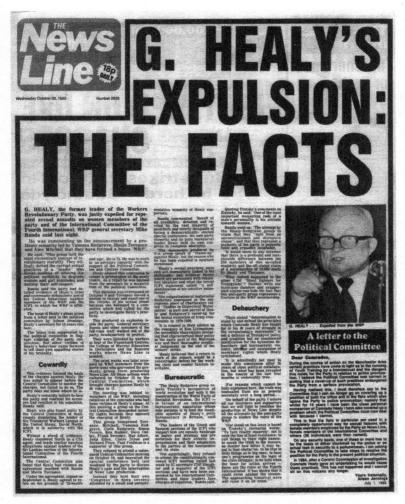

Figure 4   News Line, 30 October 1985

WRP life and had flown home to Australia to visit his children.[5] He returned early the next year, with party disquiet still boiling over.

Sheila Torrance, the Assistant General Secretary and one of the few women to take a leading role in the party, was finding herself increasingly at odds with Healy; the latter was critical of her inability to repair either the party's finances or its membership levels. The sense of disillusionment on the British left after the defeat of the miners' strike in the spring of 1985 played a role here too, even if the WRP officially claimed that the miners remained undefeated. By April, Healy was, more so than usual, using party meetings to personally harangue WRP members who had annoyed him in some way or another. Within the staff of the WRP, secret opposition to Healy coalesced around five full-time party activists: Dot Gibson, Clare Cowen, David Bruce, Charlie Brandt and, most importantly, Aileen Jennings, Healy's secretary.[6] Brandt, a German member of the party and a highly capable electrical engineer, bugged Healy's office at this time, so that the five could gain access to otherwise secret factional discussions.[7] They had been planning their move against Healy for about a year and knew they had to move slowly and cautiously to prevent being expelled.[8] These five members would later be accused of both hiding the true extent of the party's financial problems as well as selling off or mortgaging party assets for personal gain, though these accusations were almost certainly false. Two other trusted long-standing workers, Robert Harris and Norman Harding, were aware something was in preparation but not directly involved.

By the end of April, Healy was attempting to isolate Sheila Torrance within the WRP. Intra-party machinations continued to simmer throughout May and June. But then, at the very end of June, the strife within the WRP became about something far more than personal grievances or party finances.

Clare Cowen had spent long periods in 1984 as a driver for Aileen Jennings, during which time Jennings shared disturbing revelations about Healy with Cowen, eventually to be made public.[9] Prior to this, Jennings had felt there was no one she could talk to about the revelations, because of the authoritarian internal culture of the WRP.[10] On 30 June 1985, Aileen Jennings wrote a letter to the Political Committee of the WRP that would also later be shared widely within the party. At first it was only shown to party leadership, at a Political Committee meeting at 8 a.m. on 1 July.[11] The letter made major accusations about Healy, even if they were couched in euphemistic language and paranoia about state surveillance:

for 19 years I have been the close personal companion of Comrade Healy [and] I have also covered up a problem which the Political Committee must now deal with because I cannot. This is that the flats in particular [properties owned by the WRP] are used in a completely opportunist way for sexual liaisons with female members employed by the Party on News Line, female members of the International Committee and others. On any security basis one of these or more has to be the basis of either blackmail by the police or an actual leak in security to a police-woman. I am asking the Political Committee to take steps to resolve the position for [the] Party in the present political situation. In 1964, after the Control Commission of Investigation Comrade Healy gave an undertaking he would cease these practices, this has not happened and I cannot sit on this volcano any longer.[12]

The letter was like a 'hand grenade', such was the shock with which it was greeted. As it was first read out at the meeting, Healy sat in stony silence, perhaps in anger, perhaps indifference.[13] Cowen thinks today he was looking and listening as an experienced political operator, to see who on the Political Committee was responsible.[14] At the same time that she wrote this letter, Jennings also revealed to a small number of party members that the spinal injuries she had suffered two years previously, and which left her permanently disabled, were the result of a physical assault by Healy. During one of his regular tantrums, he had allegedly broken a chair over her back. Simultaneous with the release of the letter, Jennings disappeared. Rumours soon spread about her: that she had absconded with party funds, that she had been hospitalised, perhaps even that she had been murdered.[15] In reality, she was in hiding at a cottage in Derbyshire, not far from the party's college.[16]

As the letter made clear, Gerry Healy, by then in his early seventies, was using his position within a profoundly hierarchical and authoritarian organisation to coerce women, many of them in their twenties, into having sex with him. He carefully groomed female comrades within the WRP, avoiding those that he suspected were too independent-minded. Healy himself tended to dislike women that he saw as too free-thinking or who were not afraid of him.[17]

Healy was 'remarkably cunning', Dave Bruce says today, in identifying women for abuse but also keeping them separate from each other and ensuring they all did not know about each other.[18] But the shocking extent of Healy's sexual abuses now came into the open. Gibson, Jennings and Cowen had moved cautiously in the previous months to identify these women. Any attempt to openly accuse Healy was liable to be met severely. They would instead use coded questions to other female party members to see if they had been abused by Healy.[19]

In Jennings's original letter, 26 women were named as victims of Healy. Their names were redacted from all publicly circulated copies. Party members were told to never reveal the names, a direction that not all abided by.[20] Three of the women named were full-time party workers and were soon made redundant in a round of staff lay-offs, as also was Aileen Jennings.[21] Jennings had previously told Cowen that Healy 'views all the young women at the Centre [party headquarters] as potential sexual partners. He's done it for years.'[22] The view that would later circulate among many party members was that Healy had targeted far more than the 26 women named in the letter. Indeed, starting in the early 1980s, Healy had begun to pressure Clare Cowen herself for sex. Cowen does not use the word 'rape' to describe her sexual encounters with Healy, because of the fact that she did give tacit consent. But she also recognised the power disparities within the WRP that allowed him to take advantage of her.[23] This fuzzy grey area between mutually consenting sex, on the one hand, and rape or sexual coercion on the other is, of course, a common phenomenon.[24] And it was clearly an abusive relationship; even after Cowen had been badly injured in a car crash, Healy still attempted to have sex with her.[25] Jennings had a similarly abusive relationship with Healy; when she said she would no longer have sex with him, he verbally attacked her at a party meeting.[26] A report that the WRP tasked Norman Harding with writing at the very end of 1985 confirmed that Jennings's and Cowen's experiences were part of Healy's general pattern; using his position to force women into sexual relations, threatening them verbally if they suggested they would refuse, and the regular use of violence.[27] Jennings believed Healy had an unrequited desire for Vanessa Redgrave and that Sheila Torrance had some kind of ability to keep Healy at a distance, 'as if she knows something he wants to keep secret'.[28] Healy may also have feared Torrance's husband, an industrial organiser for the party but 'a shadowy figure' whom he distrusted.[29] One woman that Cowen and Jennings talked to just before revealing the letter said that Healy had attempted to force himself on her but 'backed off when he realised she was under the legal age'.[30] Another woman that Healy abused had attempted suicide.[31] David North later produced evidence from two female members of the ICFI who said they had been abused by Healy.[32]

Tariq Ali says rumours of Healy's sexual abuses were already circulating on the British left in the late sixties and early seventies.[33] Kate Blakeney, a particularly active member of the WRP in Reading in the early 1970s, had been singled out by Healy when her branch's paper sales fell below quota; when he invited her to his flat in Clapham, he attempted (but failed) to force himself on her. At the next meeting of the WRP's Central Committee, Healy verbally attacked her for her supposedly wayward politics and soon after she left the party, later moving to Australia.[34] Blakeney sided with Alan Thornett during the 1974 split and she may have told people then about Healy's attempted assault. Garth Frankland, another supporter of Thornett, claims he had known of such accusations from about 1972 or 1973 onwards.[35]

Linda Neville's account exemplifies the patterns of the abuse in which Healy engaged, as well as the experiences of the women he targeted. She was a one-time CPGB member but had become disillusioned with Soviet Communism after 1956. Having been expelled for questioning Stalinism, Neville joined the Young Socialists (when they were still part of Labour) and was expelled from that too. She then moved to the SLL and fairly soon after joining, she met Healy who said he wanted to meet with her privately. At the SLL headquarters in Clapham, he took her into a side room and offered her a glass of whiskey, which she refused and tried to break the tension with humour. She remembers him then saying 'Never mind that. My plan was I was going to sleep with you tonight.' Neville was struck dumb by the bizarreness of this and assumed Healy was drunk. He regularly targeted her for sex after this; as with Cowen, the boundaries between consent and coercion were blurred. Attending one of the SLL camps, Neville was refused permission to share a tent with her then boyfriend and was instead told to share a tent with Healy. She was targeted at party conferences and it does seem that some comrades knew (she remembers a male member of the party who apparently knew why she was being told to go to Healy's hotel room). On another occasion, travelling back by train from a demonstration in Belgium, Healy instructed her to come to his carriage. She knew this would mean he wanted to have sex with her, so she instead went to a different carriage and sat with a young male member hoping this would protect her; Healy later told her she 'was a very subjective person' for not obeying his instructions. She today wonders why she did not resist; one explanation she has reached is that having been expelled from the CPGB, Labour and the YS, she feared being expelled again. She believed that Trotskyists were the correct party of revolutionary leadership and did not want to walk away from that. She felt she would be turning her back on everything in which she believed and turning her back on the global revolution. Neville said Healy once told her 'I take it [sex with women] where I want it, like Lenin did.' She looked up to Lenin and clearly disagreed with this comment (and to be fair, Lenin was nothing like that); 'I didn't argue [about this comment] but nobody argued with him.' Confirming what many other female members later said, Neville saw that Healy had a way of keeping women that he assaulted separate, but she thought at the time that she was alone in being assaulted by him. She also felt that she could not tell anyone what Healy had done, whether in the party or outside of it.[36]

Another woman, who had endured Healy's abuses for two decades, told a WRP meeting in October 1985 that 'He wore down my self-esteem. I had to separate myself from the abuse till my body didn't matter to me anymore.'[37] A young woman abused by Healy quoted in an article for the London *Time Out* magazine in 1988, stated that 'It wouldn't have mattered if he could have led us to power.'[38] Healy exploited female comrades' devotion to revolutionary socialism and that devotion in turn became a kind of psychological defence mechanism for these women.

As with his violent leadership, Healy's sexual abuses were a known phenomenon, at least at the top levels of the party. Already by the early 1950s, he had attempted to proposition the daughter of a high-ranking member of the Fourth International. As Jennings points to in her letter, a 'control commission' had to be arraigned within the SLL in 1964 to investigate Healy's 'relationship' with a member of the Young Socialists, the Labour Party's youth wing, after which Healy tactfully promised to 'cease these practices'. The final catalyst for the 1974 split in the WRP had allegedly been Healy's sexual harassment of Alan Thornett's wife, though other party veterans don't recall this allegation and question its veracity.[39] One female member said that rumours of Healy's behaviour was circulating among other female comrades since at least the early 1970s, including rumours about a relationship with Aileen Jennings as well as stories about two sisters in the party who were suspected to be having some kind of sexual relationship with Healy.[40] Geoff Barr, a member of the Exeter branch of the party, heard stories of Healy sexual harassing a woman in the 1960s but seems to have compartmentalised these accusations as being non-political in nature (and yet also says he was 'shocked' and 'baffled' by the revelations about Healy in 1985).[41] Paul Henderson, a member in Nottingham, already knew of one woman who had been assaulted by Healy. This, coupled with the 'uncomradeliness' of how party activists were treated, was already causing him to question the WRP by 1985 and meant he was receptive to those moving against Healy.[42]

A male former member of the party never heard such rumours and recalled a general sense of shock when the letter was released. Yet the same member also recalled a specific incident that belies the idea that no one knew:

A particular incident stands out in my mind. A fourteen-year-old went home to tell her father she had been sexually assaulted by Healy. This produced a brainstorm in the man because his wife had made a similar complaint to him many years previously, he had not believed her, and they had divorced over it. Now he realised she had been telling the truth, he went into the Clapham HQ, encountered Healy crossing the quad, shouted 'hey, Healy' and flattened him with a haymaker. Healy never appeared in public after that without a guard by his side. Of course, these were criminal activities, as was covering them up. He should have been reported to the police, arrested, charged, and jailed for these crimes. He certainly would be today. But those who should have done that could have been charged themselves with aiding and abetting an offender, so nothing happened.[43]

Clare Cowen agrees that some members may have known of individual cases of women that Healy targeted, but that the scale and systematic nature of his abuse was not known: 'It happened under our eyes and yet we didn't see it.'[44] Dave Bruce, who claims he was the one who encouraged Jennings to write the letter, also said Jennings and Dot Gibson had told him about the sexual abuse 'a couple years' before 1985.[45] *Redemption*, Tariq Ali's 1990 *roman à clef* satirising the struggles of Trotskyist leaders attempting to adjust to a post-Cold War world, is shockingly open about the nature of Healy's sexual abuse. Ali spoke sarcastically, but grimly, about the 'leader's special needs' and the 'perfectly normal and natural carnal instincts of Comrade Hood [Healy]'.[46] Women were 'pressurised' into having sexual relations with Healy, 'every pressure was brought to bear on them' as they were told that the revolution required them to make 'the most personal sacrifice of all' for their leader.[47] Even though Mike Banda would later aggressively turn on Healy, he would be accused of having known of Healy's abuses for years.[48] Andy Blunden, who oversaw the distribution of *News Line*, had been 'expelled' from the party after defending a young Jewish party member who had made an off-colour Jewish joke; the official charge against him was that he was guilty of antisemitism. But even as an expelled member, he was still expected to devote himself to party work.[49] He was thus souring on the WRP when, one day in September 1985 he was delivering copies of *News Line* to a female comrade at Liverpool Street Station in London. She told Blunden about the accusations against Healy. 'The funny thing is I immediately believed that. It just made sense.'[50] Robert Myers similarly was not at all surprised by the revelations in 1985; he feels now that he had lots of disparate pieces of evidence in his head but had never connected them until then. His half-formed suspicions now fell into place.[51] It is also quite likely that Jennings's well-known status within the party and her years of service, as well as the fact that both of her parents were veterans of the SLL, gave her accusations a seriousness they might not have otherwise had; she could not be easily dismissed.[52]

Clare Cowen, Aileen Jennings and those that acted alongside them were motivated by a genuine desire to save the WRP; having seen the party's finances, they were all aware of the existential crisis facing the party. For people like Banda, though, there appears to have been a certain amount of opportunism to this scandal and its timings. It was not so much that the leaders who slowly joined the opposition to Healy *cared* about his victims; if they did, they would have stepped in much earlier. Rather, the opponents of Healy could use this as a convenient cudgel (albeit an obviously horrifying one). Jennings's letter also spoke disapprovingly of a 'homosexual' who had been allowed to run a party youth training centre (a homophobic line of attack she would later regret).[53] And while Jennings rightly condemned Healy for physically assaulting her, her then-husband, Paul Jennings, would later be accused of standing guard outside of a small room in the party headquarters on 1 October 1985, while Mike Banda gave 'a violent beating' to Corinna Lotz, a Healy loyalist.[54] Mike and Tony Banda were both accused of physically assaulting a female party member in Manchester and throwing her down the stairs 'because of criticisms she had expressed' at a meeting. Mike Banda allegedly also attempted to have this incident covered up.[55] There are many crimes here, and many victims, but very few heroes.

Initially, the political committee of the WRP voted by 13 to three (with two abstentions) to treat Jennings's letter as a 'provocation' but by the next day an internal investigation had been started.[56] Vanessa Redgrave angrily denounced the entire set of accusations. Mike Banda accepted their veracity but also initially excused them as the 'little vices' in which 'great leaders' often engaged; he named Tito and Mao as womanising precedents, in a crass conflation of consensual romance and sexual coercion.[57] In his lengthy autobiography, published in 2011, Alex Mitchell remained dismissive of the claims: 'I knew and had worked with all 26 women named in the letter, but none of them had ever given me the slightest indication of sexual advances by Healy.' Though given his closeness to Healy and his own attitudes towards women, why would they have told him? Unsurprisingly, Mitchell calls those who broke with

Healy over his sexual violence, 'the moral outrage brigade'.[58] Corin Redgrave was apparently unmoved by the letter and dismissed discussions of Healy's abuse as 'middle-class moralising'. Clare Cowen alleges that when some party members later confronted Redgrave about the accusations against Healy, he listed off the various achievements of the party before saying 'If this is the work of a rapist, let's recruit more rapists'.[59] Another WRP member recalls Redgrave saying he was 'neither for nor against rape' but only 'for the social revolution'.[60] In other words, he refused to address the sexual assault accusations, instead taking rhetorical refuge in a purist Marxism.

Behind the scenes, though, agreements were being quietly reached to sideline Healy, force him into retirement and control the damage to the party. By early July, Healy had signed a letter undertaking, in coded language, 'to cease immediately my personal conduct with the youth'. Healy had apparently wanted to include a caveat that 'youth' would only mean those under the age of 25, because otherwise 'it'll ruin my lifestyle'. Contriteness and even just basic human empathy were clearly not Healy's strengths. Sheila Torrance exasperatedly told him to leave out these conditional qualifiers.[61] Phil Penn, a member of the WRP's central committee, wrote an open letter demanding that Healy be prevented in the future from teaching 'rubbish' at the College of Marxist Education, a valid criticism that had been a long time coming.[62] Healy began to be accused of violating 'revolutionary morality'.[63]

On 3 September, Mike Banda called David North in Michigan, who was already hostile to Healy, to not only tell him about the scandal but to also seek his support in moving against Healy.[64] Banda had apparently spoken to the father of one of Healy's victims and was so disturbed by what he learned that he had finally turned on him. Banda began to insist that retirement was not enough; Healy should be banned from party premises.[65] Banda had by now apparently decided that Healy, to whom he had previously shown intense loyalty, was actually just 'an ignorant Irish peasant' whose supporters were 'neo-fascists'.[66] The next day, after discussion with Banda and Sheila Torrance, Healy agreed to retire from the leadership of the WRP.[67]

By September 1985, the news about Healy's sexual violence was spreading throughout the WRP ecosystem, though the party leadership still sought to suppress any open criticism; when one of Healy's assault victims called for him to investigated, she was expelled from the WRP.[68] But with condemnation of Healy coming more and more into the open, the party was unable to stop both the scandal about Healy and the fracturing of the party. At a mammoth meeting at party headquarters in London on 12–13 October, the central committee of the Workers Revolutionary Party voted, by 25–11 to 'charge' Healy with sexual assault. Those voting at the meeting were intensely lobbied by the different pro- and anti-Healy factions as well as by the relatives of Healy's victims.[69] Inviting the relatives, who had a clearly emotive presence, was Mike Banda's idea.[70]

At this meeting, Banda gave a 90-minute speech in which he recounted a litany of Healy's sexually abusive actions, thus tacitly admitting that he had probably known of them all along. According to one eye-witness, Banda became severely agitated during his speech: 'he swept his hand across the table with such force that he flung a glass into Sheila Torrance's face. She suffered cuts around her eyes as the glass shattered and was only saved from serious injury by the fact she was wearing spectacles. Banda said she had "asked for it" for daring to defend Healy's political record.'[71]

Torrance, in turn, dismissed the accusations against Healy as 'bourgeois ideology' and those spreading the accusations were, she said, 'a lot of Mary Whitehouses', in reference to the notoriously prudish media campaigner. Torrance was fired from her full-time job with the party at this meeting, as recompense for her lingering loyalty to Healy.[72] Healy himself was absent from the meeting; having been living in a flat owned by the party, and probably seeing the writing on the wall, he had moved out of the property the night before, 'taking only two clean shirts and three books'.[73] As his role in the party was being decided, he hid out first in Corinna Lotz's apartment, later moving to a hotel after Torrance called him and warned him that he might be attacked by former comrades.[74]

Various leaders from the International were invited to come to Britain to take sides in the faction-fighting. Healy refused to co-operate in these proceedings, such that the only recourse left for the

WRP leadership was to expel him from the party on 19 October. The vote to expel him was unanimous, partly because Healy and his supporters boycotted the meeting. His expulsion was for four offences: 'sexual abuse of female Party members; continual use of physical violence; violating his retirement agreement; and slander of an international comrade'. This last charge was due to an accusation that Healy made around this time that the American Workers League may have been infiltrated by American intelligence.[75] Concurrent with the charges against Healy, the WRP passed a resolution that 'Any comrade who reveals details of the Party crisis to the bourgeois or revisionist press or anyone outside the Party will be charged immediately under the Constitution.'[76] Exactly a week later, those who remained in any way loyal to Healy were also expelled, a group that included Sheila Torrance and the two Redgraves. And on 25 October, Healy was expelled from the ICFI.[77]

With Healy dethroned, recriminations and condemnations began to be tossed in every direction. While the Healy loyalists would soon claim that the sexual assault accusations were a lie, *News Line* were able to point to Healy's signing of a written agreement 'that he would cease these practices',[78] a damning piece of evidence. Vanessa Redgrave was already, by this point, starting legal proceedings to gain control of some assets assumed to be owned by the party.[79] Inevitably, the story soon spread to the outside world; on 24 October, both the *Guardian* and the *Times* both ran relatively tame articles on Healy's expulsion. On 27 October 1985, an article appeared in the *Observer* which talked about a 'sudden coup d'état which has left the members of the organisation reeling'. The use of such coded phrases would soon fall by the wayside, as the infamously crude British tabloid press opened the floodgates. The *Mirror* ran a story on Healy and Jennings on 31 October titled 'Red in the Bed'. *The Daily Star* and the *Sunday Mirror*, the *Sun*, the *Express* and the *Daily Mail* also ran articles, written in the same scandalised but salacious tone. The *Sunday Times* sarcastically said *News Line* had become Britain's fastest-growing tabloid because of interest in the scandal, with its circulation supposedly trebling. The *Express* described Healy as 'the envy of many a geriatric', despite the fact that what they were describing was coercive sexual assault. And indeed, changing tone rapidly, the *Express* went on to quote

John Spencer, deputy editor of *News Line*: 'You are talking about somebody who has got a deep hatred of women, who feels compelled to humiliate and dominate them... He is a sick man.' And even the quote from a female victim of Healy's, who compared the abuse to incest, because of his father-figure status in the WRP, did not seem to make an impact on the *Express*'s prose stylings.[80]

Cliff Slaughter publicly observed in November that Healy had treated the WRP as his own 'private brothel'.[81] Other former Healy-ites were not willing to be so frank. The 'Workers Press' grouping emerging out of the WRP called out Healy for his 'entirely non-communist and bureaucratic relations inside the party',[82] a weirdly occluded way of phrasing it. Though a few days later, the same group was far less circumspect: Healy 'was justly expelled for repeated sexual assaults on women members of the party and of the International Committee of the Fourth International'.[83] The WRP's youth wing, the Young Socialists, crudely embedded their criticisms of Healy's abuses in a vulgar Marxism: 'The actions of Healy and his supporters had more in common with Stalinist degeneration and bureaucracy than Trotskyism... The sexual abuse of women represents a fundamental class position dominated by imperialism and its reactionary ideology.'[84] The *Communist Forum*, the group and journal that later coalesced around Mike Banda, reprinted copies of hotel bills run up by Healy during the miners' strike – an average of £44 a night (£130 in 2024) – and charged to the WRP's publishing company, making the obvious case that Healy was nothing but a self-serving grifter.[85] The ICFI issued a statement denouncing Healy's 'self-glorification' and also charged him with the sins of being 'a thorough-going subjective idealist and pragmatist'. And as Healy degraded politically, so also his 'personal life-style underwent a corresponding degeneration'.[86] The Healyite remnant of the WRP, in a resolution signed by Corin Redgrave, Vanessa Redgrave and Sheila Torrance among others, accused Mike Banda and Cliff Slaughter of 'subjective idealism', 'rank and fileism', and allowing 'freedom of criticism' and 'rule from below'.[87] Rather than accepting that the split had weakened them, the Healyite rump said that they had been 'theoretically strengthened' (i.e. stronger in their Marxist theories) and had their 'fighting traditions' upheld by the experience, whereas Banda and Slaughter were left, they alleged, with only a 'rump of politically deranged malcontents'.[88] Banda said of Healy and his followers after the split that they had degraded into a politics of 'positivism and pragmatism'.[89] There is an obvious irony that all the pro- and anti-Healy factions zealously denounced each other using the very terminology they had directly learned from Healy.

Commentary and criticism soon spread across the Trotskyist world.[90] The Workers Socialist League, the group formed by Alan Thornett after splitting from the WRP in 1974, made the comment that Healy's expulsion had 'lifted the lid on a Pandora's box of corruption, intimidation and political bureaucracy'.[91] Tony Cliff of the SWP sidestepped the sexual issues completely, instead appraising the WRP's fracturing in very Trotskyist and masculinist terms:

> Because of the wrong perspective about the miners' strike, expectations rose, and when those expectations were not realised then they started tearing one another to pieces... When conditions are tough, people who don't fit disintegrate. They fact that we [the SWP] didn't [disintegrate] shows that we were right. It's nothing to do with psychological toughness – in terms of toughness the WRP are the toughest in the world, but they disintegrated completely because they issued statements which didn't fit the situation at all.[92]

Tariq Ali said he kept the *News Line* front cover about Healy's expulsion from the WRP as a memento: 'It was high time that happened.' He said he was not surprised by the revelations, given the internal regime of the WRP. He compares it to clerical child sex abuse, in terms of how an ultra-hierarchical system can fuel abuse.[93]

Six groups – and in time ten separate groups – would emerge out of the wreckage of the WRP.[94] Sheila Torrance, despite being somewhat critical of Healy, still claimed that the sexual abuse accusations were a 'Trojan horse for revisionism'.[95] Torrance and the Redgraves had a brief truce, with both staying active in a party that styled itself 'Workers Revolutionary Party (Healyite)', though this only lasted a year. The two blocs parted ways at the end of October 1986. Officially, the faction that formed around Torrance remained loyal to Healyism and retained the name Workers Revolutionary Party, even as they cut all ties with Healy himself. By June 1987, they were naming Healy an 'ex-Trotskyist' who was 'doing everything possible to hi-jack the Trotskyist movement and liqui- date it into the Gorbachev Stalinist bureaucracy'.[96]

The Redgraves and their supporters formed another faction, remaining intensely loyal to both Healyism and Healy. When the Redgrave faction reformed as The Marxist Party, the bulk of the first issue of their journal, *The Marxist*, was taken up with letters between Sheila Torrance, Gerry Healy, Vanessa Redgrave and others involved in the split, mainly pointing fingers and engaging in charged recriminations.[97] Other than a handful of supporters who formed the International Communist Party (later renamed the Socialist Equality Party), the various factions all split from their former International, the ICFI, which was now dominated by David North, who was by then vociferously hostile to Healy the person but still Healyist in tone and thrust.[98] Confusingly, Healy's faction also claimed ownership of the name ICFI.

On 11 October 1985, two days before Healy was charged by the WRP leadership, Corin Redgrave took personal possession of the deeds of the College of Marxist Education but was forced to return them to Cliff Slaughter, a leading member of the anti-Healy faction.[99] Disputes over the ownership of this house, a useful polit- ical asset as well as a prime slice of real estate, lingered on; this may have contributed to the final break between Sheila Torrance and Gerry Healy. Corinna Lotz recalled attending a meeting of the Healyite ICFI at Vanessa Redgrave's flat in the later summer of 1986: 'Since I was not a committee member, I waited in the kitchen. Suddenly I heard angry shouting. Torrance stormed out of the flat. ICFI secretary Michael followed her down into the street, and per- suaded her to return. I later learned that Torrance had flown into a rage over a proposal to look into the ownership rights of the party's school in Derbyshire.'[100] Corin Redgrave began a long process of attempting to regain full control of the house. Both he and one of the WRP factions claimed to have documents proving legal own- ership. By 1990, a group of new age travellers was squatting on the property, having apparently received an invitation from the WRP to do so. Since Redgrave could not satisfactorily prove legal own- ership, he could not obtain an eviction order. Eventually, in 1993,

Redgrave was able to sell it privately to a local businessman, having also agreed to hand over some of the proceeds to liquidators of other WRP assets.[101]

Commensurate with the party's fracturing, the WRP's finances were in crisis and party assets were being seized by the differing factions. The Banda faction were accused of locking out Healy supporters from the printing works in Runcorn as they claimed ownership over its valuable equipment.[102] Two members of the Young Socialists, signatories to the party's bank account, emptied the account before allying themselves to David North.[103] According to another allegation, German allies of David North raided the WRP's offices in Clapham in search of Trotsky's death mask, supposedly securing it for the ICFI in the name of 'revolutionary continuity'.[104] There had been discussions of selling the mask to a museum, as part of a general re-ordering of party assets and shoring up of finances after the split.[105] It is not actually clear where the mask ended up. Even though the WRP received a pledge in August 1985 of £82,000 from international sections of the ICFI, intended to solve the party's financial crisis, party employees in London were made redundant (though they were expected to continue working for the party while signing on for unemployment benefit).[106] The post-Healy WRP soon organised a 'Defend the WRP' appeal that raised £60,000, though £21,000 was allegedly handed over to Vanessa Redgrave to repay a loan she had given the party before her expulsion.[107]

This is perhaps the same loan that was mentioned in a petition to the Companies Court of the High Court on 30 October 1985. Redgrave had loaned £29,000 (not £21,000) to Astmoor Litho, the legal owner of the WRP's printing works. With the loan being unpaid, Redgrave legally requested, with Healy's support, to have Astmoor Litho compulsorily wound up.[108] The WRP members who retained control of the company unsuccessfully sought to prove that the 'loan' was in fact a gift and did not have to be repaid. Redgrave, though, was able to provide documentary evidence that this was, indeed, a loan.[109] Astmoor Litho was wound up by December 1985. Since Astmoor Litho technically had no assets there was not much to gain from this. The high-tech printing equipment was the property of the party, and that ended up having to be sold off on the cheap by auction to pay creditors.[110]

Around the same time, it was discovered that two of the WRP's Youth Training Centres had been sold and that mortgages had been issued on other party properties.[111] In general, the 1985 split in the WRP was the occasion for a fair amount of financial carpetbagging. However, the generally chaotic and convoluted nature of the party's finances make it difficult to know who was actually stealing what. Alex Mitchell claimed that at one early point in the mid-1970s the WRP did not even have a bank account[112] and so party funds would presumably have been held in members' personal accounts. Whether or not that was true, Healy certainly had an indifference to the party's financial woes; attempts to get him to care would trigger one of his regular temper tantrums.[113] Clare Cowen, whose family had amassed wealth from South African and Rhodesian mining, had allowed her trust fund to be used by the party. She was the legal owner of some of the party's offices in Clapham and one of the party's youth training centres.[114] Even at the height of the split, when Cowen had already come out against Healy, he was still trying to get her to buy some of the party's bookshops.[115] All of this was generally kept secret, which is probably the reason why she could later be accused of stealing wholesale from the WRP;[116] rather than ransacking party assets, though, she was merely taking repossession of what was legally hers. Dave Bruce confirms Cowen's account; he agrees that Cowen acted honestly but thinks it was a mistake to make these financial deals in private, for which he blames Dot Gibson. Bruce and Gibson soon had a falling out and he today feels she is 'a very nasty piece of work'.[117]

The shares in New Park Publications, the WRP's publishing firm, also became a factor in the split. As the different individual shareholders formed new political entities, they took their shares with them, effectively ending the company's existence. The WRP's finance committee unsuccessfully demanded that ex-members return the shares.[118] Some of the most lucrative of the WRP's assets were held under the umbrella of New Park Publications, including its various publishing operations as well as Copescroft Ltd, which owned the party's youth training centres around Britain. It had amassed debts of £450,000 by 1985.[119] The properties held by

New Park, as well as the Runcorn printing facility, were quickly sold after the split, at below market rates in something of a rushed fire sale. The accusation that one faction or another had personally profited from the split would recur again and again.[120]

Corin Redgrave was commissioned to write a report 'under Gerry's guidance' which alleged that opponents of Healy within the WRP 'had systematically sabotaged the WRP's finances' over a period of years. Redgrave's report was more of a polemic against opponents rather than any kind of serious accounting: 'He has no financial training – but of course he's read *Volume 38*' was one contemporary view of this stitch-up.[121] The 15-page report had very few figures, and little discussion of accounts, company ownership structures or the source of party debts.[122] But it did duly present a picture of forged documents, illegal mortgages, illicit property sales and a cover-up of the developing crisis.[123] As with so much else in the story of the WRP, it is hard to separate out facts here from invective and charged allegations. And one set of financial allegations – that the party was a massive conduit for illicit funds from Middle Eastern dictators – would define the afterlife of the Workers Revolutionary Party, along with various allegations about intelligence agencies sabotaging the WRP, all of which is discussed in the next chapter.

8

Spycraft

After Gerry Healy died in late 1989, his remaining supporters organised a public tribute to him, held at the Adelphi Theatre in London on 4 March 1990. One of those who spoke about his legacy was Ken Livingstone, by then a Labour MP. He had previously been the leader of the Greater London Council (which is where he first met Healy) and would later be the Mayor of London and a prominent voice on the left of the Labour Party, until a number of ill-considered comments about Jews and Zionism led to his expulsion from Labour. Much of what Livingstone said that night about Healy was fairly unremarkable – Healy's commitment to the Palestinians, his dedication to left-wing causes in general, Livingstone's personal friendship with him – until at the end, when Livingstone announced 'I don't want to finish what I'm saying without having a word to say about MI5' and then proceeded to level a very serious charge against British military intelligence:

> I haven't the slightest doubt that the upheavals that split apart the Workers Revolutionary Party, were not some accident or some clash of personalities. They were a sustained and deliberate decision by MI5 to smash that organisation, because they feared it was becoming too pivotal in terms of domestic politics, linking too many international struggles with progressive elements both inside and outside the British labour movement. Nothing that I have seen causes me to question that basic assumption, and it may very well be that one day we will see evidence drawn out, that shows the work of MI5 agents that was put into actually damaging, and trying to roll back so much of what had been done.[1]

Figure 5   Solidarity, Issue 16, Spring 1988

In letters that he later exchanged with ex-WRP members, first published in the *Bulletin* of David North's Workers League, and then reported on in *Lobster*, a muck-raking magazine focusing on the British intelligence services, Livingstone claimed to have acquired copies of Special Branch reports on the WRP. *Lobster* generally took the accusations of MI5 interference seriously, seeing this as resulting from the WRP's Middle Eastern connections.[2]

In the most narrow sense, Livingstone's claim was absurd; the WRP was a paranoid entity, riven by personal animosities. And the immediate catalyst for the 1985 split, Gerry Healy's sexual abuse of female party members, was undeniably horrific. In such a situation, there is no need for a deep state *deus ex machina* to explain how and why the organisation fractured.

Even if there is scant evidence that MI5 played a stealthy role in splitting the WRP, though, Livingstone's claims do have a certain basis in reality. For a start, there is a well-documented history of political interference by British intelligence agencies and the police, mainly targeting the left, from shenanigans targeting Prime Minister Harold Wilson in the 1960s to infiltration of the Labour movement during the miners' strike to senior generals openly saying they would refuse to obey orders had Jeremy Corbyn become prime minister.[3] All of these should have been bigger scandals. The observations of the historian Daniel Chard about accusations of FBI interference in the American New Left and Black Power movement are apposite for the WRP; the interference was real, but relying on this as the sole explanation for why these groups disintegrated or tore themselves apart becomes 'a way to avoid reckoning with their own role' in these sometime violent conflicts. And it overemphasises the state's abilities whilst underestimating how much the left can resist this state interference.[4] As Ken Livingstone himself later commented, in a letter to Cliff Slaughter, 'democratic centralist organisations are particularly vulnerable to internal disruption by MI5/Special Branch because of their traditions of expulsions and their secretive style of operations'.[5]

Tariq Ali, still a leading voice on the British left, today has 'no doubt' that the WRP were infiltrated by the British state.[6] Even party members who had clearly split from Healy suspect some level of state infiltration could have played a role in the breakup of the WRP, albeit remaining suitably cautious about this.[7] Already, in January 1954, Healy was the subject of MI5 monitoring because of an ongoing surveillance of Charles Van Gelderen, a South African Trotskyist of Dutch Jewish ancestry. Healy at this time was setting up a company named Westminster Publications LTD, of which Van Gelderen was listed as secretary. Healy was again under state surveillance in 1957, because of contacts he and Peter

Fryer were having with Hyman Levy, a mathematician and Communist.[8] Such MI5 surveillance continued into the 1960s.[9] From evidence recently released by the Undercover Policing Inquiry, it is empirically true that the Workers Revolutionary Party were under police monitoring and that there were police informants within the party providing information on multiple aspects of the WRP's activities.[10] Infiltration of the WRP by undercover police lasted for about two years in the mid-1970s.[11] And multiple former members have clear memories and strong evidence of being spied on by the police.[12]

Deirdre Redgrave believed her and Corin's phone was bugged, whether by the police or by the intelligence services.[13] Tim Wohlforth was under FBI surveillance almost as soon as he became an active Trotskyist. He was later able to make requests under the Freedom of Information Act to view the files kept on him; information about his trips to Britain was shared with British intelligence.[14] In his infamous 1987 memoir, *Spycatcher*, Peter Wright recalled that MI5 were monitoring the Workers Revolutionary Party and the Socialist Workers Party in the 1970s, acting on direct instructions from the Tory Prime Minister, Ted Heath, and the Home Office, who had been very clear with the then Director-General of MI5, Michael Hanley, that 'they wanted a major increase in effort on this target'. Wright remembers attending a seminar on the WRP and SWP led by 'a young and ambitious F Branch officer, David Ransome', in about 1972. Wright claims that the general view within MI5 was that these 'left-wing splinter groups' were not all that dangerous, though of course that belies the perceived need to monitor them in the first place.[15] As one historian of the agency has said 'Communist subversion was the perceived Satan of MI5's political theology.'[16] Whatever about the veracity of his other claims, Livingstone was definitely correct to state that 'MI5 considers even the smallest left organisation worthy of close surveillance and disruption.'[17]

The WRP was enough of a police interest to have its Derbyshire school raided by the police in 1975, even if the raid became the catalyst for a bout of paranoia within the party. One Healyite loyalist's claim that MI5 were complicit in organising this raid is extreme but certainly not impossible or out of character for that agency.[18] In the aftermath of their related libel trial with the *Observer*, the WRP acquired a copy of a Special Branch report on the raid which does seem to confirm that the police and the newspaper were cooperating at some level.[19] The journalist and academic Stephen Dorril, a specialist in the workings of the British intelligence services, said that the 'circumstantial evidence' does corroborate MI5's role in both the 1975 raid and in the 1985–86 split; the party's financial connection to Libya, Dorril claims, would have been seen as justification for this.[20]

Paranoia had been a part of Healyist Trotskyism from an early point. Brian Behan recalls so paranoid an atmosphere prevailing within the SLL that when Healy said a new MI5 technology allowed for surveillance recording based just on the sound-wave vibrations in glass windowpanes, party members duly sat with their backs to the window to prevent their 'vibrations' from being detected. 'People who could believe this lunacy,' Behan said, 'could well be capable of anything.'[21] In 1978, Mike Banda claimed an ex-soldier who had recently joined the party was being regularly visited by police and army officers asking him to spy on the WRP. According to the soldier, not only were agents of the state using high-powered microphones to spy on the WRP but they were allegedly also planning for an 'accident' to happen to a leading WRP member.[22] It is, of course, impossible to know how real was any of Banda's story.

Healy certainly appeared to have shared the view that British intelligence played a hand in the 1985 split, though he also gave this an idiosyncratic spin. His most sympathetic biographers say that there 'was no doubt in Gerry's mind' that his insistence on 'collective theoretical work' and correct training in 'materialist dialectics' had broken the resolve of intellectually weaker members of the WRP, who thus became willing marks for MI5.[23] By 1988, he was accusing Cliff Slaughter and David North of being police agents and part of a CIA-led conspiracy, that apparently incorporated five other intelligence services, all aimed at destroying the WRP.[24]

Adding to all this intrigue, an incendiary article was published in the spring of 1988 in *Solidarity*, a magazine produced by a group of the same name, whose origins lay in the old SLL but who had since moved to something closer to anarchism. The article was a distillation of a report originally commissioned by the ICFI but which that same group subsequently self-censored. A ICFI 'Commission' on Healy and the WRP had been demanded by David North as well as the anti-Healy faction around Mike Banda and Cliff Slaughter. The report produced by this commission alleged, among other things, that the WRP had been the recipient of over a million pounds 'from Arab regimes and the Palestine Liberation Organisation' starting from at least as early as 1975, when the first contact with the PLO was established, until 1983; that the WRP acted – through Gerry Healy, Alex Mitchell, Corin and Vanessa Redgrave, and a number of others – as a collector of information for Libyan Intelligence; and that just under £20,000 was received from the Iraqi government, as payment for similar intelligence services. *Solidarity* also alleged that the WRP adapted its political positions on various issues to align with dictates from the Libyan government and also imbibed an antisemitic worldview from the Gaddafi regime.[25] The *Solidarity* article was later recycled into a piece in *Time Out*, a London-based listings and muck-raking magazine, and was also featured in the rightist *Daily Mail*, helping the story find an audience outside of the small world of Trotskyist polemics.[26] This was to become one of the most enduring allegations about Gerry Healy and the Workers Revolutionary Party, that they were not only in contact with a raft of Middle Eastern dictators but were also recipients of their generous financial contributions.

In 1983, the BBC identified 'persistent suggestions and rumours' of links to Libya. Without providing sources for this, the BBC claimed that Vanessa Redgrave had 'visited Colonel Gadaffi on a number of occasions and he once greeted her with the words "How is my party?"'.[27] As early as 1979, *Time Out* was focusing on these Healy–Tripoli connections.[28] The *Sunday Telegraph* claimed, in September 1981, that the WRP had already received £50,000 from Gaddafi, funding the printworks in Runcorn, prompting a sarcastic response from *News Line*.[29] Again, as with the assertion that MI5 was conspiring against the WRP, these allegations mix the factual with the unfounded and the downright implausible. The ICFI report from which the *Solidarity* allegations were derived, was itself the product of an emotionally charged split in a party that was already given over to paranoia and the use of bombastically over-the-top allegations. Least credible in all this is the idea that the PLO, caught in an existential struggle with the State of Israel and at the height of its crises in Lebanon, would have handed over money to a tiny group of Trotskyists in the UK. The Libyan and Iraqi connections have more truth to them (though whatever the nature of the connections with Iraq or Libya, it is difficult to know how much it actually extended beyond mere rhetoric).

The WRP was unusually praising of Saddam Hussein's Ba'ath Party regime in Iraq, going so far as to publish a pamphlet that lavished praise on his government. In February and March 1979, *News Line* published articles condoning the recent governemnt execution of 21 members of the Iraqi Communist Party.[30] Former member Robin Blick claimed that the WRP's Central Committee approved (with only one dissension) a resolution approving the executions.[31] The WRP certainly made efforts to provide coverage for the Iraqi government, speaking out against anti-Ba'ath sentiments within the TGWU union and the National Union of Students.[32]

In early July 1979, Talib Suwailh, an executive member of the Ba'ath-backed Federation of Trade Unions in Iraq, was the WRP's guest at a trade union conference in London. *News Line* uncritcally reprinted his overly positive views of working-class life in Ba'athist Iraq.[33] Suwailh was allegedly executed a few weeks later, during a purge said to have followed the deposing of President Ahmad Hassan al-Bakr and his replacement by Saddam Hussein, which *News Line* never mentioned in any subsequent articles. The details of Suwailh's murder are murky. The main source for the accusation is a statement released by David North's ICFI in the summer of 1986, after he had broken with Healy and was engaged in charged polemics with former comrades. That some key empirical details in the ICFI statement are faulty – such as the claim that Suwailh was murdered alongside al-Bakr in 1979, even though the latter died in 1982 – adds to this.[34] Other WRP members seemed to think Suwailh was a communist, not a Ba'athist.[35]

In any case, it is not clear if the WRP's pro-Ba'ath statements in 1979 went beyond rhetorical support. Moreover, the purported role of the WRP in the late 1970s crackdown on the Iraqi Communists or on opponents of Saddam within the Ba'ath Party is not mentioned in any of the standard histories of either parties.[36] It is, indeed, highly questionable if the Iraqi government would have cared about the activities of a small Trotskyist group in Britain.[37] More likely is that the Healyites sought to boost themselves with tales of international influence, and their detractors denounced them with exaggerated (if not fully fabricated) stories that they were accomplices in the murder of opponents of Saddam.[38] Whatever the truth of these accusations, the Iraqi government appeared to have had enough sense to avoid sending too much money to Healy, particuarly as the WRP suffered embarrassing electoral defeats.[39]

Likewise with Healy's dalliances with the Libyan government, it is hard to separate out fact from fantasy. It definitely seems to be true that the WRP had contracts with the Libyan government to mass-print copies of Gadaffi's *Green Book* (Andy Blunden remembers delivering copies of them) and probably also the state newspaper, *Al-Zahf Al-Akhdar (The Green March)* and *the Jamahiriya International Report*, an English-language gazette. But this appears to have had little to do with international intrigue and far more to do with the fact that the WRP could lowball the rates of other printing companies (not least because much of their printing work was done for free by party volunteers, rather than by paid employees). The BBC claimed in March 1983 that the WRP had received an overly generous £1.5m from Tripoli for this publishing, though incongrously Astmoor Litho appears to have been a loss-making enterprise.[40] Healy did apparently write obsequious begging letters to Gadaffi. David North quotes a letter of 17 May 1981 to Gaddafi which Healy wrote following a trip to Libya. Healy thanked Gadaffi for being 'kind enough to grant us an interview, and to listen patiently to my report on the political developments in Britain'. Healy then presented 'with great respect' an appeal for financial support: 'We greatly regret having to approach you with such matters, since you have so many more important affairs to contend with.' Another 'private and confidential' letter to Gaddafi assured the Libyan strongman:

> The alliance between the Socialist People's Libyan Jamahiriya and the Workers Revolutionary Party has never been more vital, and we are proud to restate that our party is your base in Britain

to fight against this international imperialist conspiracy. We resolutely place our party and all its material resources at the service of the Jamahiriya to wage this struggle in defence of the whole Arab revolution and the oppressed peoples of Africa, Asia and Latin America.[41]

Rumours have often abounded about Gaddafi's largesse to revolutionaries around the world. At a ceremony in June 1972 to mark the two-year anniversary of the US withdrawal from the Wheelus Airforce Base just outside of Tripoli, Gaddafi announced his intention of giving support to American Black Power activists, Muslims in the Philippines and the Provisional IRA. He later promised to also support Native American activists.[42] In a report on 11 August 1972, the Lebanese *Al-Bayraq* (*The Flag*) newspaper claimed Gaddafi had given $50m to Arafat's Fatah, $13m to the Tunisian opposition, $20m to Moroccan opposition forces, $10m to revolutionaries in Chad, $24m over three years to Black Power groups in the US and $10m to the IRA.[43] (Irish government documents released at the very end of 2021 confirm this latter amount – $12.5million, in three cash payments, between 1973 and 1990, along with a staggering array of weaponry.)[44]

Some of the amounts thrown around in these stories are almost certainly exaggerated but they do still show how the five-figure sums Gaddafi was allegedly giving the WRP were really only a drop in a much larger ocean. And certainly, Gaddafi had no love for the British government, evidenced by both his support for the IRA as well as in a hostility that grew worse throughout the 1980s. When a British police officer, Yvonne Fletcher, was shot and killed by Libyan embassy staff during an anti-Gaddafi protest in London in April 1984, the British government severed diplomatic ties with the country. American F-111 planes that bombed Libya in 1986 took off from Upper Heyford in Oxfordshire, which became one more reason for Gaddafi's hostility towards the British government.

But as with his Iraqi counterpart, the Colonel was probably not eager to open the purse strings too widely for the WRP. The literature on Gaddafi is often sensationalised and Orientalist, reliant on images of a 'mad' Arab potentate, eccentric at best, drunk on oil money at worst, throwing his wealth at radicals and revolutionaries.[45] And yet, in the various studies of Gadaffi, the WRP goes unmentioned; the authors of these books are often of an ideological bent such that they would have happily discussed the Colonel's connections to a marginal Trotskyist group; the best we can say, is that the WRP's connection was too insignificant to warrant a mention. More realistically, those connections probably consisted of printing contracts and some small-scale donations to the WRP. In general, it is rarely clear if Healy's desires to build relationships with decidedly non-Marxist leaders in the Middle East achieved much for the WRP.[46]

Additionally, linking Healy to Gadaffi was another useful stick with which to beat him and his supporters. Already in January 1980, Sean Matgamna was alleging in *Socialist Organiser* that the WRP was taking money from Gaddafi and possibly other governments in the region; Vanessa Redgrave attempted to sue Matgamna for this accusation, as well as a claim that the WRP was a cult, but later dropped the case.[47] The BBC's *Money Programme* accused Healy of taking money from Libya, after which Healy wrote a response in *News Line* that claimed this accusation came from 'Zionists' active in Labour, in Thatcher's government and at the BBC, his paranoia here crossing over into classic antisemitic tropes about Jews controlling the government and the media.[48] For sure, the BBC documentary was, at times, tendentious and overly hostile, but as Sean Matgamna pointed out soon afterward: 'Bluster as you will, however, the important question in this matter – whatever the BBC's intentions – is this: are the allegations true? Do you get money from Libya?'[49] In 1985, Alan Thornett's Workers Socialist League published *An Open Letter to WRP members following the expulsion of Gerry Healy* which was accompanied by a large photo of the Libyan dictator, even though Gaddafi was never actually mentioned in the letter.[50]

The ICFI's 1985 investigation, eventually printed under the title *Corruption of the Workers Revolutionary Party: Interim Report of the International Committee Commission*, has since become a key source for these accusations about Arab gold. The investigators claimed to have found seven documents detailing secret donations from the Iraqi government, apparently made in return for photos of London-based Iraqi Communists who opposed the regime.[51] At

the time of the 1985 split, a party member named Ray Rising allegedly confessed to being the photographer tasked with taking these
photos, after which Alex Mitchell is said to have delivered the photographs to the Iraqi embassy, receiving a payment of £200 for the
WRP.[52] The total alleged sums from Iraq came to at least £19,967,
possibly more, and may have not lasted past 1980, when the Iran–
Iraq war started. The ICFI inquiry then claimed to have acquired
a further 28 documents claiming the Libyan government gave
up to £500,000 which supposedly paid for the printing works at
Runcorn. In keeping with an agreement allegedly signed by Corin
Redgrave and Roy Battersby, the WRP was expected to give intelligence reports on 'Zionists' to the Libyan government in return, here
used as an antisemitic synonym for 'Jews' more broadly. According
to this tranche of files, Healy visited Libya in August 1977 seeking
£100,000 for *News Line*: 'The Commission was not able to establish if any of this money was received.' The investigators also said
that Healy destroyed many incriminating documents but they
claimed to have established that Healy had received £1,075,163
from foreign governments, mainly in the Middle East (£542,267
from Libya, £156,500 from Kuwait, £50,000 from Qatar, £25,000
from Abu Dhabi, £19,997 from the PLO, £19,697 from Iraq, with
£261,702 coming from unknown sources).[53] These are shocking
allegations and there are certainly some genuine discrepancies
and oddities in the WRP's finances.[54] The large sums here would
go a long way to explain how a party as small as the WRP was
able to afford so large a portfolio of capital assets, from the Derbyshire school to the Runcorn printing works (even if, in reality,
donations sweated from party members were probably always
the main revenue stream for these expensive purchases). Yet, it
has to be remembered that this is one sectarian Trotskyist faction
using a politicised report to condemn another faction – this not a
clear-headed report, much less an impartial one. Some of this was
almost certainly fabricated out of whole cloth; some of the sums
were probably payments made for broadcast rights for the *Palestinian* documentary or for printing jobs.[55] The idea that the PLO
would give £20,000 to a small Marxist group in Britain is absurd
as is the general claim that Healy had personally amassed over a
million pounds. *Time Out* magazine alleged in 1988 that the PLO

was paying £5 for every WRP member attending pro-Palestinian demonstrations, almost certainly crossing over into conspiracy theory territory.[56]

The WRP undeniably had connections with various regimes and political movements in the Arab world as well in the Middle East and Global South more broadly. A number of WRP publications wrote with sympathy for Khomeini's Islamic Revolution and for the emerging post-Rhodesian regime in Zimbabwe.[57] The WRP at one point attempted to open an office in Lebanon, ran by a hapless Malian party member named Ali who was confused as to why he had even been dispatched there.[58] Mike Banda had defended the Suharto regime in Indonesia during its invasion of East Timor.[59] Healy had long-standing connections, from well before the founding of the WRP, to Lanka Sama Samaja Party (LSSP), a major force on the Sri Lankan left, and one of the few Trotskyist parties to gain actual governmental power.[60] The WRP was clearly proud of its links to Abu Jihad (Khalil al-Wazir), a leading PLO militant.[61] Abu Jihad's wife, Intissar al-Wazir, herself a member of the Central Committee of Fatah who would later serve as Social Affairs Minister of the Palestinian Authority, gave a eulogy message for Gerry Healy pronouncing:

> We mourn with you the death of our comrade, fighter and friend, Gerry Healy. Gerry was a man of principle, a great revolutionary leader, a Marxist, who devoted his life to teaching revolution-ary ideas and theory to all who struggle against imperialism, Zionism and racialism. He was an unswerving friend and ally of the Palestinian Revolution, and a true friend and brother to every liberation movement throughout the world.[62]

The General Union of Palestinian Students also delivered a message of condolences for Healy.[63] The WRP appears to have inflated these connections, and in some cases outright invented them, knowing that they added to the party's prestige and self-im-portance. Ken Livingstone claimed in 1994 that Healy maintained regular contact with Yasser Arafat, 'through the WRP's use of the latest technology', and that this was at the root of MI5's ostensible campaign against him;[64] this is a downright silly allegation.

Several WRP members were later quite open about their connections to Gadaffi, some making unbelivable claims about their connections, others more credible.[65] Alex Mitchell's 2011 memoirs are filled with accounts of his visits to various Middle Eastern countries – including Libya and Iraq – as an official representative of the WRP. Parts of this recounting are certainly true.[66] But some of his claims read as sheer fantasy; that Ahmed al-Shahati, Director of the International Center for Green Book Studies and Research handed him $15,000 in cash on one trip; that Yasser Arafat gave £15,000 to Ted Knight to fund the *Labour Herald*, supposedly as recompense for Knight's work in steering the Labour Party in a more pro-PLO direction; that at a conference in Tripoli, Yasir Arafat came straight up to Mitchell, ignoring other Western journalists, to ask 'How is the Old Man [Healy] and Vanessa? Give them my greetings.'[67] Healy supposedly accompanied Mitchell on a number of these trips, meeting Gadaffi to discuss British and Irish politics. On a trip to Iraq with Redgrave, Aileen Jennings and Mitchell, apparently to cement the WRP and Iraqi government's shared pro-Palestinian stance, Healy hated the heat and dust. When Redgrave contradicted him in front of their Ba'athist hosts, Healy berated her until she was in tears. The visit ended better when Saddam – then 'number two in the regime but effectively its strong man', which dates the trip to sometime before 1979 – invited Healy and Redgrave to meet him and 'said he had received reports from London and Beirut about the party's commitment to the Arab revolution'. Mitchell claims that Saddam discussed his plans to develop nuclear weapons with Healy, which is hard to believe. On the other hand, the way that Mitchell presents the story points to the masculinist posturing that so often defined the WRP: 'After hearing Healy's report of the conversation, I asked whether he thought Hussein was serious [about developing nuclear weapons]. "Oh, he meant it all right", he [Healy] said. "It was in his eyes. The guy's a fighter."'[68] (It is interesting that none of these visits are dated, either because they never happened or because Mitchell cannot mention the dates for security reasons.) In another travel account, Mitchell says that

When Healy, Aileen Jennings, and I arrived in Baghdad [circa 1979 or slightly thereafter], it was obvious that reports of our effusive support for the Iranian revolution had preceded us. Appointments with senior Ba'athist officials were impossible to secure, and we were left in the hands of minders who were little more than junior functionaries determined to take us on guided tours of the city's tourist venues. In volcanic exasperation, Healy told our young host that unless a top-level meeting was arranged that day, the WRP's agreement with the Ba'ath Party was finished and we were leaving for London on the next plane. His theatrical brinksmanship worked, and within two hours we arrived at the party's palatial regional headquarters to meet three Ba'athists, including one of Saddam Hussein's cabinet ministers, named Moalla.[69]

This is a delusional story; it requires us to believe that leading politicians in Iraq were reading *News Line*, and thus saw there that the WRP was writing uninformed commentary about the Iranian Revolution being a quasi-socialist revolution. It also requires us to believe that the WRP had such leverage over the Iraqi government that it could strong-arm them into granting Healy a high-level audience.

Less fanciful is Norman Harding's account of attending an agricultural conference in Iraq in December 1980, held under the auspices of the Ba'ath government's Ministry of Agriculture. This seems to have been a mostly uneventful event, though Harding says he was granted an audience with Saddam Hussein at the tail end of their seven-day visit.[70] Mitchell says that links with Libya ended in the early 1980s, when Gaddafi was seeking to normalise relations with the British government.[71] The WRP/Iraq connection was broken by 1982, according to Mitchell, as Saddam courted American connections and supposedly lost interest in British Trotskyists.[72]

As with so much else in the small, enclosed world of the Workers Revolutionary Party, fact was tossed into fiction, accusations were thrown around with abandon, tall tales were used for reasons of political self-aggrandisement, and a clear understanding of the truth becomes almost impossible to achieve.

9

Legacies, After 1985

By the end of 1985, Gerry Healy had disappeared from public view and was sharing a flat with Corinna Lotz who also served as his new secretary.[1] His previous secretary, Aileen Jennings, was obviously no longer working for him. Healy and some of his lingering supporters attended a small private party at the home of the actor Frances de la Tour, just before Christmas 1985, one of their first chances to regroup. 'Everyone greeted him warmly, commiserated over the violent damage done to the party and discussed our next steps.'[2] When Healy did travel outside of his flat, he requested that they always take different routes, out of a fear that he was being followed by his post-split enemies.[3] Fears of violence on Healy's part were certainly not misguided. In the aftermath of the split, some members of the fragmenting WRP apparently took to burglarising the possessions of other members; the warring factions were also attempting to take control of a party bookshop in Liverpool.[4] Most seriously, an altercation between Eric Rogers, who supported the Torrance faction, and Phil Penn, a follower of Cliff Slaughter, led to the partial blinding of Rogers and a three-month prison sentence for grievous bodily harm (GBH) for Penn. The Slaughter faction was unrepentant, saying Penn had been defending himself from an assault by Healy's supporters and described him as a victim of state repression because of his imprisonment.[5]

Healy slowly began to come out of hiding in 1986, returning to giving interminable philosophy lectures to comrades in affiliated Greek and Spanish parties.[6] As Healy re-emerged into the public, he formed a new grouping with the Redgraves in the middle of 1987, entitled simply The Marxist Party:

The launching of the Marxist Party, embodying the continuity of the Workers Revolutionary Party as the British Section of the

ICFI, is an event of international significance. It manifests the undestructible [sic] character of the world Trotskyist movement represented by the ICFI and the defeat of the 1985 conspiracy to smash our movement.[7]

In truth, it remained tiny to the point of insignificance.[8] Tariq Ali provided a sarcastic and devastating (but coded) description of it:

Figure 6   News Line, 31 October 1985

The membership of [The Marxist Party] was, at the last count, fifty-three, not counting the ten members of the Youth wing, most of whom were [Redgrave] children of one sort or another. Half the organization consisted of the Central Committee. This body included [Corin and Vanessa's] paramours at the time, as well as the cook, maid, chauffeur, the full-time gardener and the man who came to prune the roses. The Transport Workers were represented by the milkman. The others were all aspiring young singers and musicians, desperate for a leg-up in the industry. Their only function was to rubber-stamp any and every [Redgrave] fantasy.[9]

It perhaps represented the purest distillation of Healy's preferences for top-down party structures and pseudo-philosophy. Prospective members had to serve a three-month probation period before being allowed to become full members.[10] Its journal, unambiguously entitled *The Marxist*, was the venue for some of Healy's final writings.

On a trip to Greece in September and October 1989, Healy suffered a seizure probably related to his lingering heart problems. His 76th birthday was on 3 December of that year, but having not fully recovered, it was a quiet affair. He died on 14 December and was cremated two weeks later; the funeral was mostly attended by his loyalist remnant, though two former supporters did try to stage a 'provocation' at the crematorium by picketing the funeral. His ashes were interred in a small plot not far from Karl Marx's imposing grave in Highgate cemetery in north London. Obituaries appeared in some of the major British papers as well as Ireland and, incongruously, the centre-left Greek satirical paper *To Pondiki* (The Mouse).[11] The *Irish Press*, the newspaper of *Fianna Fáil*, political hegemons of twentieth-century Ireland, ran an obituary that focused on Healy's sexual scandals and mistakenly said his hometown was Cork.[12]

Corinna Lotz was initially also a member of the Marxist Party but was expelled in November 1990 for 'subjective idealism'[13] and then accused of being an agent provocateur.[14] She claimed that her expulsion was accompanied by an intimidating encounter with the Redgraves after which she received a lawyer's letter dismissing her from her paid employment with Vanessa Redgrave as well as instructing her not to contact Redgrave.[15] Lotz's later comments were classically Healyite: she denounced the 'nationalism' of the Marxist Party, declaring that 'The degeneration of the Marxist Party leadership and its attack on C. Lotz as well as its own membership, is inseparable from the transition of Thatcherite Bonapartism to more open forms of dictatorship.' In a further polemic, she declared that the Redgraves 'refused to recognise the dialectic of history, but the dialectic recognised them'.[16] Lotz later established a journal with Paul Feldman, entitled the *Movement for a Socialist Future*. It had little in the way of mentions of Healy; the tone was more humanistic and clearly plugged in to contemporary anti-globalisation politics. Though advertisements for Lotz and Feldman's overly praising biography of Healy did regularly appear, as did some periodic invocations of Trotsky and Trotskyist ideas.[17] The Marxist Party continued to exist until about 1995, with Corin Redgrave taking a dominant position. Commensurate with the Marxist Party's demise, Redgrave returned to acting; his career had stalled throughout his time with Healy, partly because his devotion to the cause took over, partly because his less-politicised colleagues had given him a wide berth.[18] Corin Redgrave died in 2010. His sister seems to have moved away from far-left politics and generally refuses to discuss her time supporting Healy. Incongruously, she was made a Dame in January 2022, receiving a CBE (Commander of the Order of the British Empire) in the New Year's honours list, alongside such mainstream figures as the actors Daniel Craig and Joanna Lumley and the director John Boorman, as well as Tony Blair. Her past notwithstanding, Vanessa Redgrave has clearly become acceptable to the British Establishment.

Sheila Torrance retained the name 'Workers Revolutionary Party' and the *News Line* title, and in theory that group and its newspaper still exists today, but has dwindled to only a handful of members and retains its dedication to an orthodox Healyite line. One scholar has suggested this WRP has, as of 2017, 120 members, with the Socialist Equality Party (the only other functioning remnant of the WRP in Britain) having 50 members. Both figures are probably inflated.[19]

Cliff Slaughter also led a group that styled itself the Workers Revolutionary Party. The two rival groups were usually referred to by outsiders as, respectively, 'WRP (News Line)' and 'WRP (Workers Press)', using their newspaper titles to distinguish them. The Slaughter faction of the WRP was probably the largest to emerge from the split and it stayed more-or-less loyal to Trotskyism, but slowly began to grow away from Healyism and searched for new international allies, though a grouping led by Dot Gibson remained wedded to Trotskyism and continued to act as if it were operating under revolutionary conditions.[20] Robert Myers, who sided with Slaughter, talks with genuine excitement about the critical debates that could now happen. Debates did not happen under Healy but now 'politics was exciting again'. He has spoken of 'amazing party meetings' as the previous façade of homogeneity and party discipline disintegrated. One of the most impressive actions of the WRP (Workers Press) was a campaign in the mid-1990s to bring aid convoys to a multi-ethnic area of northern Bosnia. Workers Aid for Bosnia connected the party to trade union activists in Britain as well as a diverse assortment of British working-class people who volunteered to help. The group Workers Power, products of a different strand of Trotskyism, was also involved.[21] The campaign grew in time to include activists in France, Italy, Germany and Spain; not uncoincidentally, some members of the WRP (Workers Press) moved away from the elitism of Leninist vanguardism as this time. Robert Myers today says that if there is one thing in his life that was genuinely worthwhile, it would be Workers Aid for Bosnia. Conversely, he says his time in the WRP was a 'nightmare', that party members' enthusiasms were abused and 'in effect, I don't think anything we did was of any lasting value'.[22] The *Workers Press* ceased publication in 1996 and that iteration of the WRP folded alongside it.[23] In a 2006 work, *Not Without a Storm*, Slaughter thought through the experiences of Workers Aid of Bosnia as well as his evolving understanding of socialism, highlighting how much his politics had evolved since 1985.[24] He died in May 2021.

Mike Banda was also initially a member of the Workers Press faction but was soon expelled. Banda then formed a group named Communist Forum – a small group of perhaps only 25 members – ultimately breaking with Trotskyism and embracing Stalinism.[25] The Communist Forum would eventually come to label the Workers Revolutionary Party as 'an obstacle to building a revolutionary leadership in Britain', describing Healy, not inaccurately, as 'an opportunist and a sectarian' as well as morally corrupt and degenerate.[26] Banda died in 2014. In one example of the Communist Forum's reckoning with the legacy of the Workers Revolutionary Party, a former WRP member wrote with genuine poignancy about the cul-de-sacs of the group:

> What have you got to show for these decades of 'revolutionary' politics? The best and most self-sacrificing recruits, females [sic] in particular, were enslaved, abused, and either corrupted or driven out. Their injuries, physical and psychological, are a deep wound on several generations of potential revolutionists. The best and most honest layers of workers and intellectuals were battered and driven out in one way or another.[27]

The fact that hundreds if not thousands of otherwise idealistic leftists joined the SLL and WRP over the years, only to quickly become burned out by the pace of work demanded, and then fade away from political activism in general, is one of the great tragedies of this story. As Theodore Draper once lamented: 'The revolution devours its children. But there are always more children to devour.'[28] And Communist Forum were not alone in lamenting the existence of the WRP. Alan Thornett, an early critic within the WRP, retains a hostile attitude to Healy. In early 2022 he said: 'Healy was not just abusive, he was a thug and a serial rapist of women comrades and this is what defines him.' Thornett feels Healy left a wholly negative legacy.[29] Other former members retain a slightly more mixed view. Gerry Downing, an Irish-born member and one-time parliamentary candidate for the WRP, is certainly critical today of Healy but also feels that the party's emphasis on Marxist education was serious and beneficial (even if 'Healy himself was no great theoretician' and his efforts to establish himself as such failed) and that those who faded away from formal left politics retained a left-wing understanding of the world.[30]

Another member said the education for youth members was such that she was strongly prepared when she later went to college;

in her case, a Monday evening Marxist classics reading group introduced her to works such as Engels's *History of the Family, Private Property and the State*.[31] Leaders of the WRP had a notorious tendency to see their own brand of Marxist theorising as the font of all true knowledge, with a disdain for all others. Nonetheless, party members did gain an intellectual confidence, even if confidence can often be the first cousin of arrogance. Gary Younge, today a leading journalist, was a WRP youth member in 1984. He soon came to see the WRP as 'delusional' but still speaks with a certain very qualified respect for the party's vision of a socialist revolution. But even that coexisted alongside a realisation that they were a deeply homophobic organisation and with a political analysis stuck in 1917. Younge says that his experiences within the party were 'useful' for his own political development even if he has no desire now to repeat them.[32] Gerry Downing talks positively of the sense of camaraderie engendered within the party.[33] Younge echoed this to a degree, but also talks of the verbal aggression he regularly saw meted out to comrades.

Andy Blunden says his time in the WRP was a 'pretty miserable experience' and he does not have much positive to say about them. While he does see the WRP as having some of the traits of a cult, he also observes that few if any of the members were lost souls in search of religious solace. There was a high turnover of party members but the ones who remained were, he says, highly effective people and clearly capable of running a national newspaper; he talks with pride of how his party branch in east London could sell 110 copies *of News Line* a day.[34]

It should also be recalled that the flipside of Healyite 'crisisism' was a willingness to lend support to multiple left-wing actions. Dedication to the cause is not a bad thing, even if here it slipped into something more negative and Healy exploited members' idealism. The other aspect of the WRP's 'crisisim' worth noting is that there were many members who did genuinely believe that a socialist revolution was both possible and necessary and were willing to struggle for it. For sure, the leaders of the WRP took advantage of these people but the strength of their convictions should not be dismissed. Any organisation should be defined as much by the decent views and actions of its rank-and-file members as by the crimes of its leaders. And yet Blunden's ultimate assessment, grim but evocative, focuses on the exploitation of members and the party's inability to face reality. He has come to see the WRP as being 'utterly divorced from the real world', though he also sees his initial faith in them as being a product of post-1968 excitement about the imminent victory of socialism. A person like Healy could exploit that excitement; 'I was part of a generation that was vulnerable to that call to be a revolutionary. I was served up on a plate for someone like Healy.'[35]

Aileen Jennings remained in hiding after the split. She then moved to the north of England and became involved in labour union activism while working as a secretary at the University of Sheffield. Dot Gibson remained for a time in the Cliff Slaughter wing of the WRP but soon left. For a time, she had a leadership role in another Trotskyist group, the Workers International to Rebuild the Fourth International, and later became involved in the National Pensioners Convention.[36] Clare Cowen did remain active in Trotskyist circles, but began to look more and more to feminist currents, recognising that the WRP had a profound misogyny that facilitated Healy's abusiveness.[37] Likewise, Norman Harding, who had devoted an inordinate amount of his adult life to the SLL and WRP, remained politically active but now embraced a far less doctrinaire view of things. In the mid-1990s he began to suffer from debilitating panic attacks, which, after visiting a psychiatrist, he ascribed to both the abusiveness of the WRP and his guilt at not being able to stop Healy's attacks on female comrades.[38] He died in December 2013.

Alex Mitchell returned to Australia and to a fairly mainstream journalism career shortly after the split and, as evidenced by the tone of his autobiography, remains generally unrepentant – proud, even – of his time in the WRP, though he never again maintained the same level of political activism after leaving Britain. Andy Blunden also returned home to Australia after the split. He initially stayed active in Trotskyism, joining the Australian SLL where a new culture of debate was at hand following Healy's downfall. But after 1991, Blunden began to question whether Trotskyism could have any real relevance following the collapse of the Soviet Union. He today identifies as a Marxist Hegelian, having felt that a return to the philosophical origins of Marxism had become necessary and has since become an astute interpreter of Hegel.[39]

Trotskyism in general has floundered since the early 1990s. The dream that the collapse of Stalinism would create a vacuum that only Trotskyists could fill never came to pass. Trotskyism also declined alongside the decline of Soviet-style communism. It is today overshadowed on the left by a more free-thinking democratic socialism or by Latin America's pink tide. The Golden Age of British Trotskyism that started at the end of the 1960s came to a halt in the mid-1980s, partly a result of the despondency at the crushing of the miners' strike. The International Marxist Group imploded at this point and the Militant Tendency, a Trotskyist entryist group led by Healy's one-time comrade in the RCP Ted Grant, were systematically expelled from the Labour Party across the second half of the 1980s. Despite a few momentary upticks, such as the Militant-led Poll Tax protests that eventually forced Thatcher from office in 1990, British Trotskyism has dropped exponentially. A 70 per cent drop in membership numbers would not be an exaggeration.[40]

Gerry Healy's son Alan died in early 1991; he had played little if any role in Healy's political career. Alan Healy had had psychiatric problems, probably schizophrenia, and died from an overdose of his anti-psychotic medication. It was not clear if he had overdosed intentionally. The funeral provided a sombre occasion for one more reunion of WRP members. Betty Russell, Healy's widow, had long remained at a remove from her husband's politics. They had been mostly estranged since the early 1970s; Betty had supposedly once told Mike Banda that Gerry Healy was 'a madman' and felt some sense of guilt that, by supporting him financially, she had enabled him.[41] According to Dave Bruce, Betty Russell 'roundly despised' Gerry, 'but not as much as she roundly despised his supporters' and she tried in a coded way to warn people about him. Bruce says he has fond memories of Russell.

Dave Bruce remained in the WRP for a short period after the split but soon left, lamenting both the Healyites who carried on as if nothing had happened, naming David North as an example of this, as well as those who drifted to the right. Drawing on his work for *News Line*, he was able to find work as a printing technician,

moved home to Scotland and became involved in environmentalism. Bruce still identifies as a Trotskyist whilst simultaneously
wanting nothing to do with organised Trotskyism. In his view, no
one from this milieu wants to face up to the fact that Healy was a
product of his party as much as the party was a product of him.[42]
Simon Pirani has made a similar claim, that even if WRP members
did not know of the sexual abuse:

> we unknowingly created the conditions for it by our acceptance
> of things we *were* aware of: a hierarchical structure; tolerance
> towards bullying by individual leaders; intolerance towards
> people who were outside the group; the deliberate ritual humil-
> iation of members in large meetings – particularly senior
> members with whom Healy was picking a fight for one reason
> or another; the expulsion of all those who voiced substantial
> political disagreement and some who did not – that goes almost
> without saying; and the use of violence.[43]

When Tim Wohlforth left the Workers League, the WRP's
American subsidiary, in 1974, he eventually drifted back to the
Socialist Workers Party, of which he had earlier been an active
member. And yet later in life Wolhflorth seemed to disavow Trotskyism altogether and recognise the need for a broader and more
fluid party for the American left: 'It is *now* very clear to me that
what was needed was a broad socialist party', he said, in the tradition of the great early twentieth-century socialist, Eugene V. Debs:

> staunchly anti-imperialist, radically democratic and pluralistic, a
> bit messy and sloppy internally, capable of absorbing and reflect-
> ing the leftist activists as they and their movements evolved.
> Such a party would have been a home for the black activists, the
> feminist movement, which was only then coming into being, and
> militants from the trade unions and would have been capable of
> 'greening' as the ecological movement developed. Yes, it would
> have been somewhat like the Democratic Socialists of America
> launched over a decade later but positioned to the DSA's left,
> reflecting the political temper of the 1960s.[44]

Alex Callinicos, a member of the British SWP, has said that the paradox of Trotskyism more generally is that by seeking to preserve 'the letter of Trotsky's theory', Trotskyists ossified it into a rigid canon of ideas incapable of responding to new events with any kind of intellectual or political flexibility.[45] That rigidity was probably attractive to some in the years immediately after 1968. But by virtue of its hardline top-down party structure, the WRP remained not just undemocratic but also unable to respond to new political developments like second-wave feminism, environmentalism or gay liberation. It remained unwilling to even properly incorporate anti-racism into its politics.[46] There were no avenues for the rank-and-file to change party policy. And the WRP's refusal to deal with 'new' issues was of a piece with its long-standing inability to deal with Healy's abuses, because both were products of a situation where the leadership could not be questioned and protection of the party's reputation was a paramount concern. It is not a coincidence that other Trotskyist groups – the International Socialist Organization, the American Socialist Workers Party and the British Socialist Workers Party – have also had shocking scandals of sexual abuse, in which party members closed ranks rather than deal with the issue.[47] The Spartacist League expelled one of its founding members, Bill Logan, for sexual abuse in 1979.[48] There is no inherent link between Trotskyism and sexual abuse – and indeed the scale of Healy's sexual abuses was far more extreme than what happened in these other cases[49] – but all political choices have consequences, and the choice to structure a party along democratic centralist lines carries many potential unintended consequences. One regular consequence is that democratic centralist parties tend to favour the centralism over the democracy.[50]

In 1960, Brian Behan, a well-known communist writer and the brother of the Irish republican playwright Brendan Behan, formed a short-lived democratic socialist party named, simply, The Workers Party. Having been a member of both the CPGB and, for a brief period, the SLL, Behan was in a strong position to critique these two divergent strands of Leninism, which he astutely did in an article entitled 'Our Revolutionary Democracy':

Both the Stalinists and the Trotskyists borrow wholesale the idea that the party must be an elite type with minimum of democratic discussion inside or outside the party... the inhumanity of the Stalinists and the Trotskyists flows directly from their idea that they are the chosen repository of all wisdom and that the working class are really their ignorant servants; they substitute an elite for the working class, then stand history on its head and say it is individuals that are decisive in history and not the class. This idealist conception leads to their worship of the strong man whether he be a Stalin, Dutt [R.P. Dutt of the CPGB] or Healy. On this basis you excuse everything in the name of the party, since the party is the highest expression of the class. You excuse the crimes of the elite from beating and murder to their contempt for human beings. Even worse you relegate the role of the working class to that of sheep, passive observers waiting for the good word.[51]

This is perhaps *the* central lesson of the Workers Revolutionary Party. The history of this party teaches us something very important about Leninist-style politics and the best and worst ways to structure political party. Leninism offers the hope that we can shortcut the difficult work of politics and the building of a socialist future if only we develop the 'correct' kind of party organisation (which happens to be a generally undemocratic type of organisation). Leninism is certainly attractive, not least because of the simple fact that Leninists erected the first socialist state on Earth. Even harsh critics of Leninism have often acknowledged its great utility as a coherent and explicit philosophy of revolution.[52] The best thing about the Leninist tradition is that it remained always radical, never prevaricating: twenty-first-century socialism needs that radical commitment, and certainly contemporary formations like the Democratic Socialists of America would benefit from having some of that discipline, but that must be coupled with a deep-rooted democratic culture, which Leninism has always lacked. As Tim Wohlforth saw, a radical non-Leninist socialism might be a little messy and chaotic but it also has a far better chance of actually building something long-lasting within the interstices of Western capitalism.[53]

Sheila Rowbotham took a political journey through Trotskyism – she was a member of the International Marxist Group, a far less severe group than the SLL or WRP – anarchism and the Labour Party, eventually becoming one of the foremost feminist historians in Britain. Looking back at her life in the 1960s, she saw both the positive sides of Trotskyism – an admirable tenacity and a sense of resolution – as well as the negative: 'Based on betrayal, forged in the bitterness of failure, Trotskyism subordinated all individuality to the calling of the professional revolutionary. For the Trotskyist, personal joy could be expected only as the faintest glimmer of sunlight on grass.'[54] This split personality – a serious dedication but a joyless lack of democracy – has always bedevilled Trotskyism. In 2021 Rowbotham observed that socialism should not be held as a fixed entity but should be open to other radical social movements and able 'to absorb wider aspects of understanding' as a result.[55] It remains difficult to see why a model of rigid and narrow-gauge party organisation initially devised to deal with Tsarist oppression is needed in the relatively freer environs of the US, the UK or the West in general.

The Workers Revolutionary Party remains a cautionary tale for the modern left.

10

Epilogue:
Twenty-first-century Healyism

In February 2022, an esteemed anthropology professor at Harvard University named John Comaroff was the subject of credible accusations of serial sexual harassment. Three doctoral students who had worked under Comaroff filed a legal case alleging not only a pattern of persistent sexual abuse but also a malicious use of his academic standing to avoid any professional or legal repercussions and to silence any accusers.[1] Other accusations soon emerged, alleging not only that this was a long-standing behaviour on Comaroff's part, but that it was more or less an open secret and that his wife, Jean Comaroff, also an academic at Harvard, helped cover up his actions, all without any impingements on his scholarly career. Amidst this, a group of 38 Harvard professors signed a letter supporting Comaroff, many of them near-celebrities like Sven Beckert, Henry Louis Gates, Homi Bhabha and Stephen Greenblatt. The power dynamics of such actions are readily apparent; an older male professor at an elite university – backed up by some of the most powerful names in their fields – who (allegedly) abused his position to not just sexually harass and coerce young female students, but to do so with apparent impunity. The vast majority of commentators on the left looking at cases like that of Comaroff, or of #MeToo more broadly, have focused on the clear and undeniable power politics of these situations, even if they are careful to also recognise that Comaroff has not *yet* been legally charged with a crime (Harvard placed him on administrative leave in August 2020 and he returned to teaching two years later).

One exception is an oddly prominent online news source named the World Socialist Website (WSWS), which published a fawning apologia for Comaroff, despite the credible accusations of sexual abuse against him.[2] WSWS is tightly overseen by the Socialist Equality Party (SEP) and that party's National Secretary, David North, a long-time Trotskyist and one-time ally of Gerry Healy. He remains today one of the few leaders within this milieu to retain a loyalty to Trotskyism.

The website's blunt defence of Comaroff is not at all out of character: they have also published exonerations of Harvey Weinstein (a convicted rapist), Woody Allen (credibly accused of child sexual abuse) and Louis CK (who admitted to extreme sexual harassment of fellow comedians) and have a general contempt for the debates over sexual harassment that followed the various #MeToo revelations.[3]

The SEP has its roots in the Workers League that had once been led by Tim Wohlforth and closely influenced by Gerry Healy. Developing the ideas it learned from the WRP, the SEP's privileging of class over all else has ended up not just downplaying race and gender, but outright sexism and racism. It is mainly known today for this online presence, which provides both ultra-leftist perspectives on current events and bad faith attacks on the recent crop of democratic socialist politicians, Alexandria Ocasio-Cortez especially, but also Bernie Sanders and Jeremy Corbyn. The WSWS is a contradictory beast. It has an undeniable presence on the American radical left; since its establishment in 1998 it has published, on average, 2,500 articles a year, a major achievement for so small a group.[4] And there has been some genuinely strong writing and analysis within all this (alongside some very inferior articles). But like *News Line* in the 1970s and 1980s, this has become an end in itself and party members are swamped with impossible to achieve journalistic targets, now moved online rather than by selling papers outside factories in London. Party members are expected to write inordinately high numbers of articles for the website.[5] As with the WRP, this achievement requires the exploitation of rank-and-file members' genuine commitment to socialism, here redirected into a dead end. For all its status online, the SEP has never converted its readership into a mass movement. Tightly centralised and with a rigid party line, it is a difficult organisation to join and seems to quickly alienate most potential recruits.[6]

Gerry Healy used to be accused of mimicking James Cannon, as if by copying his speech and mannerisms he could replicate his political prominence. David North today apes Gerry Healy; he is a copy of a copy.

Like Healy, North is circumspect about his early life. In a rare interview with a non-SEP/WSWS venue in 2017, he spoke in only broadly generic terms about being 'part of a generation that was politically radicalized during the 1960's'[7]. Even within the SEP, not much is known about his background.[8] North's real name is David Waghalter Green and he was born in January 1950 in New York to Maurice Sheyman and Beatrice Waghalter, both of whom were European Jewish refugees. His maternal grandfather was Ignatz Waghalter, a minor composer who had fled Germany with the rise of Nazism. Beatrice was herself a well-regarded opera singer. Sheyman died in 1953 but, soon after, Beatrice married a wealthy businessman, Russell Green, from whom North takes his legal last name. With her new marriage, Beatrice abandoned music and also moved into business, running her own travel agency and a fashion imports company. The family were wealthy enough to spend summers in Switzerland. From an early age, David North was blessed with cultural capital, as well as raw economic capital.

In 1967, Green/North enrolled at Trinity College in Hartford, Connecticut, where he studied history. Then, as now, Trinity was a small, and fairly exclusive institution with a WASP-y culture. It had a tradition of heavy drinking among its mostly male and white student body. Female students were only admitted for the first time in 1969, two years into North's undergraduate career. As with '68-era student activism elsewhere, Trinity had a branch of Students for a Democratic Society. While Green/North does seem to have been politically conscious from an early point in his student days, he did not play a role in SDS, and seemed to be on a more mainstream path. He was editor of the campus newspaper and, ironically, served in 1970 as a speechwriter and intern for Vance Hartke, the senior senator for Indiana and the kind of loosely left-of-centre Democrat for whom the SEP would today reserve their greatest ire: 'he fit in so well that six other senators wrote the College' asking for student interns.[9] Gerry Healy probably knew whose buttons he was pushing when he once dismissed North as being nothing but 'a representative of the United States middle class'.[10]

By April 1971, though, Green/North had joined the Trinity branch of the Workers League and by March of the following year he had adopted his pseudonym.[11] By this point, the Workers League had somewhere in the region of 350 members across the United States, representing its numerical highpoint. Men predominated in the leadership of the WL, though the grassroots membership was more balanced (and there were some female leaders). Likewise, it was predominantly white in the early 1970s but worked to recruit more Hispanic and Black members across the decade.[12] In the faction-fighting before and after Tim Wohlforth's expulsion in 1974, the League probably lost around 150 members, including leading members and dedicated youth activists.

The WL, and its newspaper, *Bulletin*, were becoming more labour- and union-focused into the early 1970s, with less discussion of the student and anti-war movements. The League's crystallising view was that union leadership were craven sellouts while rank-and-file workers are committed leftists but in need of proper socialist leadership. *Bulletin* regularly had headlines calling for a general strike in the early 1970s, without much of a plan as to how union membership could be won over to such a position. The League was also calling for the founding of a Labor party independent of the Democratic Party, a sensible idea but one that they provided no concrete plans to achieve and no admission of the difficulties of achieving.[13] They often issued such calls through their 'Trade Union Alliance for a Labor Party', a name clearly borrowed from the WRP's All Trade Union Alliance (ATUA).[14] Steve Zeltzer, expelled from the WL for questioning their Labor party policy, says the leadership never really addressed what form this party would have, whether it be a broad left party or a narrowly Trotskyist party.[15]

From its founding in 1966, the Workers League was intellectually dependent on the British. The SLL and WRP provided an encouraging model for the WL to emulate, but there was also a 'hero worship' of Healy, as one former member recalls.[16] Early issues of *Bulletin* featured regular articles by British Trotskyists or requests for funds. Adverts for subscriptions to SLL and WRP publications as well as for pamphlets by Gerry Healy *et al.* were common from the start. *Bulletin* even looked like *News Line*, adopting the same British tabloid-style red-top front page layout. Over the years, the contents of *Bulletin* show an obvious debt to the SLL and WRP; well-written articles on the Palestinians and even interviews with leading members of Fatah alongside obsequious portraits of Libya and Iraq.[17] By 1979, the paper had added the emerging Islamic Republic of Iran to the list of regimes to which it gave uncritical support.[18] Merging two of the least defensible traits of their strand of Trotskyism, *Bulletin* started to run articles claiming the American SWP was in league with the FBI in attempts to undermine the Iranian Revolution, which they called 'the greatest mass uprising since the Russian Revolution of 1917'. *Bulletin* had especial venom for the feminist writer Kate Millett who had criticised the suppression of women's rights by the Iranian Revolution. Yet the paper could, and did, publish good articles. Their coverage of the PATCO air traffic controllers strike in 1983, a moment of major defeat for the Reagan-era labour movement, was genuinely exemplary.[19] Selling *Bulletin* was a central activity for members, perhaps *the* central activity, with the same impossible-to-achieve sales quotas as in the UK.[20] Similar to their British cousins, it was hugely demanding to be a full-time activist in the WL; maintaining a healthy family life or a romantic relationship was highly difficult because of the commitments that were expected of members.[21]

Like the SLL and WRP, the WL had a long-standing contempt for 'particularist' gender and anti-racist politics, seeing universalist socialism as the cure for all ills. Even prior to Wohlforth's departure, the WL took a hard line against Black nationalism.[22] At one point the League had a ban on the recruiting of gay people (the SWP and American Communist party had similar bans going back to the 1930s).[23] By the mid-1980s, it was party doctrine that class is all that matters, such that any politician mentioning race or gender is engaging in an insidious attempt to distract the working class.[24] This kind of thinking has today led North and his followers to a politics so allergic to discussions of gender or of the problems facing Black people that it is itself essentially racist and sexist.

When Wohlforth was expelled in August 1974, the WL's newspaper, *Bulletin*, simply carried on as if nothing has happened. No public explanation about the removal of their leader, allegedly for being a CIA spy, was offered over the next year.[25] After Wohlforth's departure, the League was briefly led by Fred Mazelis, who would also stand as the League's candidate for various state and federal elections. But by 1976, Mazelis had been replaced as leader by North, probably following guidance from the WRP.[26] North also started to give public lectures for the League, another sign that he was emerging as a leader though with contents that followed a set Healyite script. He gave lectures in September 1977 on the familiar pseudo-Hegelian topics of 'Dialectics of Nature and Origins of the Solar System' and 'Practice of Cognition'.[27]

From 1976 onwards, the WL was talking of starting a daily paper that would be 'the first daily Trotskyist newspaper in the United States'. Given the party's size, this was probably always going to be an impossibility for them (at least until the internet became a functioning reality in the 1990s) but they would tout this plan for the next few years. In May 1979, the party launched a $100,000 'expansion fund' to pay for this new paper. While the money does appear to have been raised, the daily paper never materialised.[28] Like the WRP, there was a murkiness to the party's finances.

The WL also imbibed Healy's paranoia. This was not always misplaced: from at least 1967, the FBI was monitoring the Workers League, paying particular attention to their international travel, and the FBI does seem to have had an informant within the League. The WL's youth wing, the Young Socialists, were also being monitored.[29] Irving Hall, active in the WL in southern California, remembers a briefly active female member who, suspiciously, always flew to national meetings, rather than driving cross-country like everyone else. He was later told, after her sudden disappearance, that she was a suspected government agent who had been spying on them.[30] On 15 October 1977, Tom Henehan, a young Workers League member and recent graduate from Columbia University, was shot at a League event in Brooklyn, dying early the next morning at a nearby hospital. There was no clear motivation for Henehan's murder. It was quite possible it was just a street crime that escalated. The more outlandish WL theories – that the American SWP killed him, for example, or that it was a mob hit[31] – can be dismissed readily. Police involvement, on the other hand, would not be impossible. As Alex Steiner says today, 'you didn't have to be big to attract police attention'[32] in 1970s New York; the NYPD's Red Squad was always going to be suspicious of leftists looking to recruit Black people in the projects. And extra-judicial police murders undeniably happened (and happen) in America, whether of Fred Hampton in Chicago in 1969 or the police bombing of a house owned by the MOVE organisation in Philadelphia in 1985. The most common WL accusation was that Henehan was killed by American intelligence services who sought to smash the Workers League on the eve of their long-awaited expansion. Within two weeks of the shooting, the WL had launched a '$100,000 Tom Henehan Memorial Fund' that would allegedly be used to fund a daily paper.[33] For years afterwards, the front page of *Bulletin* would feature a recurring statement about Henehan and that his true killers were supposedly still at large, even after the murderers, Angelo Torres and Edwin Sequinot, had been found guilty and sentenced to prison in 1981.[34]

In the early 1980s, the Workers League relocated from New York to Detroit, where North was now living. The WL had been shrinking in the later 1970s as the left in general contracted. WL members were 'grim and pessimistic' but also trying to hide this with claims that the tempo of the class struggle was about to ramp up. The move to Detroit was partly related to a need to find cheaper rents as well as a desire to be closer to the organised working class in what was still one of the most industrialised cities in America.[35] Operating through a privately incorporated company named Vernor Distributors, the WL established a bookshop in the city, Detroit Book Center, almost a direct reproduction of the names used by WRP shops.[36] As with the WRP, the Workers League cadre had a genuine commitment and willingness to subsume themselves into party work; full-time party workers, North included, apparently lived on $50 a week in the 1970s and 1980s.[37]

Just after Healy's expulsion, North arrived in Britain and claimed that the root cause of the WRP's crisis was a kind of nationalist deviation. North said that the solution was thus to put the British party under his international control. For a time, it did seem that most WRP comrades would subordinate themselves to North.[38] But as one WRP member recalls, the vast majority of WRP members felt liberated now that Healy's domineering presence had been removed and 'most of us said "fuck off"'. A small faction did join North, though, led by a long-time WRP member, David Hyland. This small British group initially operated under the name the International Communist Party.

As the fragmentation of the WRP progressed, North downplayed Healy's sexual abuse, recasting the split as something narrowly party-political instead.[39] As a group of party intellectuals within the WRP said: 'North first opposed the expulsion of Healy and then, reluctantly, went along with it. He wanted a struggle based on abstract theoretical matters, but not a fundamental political break with Healy.'[40] Soon North and the WL were harshly condemning their former comrades; a particular sore spot was that the WRP (Workers Press) had made the wise decision to distance themselves from the 'Security and the Fourth International' accusations that the American SWP had colluded in the murder of Leon Trotsky. Truthfully, this had always been an embarrassment for the party. North, however, had been one of the original 'investigators' and to this day his party maintains that the accusations are true.[41]

Back in Detroit, the Workers League rebranded itself as the Socialist Equality Party in 1995.[42] This newly formed SEP had four international affiliates, in Australia, Germany, Sri Lanka and the UK. It has since added sections in France and New Zealand.[43] All operate under the name Socialist Equality Party, or a translated version of the same, within a highly centralised international organisation controlled by North and his closest allies. The British section, a 'tiny'[44] grouping, is today led by, among others, Julie Hyland, daughter of Dave Hyland and a former editor of the WRP's youth paper, *Keep Left*. For all its claims to have broken with Healy, the SEP still very much walks and talks in a Healyite mode. With the switch to the SEP, the Workers League's old print newspaper, *Bulletin*, was wound down and replaced with the *World Socialist Web Site* (WSWS), pompously described as 'the most important instrument for the development of socialist consciousness within the working class'.[45] The SEP is not an organisation to languish in humility and the scholar John Kelly has described North as 'an immodest and arrogant individual'.[46] Unfortunately for North and the SEP, though, other Trotskyists were also moving onto the internet.

An early web 1.0 chatroom, alt.politics.socialism.trotskyism, provided a rough-and-ready debating shop for various Trotskyists and ex-Trotskyists. One user of this site was a former member of the Workers League, Scott Solomon. Solomon had been a student member of the League's branch at the University of Minnesota in the mid-1980s. Highly active for about a year, he continued to identify with the WL for several years after this. But by the 1990s and 2000s, he had soured on North's brand of Trotskyism. At this Trotskyist chatroom, he came into contact with Tim Wohlforth, who revealed North's real name to him. Some personal detective work on Solomon's part further revealed that North/Green, a man prone to denounce all opponents as capitulators to capitalism, was actually the owner of a lucrative printing company outside of Detroit, Grand River Printing.[47] According to allegations later made by rival Trotskyists in the International Bolshevik Tendency, Grand River has gone on to become a multi-million dollar business.[48] Such allegations were, Solomon observes, 'catnip'[49] for other Trotskyist groups, only too ready to pounce on the idea that North is just a hypocrite.

That the SEP leadership are the owners of a number of high-profit businesses has become, more or less, an open secret on the American left.[50] Grand River Printing, the main business, was founded in August 1978 with an initial share value of $50,000. It began as a continuation of Labor Publications, the official printers of the WL, but according to a former member, 'at some point the business became independent of the movement'.[51] It operated out of a 12,000-square foot facility in Southfield, a suburb of Detroit, before relocating to an 84,000-square foot building in 2004. By the end of the 1990s, the company had a staff of 95 employees. Key leadership positions were held by high-ranking members of the WL/SEP. David Freund, a Congressional candidate for the League in 1982, served as the plant manager. Sheila Leburg, another one-time electoral candidate, was Vice President of Sales. Ann Porster, former business manager of *Bulletin*, was CEO. In 1998, the company had a revenue of $11.3m and by 2004 it was reporting annual sales of $16m. In 2013, Grand River's printing operation was sold for an undisclosed sum.[52] WSWS itself is also registered as a for-profit corporation; other than online advertising, it is not clear what profits it could be making.[53] The SEP's print company, Mehring Books, is likewise a privately registered corporation with sales allegedly reaching into six figures each year. One former SEP member has said that:

> Each branch in the party is also compelled to extract a minimum amount of money from supporters and members each month alongside a yearly fund drive which must easily generate over $100,000. The fact is that the *rank and file have no idea how the finances of the party, collected through the participation of all members, are being used, nor do they have any say in the utilization of funds.*[54]

North has clearly done well from his side-businesses and has developed an ability to code-switch between two radically divergent lives. As 'David Green', he is a relatively well-known figure in the business world of Metro Detroit and has also made a number of media appearances to promote a rediscovery of Ignacz Waghalter, his composer grandfather. In that latter endeavour, he has focused on Waghalter's identity and how his music became a way to explore the exigencies of Jewishness on the eve of Nazism. As 'David North' he has a parallel career as a bellicose Trotskyist, one who fulminates about the kind of particularist identity politics and bourgeois lifestyle with which David Green seems quite content. The key point is not that identity politics are bad. A properly universal socialism would find space for the joys of Jewish (and all other) particularities; it would strive to accommodate those particularisms rather than erasing them within a faux-universalism. Nor is it the case that a rich person cannot be a socialist; the history of socialism is replete with committed socialists who, through accidents of birth, were born into well-to-do families, from Friedrich Engels to Leon Trotsky to Vanessa Redgrave, even. Indeed, a good socialist should recognise that the lottery of birth is one of the things that makes capitalism so inherently unfair. What *is* the key point, though, is that by maintaining these duelling personas, Green/North quietly excuses for himself all that which he so vociferously denounces in others. And while the revenues from Grand River probably underwrite much of the SEP's work, the political results have not been encouraging.

The SEP's efforts to break into electoral politics, for example, have been highly unsuccessful; their candidate for president in 2020, Joseph Kishore, received all of 350 votes (0.0002%). It is safe to assume that this 350 represents the party's total national membership and support base. Former member Shuvu Battu is even more parsimonious. He estimates the SEP has 100 members in the US and that the entire international membership of the ICFI is today only 300 people.[55] In the Sri Lankan parliamentary election, also in 2020, three Socialist Equality Party candidates secured 780 votes (0.007% of the 11.6m who voted). Their response – 'While these numbers are still small, they are class-conscious votes for socialism and an indication of growing support for the SEP'[56] – was a classically Healyist dodge. When WRP candidate Gerry Downing obtained just 290 votes (0.76%) in London's Brent East at the 1979 general election, he reported his disappointment to Healy only to be told, 'you didn't get 290 votes, you got 290 *revolutionary socialist* votes!'[57]

Despite its electoral failures, the SEP remains a party with an implausibly inflated sense of its own importance. When former member Shuvu Battu progressed to work as an Amazon unionisation activist and was invited onto National Public Radio to discuss this, the SEP seemed confused as to how he was achieving anything outside of the party, as well as utterly confident that Battu was a stooge for union leaders who desire the end of SEP criticism (when in fact the SEP is mostly unknown to union leaders).[58] Around the same time, another soon-to-be-expelled member, Peter Ross, raised questions about the party's policies and was subjected to 'hysterical denunciations' and 'personal slanders' at a national meeting.[59] North and Joseph Kishore then released a long-winded letter denouncing Ross for supposedly exhibiting 'the viciously anti-Marxist irrationalism of pseudo-left race-sex-gender politics'.[60] 'Pseudo-left' is their preferred adjective for all those outside the SEP.[61] They have a hostility for all labour unions in the US, which even led them in 2021 to argue against unionisation in Amazon's Bessemer plant in Alabama.[62] SEP members who are active in unions are encouraged to leave and to refuse to pay union dues.[63]

WSWS infamously served as a forum for duplicitous criticisms of Nikole Hannah-Jones's *1619 Project*, thus playing an unlikely role in helping foment the far-right Critical Race Theory panic of 2021. For all their Marxist posturing, the SEP provided multiple platforms to conservative historians, such as Gordon Wood, sharing with them a contempt for organised anti-racism. North's antagonism toward Critical Race Theory is strong enough that he was willing to come out of character and to write a letter under his government name to his alma mater's alumni magazine, *Trinity Tripod*, to censure the college's racially conscious teaching methods.[64] WSWS has also targeted contemporary scholars of race, calling them 'race obsessed', and naming the Marxist historian Keeanga-Yamahtta Taylor in particular, accusing her of promoting racial division.[65] The Lebanese political scientist Gilbert Achcar was certainly not being polite when he called the WSWS 'gutter journalism' and said that North is 'a political sicko'.[66] But nor was he being totally inaccurate.

A certain kind of vulgar Marxist logic underpins the SEP world-view, based, as it is, on a claim that a true socialist should only be concerned with a narrowly defined conception of class struggle; any politics of race or gender is thus divisive, a distraction and inadmissible. A post-1968 hostility to identity politics, seen as an abdication of class consciousness, is also at play here. The SEP's very orthodox strand of Trotskyism, inherited from Healy, also has a specific problem with any social movement that does not operate within a circumscribed idea of a Bolshevik-style mass proletarian party with a Trotskyist leadership. All other political formations and movements – whether feminist activism or the large-scale protests that emerged following the murder of George Floyd in 2020 – are dismissed from the very outset and never engaged with in good faith. It is, of course, possible to have specific criticisms of #MeToo or the 1619 Project. But in painting everyone and everything with a broad brush, North and his fellow travellers dismiss not just individual thinkers and activists, but the entire projects of feminism and anti-racism. There is no nuance here. Rather than identifying the genuine problems of centrist feminism or liberal anti-racism while trying to also ascertain how to still be an anti-racist and feminist socialist organisation, they dismiss feminism and anti-racism in total. There is also a profound lack of intellectual curiosity. A huge and sophisticated literature exists that teaches how class can and should be incorporated with race or gender, that shows how capitalism requires and reproduces these other forms of human difference and how an anti-capitalist politics needs socialist feminism and radical anti-racism; Cedric Robinson, Robin D.G. Kelley, David Roediger, Stuart Hall, Angela Davis, as well as Keeanga-Yamahtta Taylor, whom WSWS directly malign. The SEP ignore all this, finding refuge in their doctrinaire, and ultimately sexist and racist, sureties. For better or worse, this is where the last politically impactful remnant of Healyist Trotsky-ism has ended up.

Sources

INTERVIEWS AND PERSONAL CORRESPONDENCE

Tariq Ali, 16 June 2022
Shuvu Batta, 5 August 2022
Andy Blunden, 14 & 27 July 2022
Dave Bruce, 1, 7 & 27 July 2022
Scotty Clark, 27 November 2022
Clare Cowen, 15 May 2023
Vincent Doherty, 8 November 2022
Gerry Downing, 12 March 2022
Philip Edwards, 16 November 2022
'Elizabeth', 14 March 2022
Paul Flewers, 10 November 2022
Bridget Fowler, 15 June 2022
Garth Frankland, 8 August 2022
Irving Hall, 3 December 2022
Barry Healy, 14 July 2022
Paul Henderson, 30 October 2022
Tareq Ismael, 26 July 2021
'Judith', 21 February 2022
Paul le Blanc, 18 February 2022
Liz Leicester, 6 June 2023
Sean Matgamna, July 2022
Chris McBride, 25 July 2023
Jim Monaghan, 4 July 2022
Marie Monaghan, 22 February 2022
Peter Money, 23 November 2022
Danny Morrison, 14 November 2022
Jacob Morrison and Adam Keller, 1 December 2022
Robert Myers, 23 June 2022
Linda Neville, 5 July 2023 (interview conducted by Dr Leonard Holden)
David Parks, 23 November 2022
Mike Richardson, 8 June 2023
Sheila Rowbotham, 19 July 2023
Peter Ross, 23 August 2022

Joseph Sassoon, 25 July 2021
'Shannon', 30 March 2023
Scott Solomon, 3 August 2022
Alex Steiner, 17 May 2022 & 4 July 2023
Paul Thompson, 22 November 2022
Alan Thornett, January and February 2022
Granville Williams, 4 January 2023
Gary Younge, 27 January 2022
Steve Zeltzer, 14 November 2022

ARCHIVAL SOURCES

Archives of Michigan
  Department of Commerce
John Bloxam, Privately Held Files
British Film Institute (BFI)
  The Money Programme, BBC, 20 March 1983
Glasgow Caledonian University Archives Centre
  Glasgow Caledonian Archive of the Trotskyist Tradition (GCATT)
  Bill Hunter Papers
  Simon Pirani Papers
Hull History Centre
  Papers of Jock Haston
  Papers of Tom Kemp
National Archives, College Park, Maryland
  FBI Central Records Center
University College London
  File on the Workers Revolutionary Party (GB 96 MS 1256)
University of Warwick Modern Records Centre
  Papers of Alan Clinton
  Papers of Bob Purdie
  Papers of David Spencer
  Papers of Chris and Ann Talbot
  Papers of Ken Tarbuck
  Papers of Alan Thornett
  Papers of E.A. Whelan
Wayne State University, Reuther Library
  John Dwyer Papers
Wisconsin Historical Society
  James P. Cannon Papers

NEWSPAPERS, MAGAZINES, JOURNALS

Australian Spartacist
Communist Forum
Coventry Evening Telegraph
Daily Mail
Daily Star
Direct Action
Forum
Fourth International
Guardian
Independent
Irish Press
Labour Review
Lobster
The Marxist
Marxist Monthly
Marxist Review
Mirror
Morning Star
New Interventions
New Statesman
New York Times
News Line
News Line (Anti-Healy)
News of the World
Newsletter
Observer
On The Issues Magazine
Revolutionary History
Revolutionary Socialist History
Socialist Future
Socialist Organiser
Socialist Outlook
Socialist Review
Socialist Viewpoint
Solidarity: A Journal of Libertarian Socialism
St Andrew's Economist
Sunday Mirror
Sunday Telegraph
Tasks of the Fourth International

Time Out
The Times
Trinity Alumni Magazine
Trinity Tripod
Weekly Worker
Worker's Voice
Workers Liberty
Workers News
Workers Press
Young Socialist

ONLINE SOURCES

angryworkers.org
BBC News
Bolshevik.org
Hansard Parliamentary Debates
Irish Left Archive
libcom.org
Marxists Internet Archive
North East Labour History, Oral History Interviews
Novara Media
Bob Pitt. *The Rise and Fall of Gerry Healy*
RTÉ News
SocialistWorker.org
Splits and Fusions
World Socialist Web Site

PUBLISHED AND SECONDARY SOURCES

Aburish, Saïd. *Saddam Hussein: The Politics of Revenge* (London: Blooms-
    bury, 2000)
Alexander, Robert J. *International Trotskyism, 1929–1985: A Documented
    Analysis of the Movement* (Durham, NC: Duke University Press, 1991)
Ali, Tariq. *The Coming British Revolution* (London: Jonathan Cape, 1972)
— *Redemption* (London: Chatto & Windus, 1990)
— *Street-Fighting Years: An Autobiography of the Sixties* (London: Verso,
    2005)
Amarasinghe, Y. Ranjith. *Revolutionary Idealism and Parliamentary
    Politics: A Study of Trotskyism in Sri Lanka* (Colombo: Social Scientists'
    Association, 1998)

Arnold, Guy. *The Maverick State: Gaddafi and the New World Order* (London: Cassel, 1996)

Banda, Michael. *Whither Thornett?* (London: New Park Publications, 1975)

Batatu, Hanna. *The Old Social Classes and the Revolutionary Movements of Iraq A Study of Iraq's Old Landed and Commercial Classes and of Its Communists, Ba`thists and Free Officers* (Princeton, NJ: Princeton University Press, 1983)

Bearman, Jonathan. *Qadhafi's Libya* (London: Zed Books, 1986)

Behan, Brian. *With Breast Expanded* (London: MacGibbon & Kee, 1964)

Birchall, Ian. *Tony Cliff: A Marxist For His Time* (No Place of Publication (London?): Bookmarks, 2011)

Black, Robin. *Stalinism in Britain* (London: New Park Publications, 1971)

Blackledge, Paul; Kelvin Knight, eds. *Virtue and Politics: Alasdair MacIntyre's Revolutionary Aristotelianism* (South Bend, IN: University of Notre Dame Press, 2011)

Blunden, Andy. *Hegel for Social Movements* (Chicago, IL: Haymarket Press, 2020)

Bornstein, Sam; Al Richardson. *Against the Stream: A History of the Trotskyist Movement in Britain, 1924–38* (London: Socialist Platform, 1986)

— *The War and the International: A History of the Trotskyist Movement in Britain, 1937–1949* (London: Socialist Platform, 1986)

Buhle, Paul. *Marxism in the United States: A History of the American Left*, 3rd edition (London: Verso, 2013)

Callaghan, John. *British Trotskyism: Theory and Practice* (Oxford: Basil Blackwell, 1984)

Callahan, Dan. *Vanessa: The Life of Vanessa Redgrave* (New York: Pegasus, 2014)

Callinicos, Alex. *Trotskyism* (Minneapolis, MN: University of Minnesota Press, 1990)

Campbell, Fergus. *Land and Revolution: Nationalist Politics in the West of Ireland, 1891–1921* (Oxford: Oxford University Press, 2005)

Cannon, James P. *The History of American Trotskyism: Report of a Participant* (New York: Pioneer Publishers, 1944)

Caute, David. *Red List: MI5 and British Intellectuals in the Twentieth Century* (London: Verso, 2022)

Connor, James E., ed. *Lenin on Politics and Revolution: Selected Writings* (New York: Pegasus, 1968)

Cowen, Clare. *My Search for Revolution: How We Brought Down an Abusive Leader* (Kibworth Beauchamp: Matador, 2019)

Dorril, Stephen. *The Silent Conspiracy: Inside the Intelligence Services in the 1990s* (London: Heinemann, 1993)

Draper, Theodore. *The Roots of American Communism* (New York: Viking Books, 1957)

Elbaum, Max. *Revolution in the Air: Sixties Radicals Turn to Lenin, Mao and Che* (London: Verso, 2002)

Frank, Pierre. *The Fourth International: The Long March of the Trotskyists* (London: Ink Links, 1979)

Fryer, Peter. *The Battle for Socialism* (London: Socialist Labour League/ Plough Press, 1959).

— *Staying Power: The History of Black People in Britain* (London: Pluto Press, 1984)

Gale, Jack. *Oppression and Revolt in Ireland* (London: Workers Revolutionary Party, 1975)

— *The Anti-Nazi League and Fascism* (London: News Line, 1978)

Gavey, Nicola. *Just Sex? The Cultural Scaffolding of Rape* (New York: Routledge, 2013)

Gilbert, Keith; David Howell (eds), *Dictionary of Labour Biography*, Volume 12 (Basingstoke: Palgrave Macmillan, 2005)

Grant, Ted. *History of British Trotskyism* (London: Wellred Publications, 2002)

Griffiths, Trevor. *The Party* (London: Faber & Faber, 1974)

Groves, Reg. *The Balham Group: How British Trotskyism Began* (London: Pluto, 1974)

Hansen, Joseph, ed. *Healy 'Reconstructs' the Fourth International* (New York: Socialist Workers Party, 1966)

— ed. *Marxism vs. Ultra-Leftism: The Record of Healy's Break with Trotskyism* (New York: Socialist Workers Party, 1974)

Hansen, Joseph et al. *Healy's Big Lie: The Slander Campaign Against Joseph Hansen, George Novack, and the Fourth International* (New York: Socialist Workers Party, 1976)

Harding, Neil. *Lenin's Political Thought: Theory and Practice in the Democratic and Socialist Revolutions* (Chicago, IL: Haymarket Press, 2009)

Harding, Norman. *Staying Red: Why I Remain a Socialist* (London: Index Books, 2005)

Healy, Gerry. *Stop This War! Hands Off the Arab People* (London: New Park Publications, n.d. [1956])

— *Stop the Tory War: Throw Them Out!* (London: New Park Publications, n.d. [1956])

— *The Future of the Labour Party* (No Place of Publication: 1960)

— *Problems of the Fourth International* (No Place of Publication, n.d. [1966])

— *Revolution and Counter-Revolution in Hungary* (London: New Park Publications, n.d.)

The Historical and International Foundations of the Socialist Equality Party (Oak Park MI: Mehring Books, 2008)

Hosken, Andrew. *Ken: The Ups and Downs of Ken Livingstone* (London: Arcadia Books, 2008)

Hughes, Celia. *Young Lives on the Left: Sixties Activism and the Liberation of the Self* (Manchester: Manchester University Press, 2015)

Hunter, Bill. *Lifelong Apprenticeship: The Life and Times of a Revolutionary, Vol. 1: 1920–1959* (London: Index Books/Porcupine Press, 1997)

Ismael, Tareq Y. *The Rise and Fall of the Communist Party of Iraq* (Cambridge: Cambridge University Press, 2008)

Kelly, John. *Contemporary Trotskyism: Parties, Sects and Social Movements in Britain* (London: Routledge, 2018)

— *The Twilight of World Trotskyism* (London: Routledge, 2023)

al-Khalil, Samir. *Republic of Fear: The Politics of Modern Iraq* (Berkeley, CA: University of California Press, 1989)

Knapp, Peter J.; Anne H. Knapp. *Trinity College in the Twentieth Century: A History* (Hartford, CT: Trinity College, 2000)

Le Blanc, Paul. *Lenin: Responding to Catastrophe, Forging Revolution* (London: Pluto Press, 2023)

Leigh, David. *The Wilson Plot: The Intelligence Services and the Discrediting of a Prime Minister* (London: Heinemann, 1988)

Liebman, Marcel; Brian Pearce, Trans. *Leninism under Lenin* (London: Jonathan Cape, 1975)

Lih, Lars. *Lenin Rediscovered: What is to be Done? in Context* (Chicago, IL: Haymarket Books, 2008)

Linehan, Thomas. *Communism in Britain, 1920–30: From the Cradle to the Grave* (Manchester: Manchester University Press, 2007)

Livingstone, Ken. *You Can't Say That: Memoirs* (London: Faber & Faber, 2011)

London, Eric. *Agents: The FBI and GPU Infiltration of the Trotskyist Movement* (Oak Park, MI: Mehring Books, 2019)

Lotz, Corinna; Paul Feldman. *Gerry Healy: A Revolutionary Life* (London: Lupus Books, 1994)

Lukács, George; E. San Juan Jr, ed. *Marxism and Human Liberation* (New York: Delta Books, 1973)

— *Lenin: A Study in the Unity of His Thought* (London: Verso, 1997 [1924])

Magid, Shaul. *Meir Kahane: The Public Life and Political Thought of an American Jewish Radical* (Princeton, NJ: Princeton University Press, 2021)

Markham, Kika. *Our Time of Day: My Life with Corin Redgrave* (London: Oberon Books, 2014)

Marxism, Opportunism and the Balkan Crisis: Statement of the International Committee of the Fourth International (Oak Park, MI: Labor Publication, 1994)

Mau, Søren. *Mute Compulsion: A Marxist Theory of the Economic Power of Capital* (London: Verso, 2023)

McAdams, James. *Vanguard of the Revolution: The Global Idea of the Communist Party* (Princeton, NJ: Princeton University Press, 2017)

McGlinchey, Marisa. *Unfinished Business: The Politics of 'Dissident' Irish Republicanism* (Manchester: Manchester University Press, 2019)

McKinley, Michael. 'Of "Alien Influences": Accounting and Discounting for the International Contacts of the Provisional Irish Republican Army'. *Conflict Quarterly*, Vol. 11, No. 3 (summer 1991), 7–35

McNamara, Conor. *War and Revolution in the West of Ireland: Galway, 1913–1922* (Dublin: Irish Academic Press, 2018)

Medhurst, John. *No Less Than Mystic: A History of Lenin and the Russian Revolution for a 21st Century Left* (London: Repeater, 2017)

Milne, Seumas. *The Enemy Within: The Secret War against the Miners* (London: Verso, 1994)

Mitchell, Alex. *Come the Revolution: A Memoir* (Sydney: NewSouth Publishing/University of New South Wales Press, 2011)

North, David. *Gerry Healy and his Place in the History of Fourth International* (Detroit, MI: Labor Publications, 1991)

— *The Heritage We Defend: A Contribution to the History of the Fourth International*, 2nd edition (Oak Park, MI: Mehring Books, 2018)

North, David; Alex Steiner, eds. *Trotskyism vs. Revisionism, Vol. 7: The Fourth International and the Renegade Wohlforth* (Detroit, MI: Labor Publications, 1984)

Nugent, Brodie; Evan Smith. 'Intersectional Solidarity? The Armagh Women, the British Left and Women's Liberation'. *Contemporary British History*, Vol. 31, No. 4 (2017), 611–635

Oakes, John. *Libya: The History of Gaddafi's Pariah State* (Stroud, Gloucestershire: The History Press, 2011)

Perreau-Saussine, Émile; Nathan J. Pinkoski, Trans. *Alasdair MacIntyre: An Intellectual Biography* (South Bend, IN: University of Notre Dame Press, 2022)

Pilling, Doria, ed. *Marxist Political Economy: Essays in Retrieval: Selected Works of Geoff Pilling* (London: Routledge, 2012)

Pons, Silvio; Stephen A. Smith, eds. *The Cambridge History of Communism, Volume 1: World Revolution and Socialism in One Country, 1917–1941* (Cambridge: Cambridge University Press, 2020)

Ratner, Harry. *Reluctant Revolutionary: Memoirs of a Trotskyist, 1936–1960* (London: Socialist Platform, 1994)

Rayner, Stephen Frank. 'The Classification and Dynamics of Sectarian Forms of Organisation: Grid-Group Perspectives on the Far-Left in Britain', unpublished PhD thesis, University College London, 1979

Redfern, Neil. 'No Friends to the Left: The British Communist Party's Surveillance of the Far Left, c. 1932–1980'. *Contemporary British History*, Vol. 28, No. 3 (2014), 341–360

Redgrave, Deirdre; Danaë Brook. *To Be a Redgrave: Surviving Amidst the Glamour* (New York: Linden Press/Simon & Schuster, 1982)

Redgrave, Vanessa. *Vanessa Redgrave: An Autobiography* (New York: Random House, 1994)

Renaud, Terence. *New Lefts: The Making of a Radical Tradition* (Princeton, NJ: Princeton University Press, 2021)

Richardson, Mike. *Tremors of Discontent: My Life in Print, 1970–1988*, Bristol Radical Pamphleteer #53 (Bristol: Bristol Radical History Group, 2021)

Ronen, Yehudit. *Qaddafi's Libya in World Politics* (Boulder, CO: Lynne Rienner, 2008)

Rowbotham, Sheila. *Promise of a Dream: Remembering the Sixties* (London: Verso, 2019 [2000])

— *Daring to Hope: My Life in the 1970s* (London: Verso, 2021)

Salucci, Ilario. *A People's History of Iraq: The Iraqi Communist Party, Workers' Movements and the Left, 1924–2004* (Chicago, IL: Haymarket Books, 2005)

Samuel, Raphael. *The Lost World of British Communism* (London: Verso, 2006)

Sandbrook, Dominic. *Seasons in the Sun: The Battle for Britain, 1974–1979* (London: Penguin Books, 2012)

Saunders, Jack. *Assembling Cultures: Workplace Activism, Labour Militancy and Cultural Change in Britain's Car Factories, 1945–1982* (Manchester: Manchester University Press, 2019)

Sayigh, Yezid. *Armed Struggle and the Search for State: The Palestinian National Movement, 1949–1993* (Oxford/Washington, DC: Clarendon Press/Institute for Palestine Studies, 1997)

Shaw, Mickie. *Robert Shaw: Fighter for Trotskyism, 1917–1980* (London: New Park Publications, 1983)

Shipley, Peter. *Revolutionaries in Modern Britain* (London: Bodley Head, 1976)

Slaughter, Cliff. *The Class Nature of the 'International Socialism' Group* (London: Socialist Labour League, n.d.)

— *A Balance Sheet of Revisionism* (London: A Newsletter Pamphlet, 1969)

— ed. *Trotskyism vs. Revisionism: A Documentary History, Vol. I, The Fight against Pabloism in the Fourth International* (London: New Park Publications, 1974)

— *Trotskyism vs. Revisionism: A Documentary History, Vol. III, The Socialist Workers Party's Road Back to Pabloism* (London: New Park Publications, 1974)

— *Not Without a Storm: Towards a Communist Manifesto for the Age of Globalisation* (London: Index Books, 2006)

Smith, Evan; Matthew Worley, eds. *Against the Grain: The British Far Left from 1956* (Manchester: Manchester University Press, 2014)

St John, Ronald Bruce. *Qaddafi's World Design: Libyan Foreign Policy, 1969–1987* (Atlantic Highlands, NJ: Saqi Books, 1987)

Suny, Ronald Grigor. *Stalin: Passage to Revolution* (Princeton, NJ: Princeton University Press, 2020)

Thayer, George. *The British Political Fringe: A Profile* (London: Anthony Blond, 1965)

Tourish, Dennis; Tim Wohlforth. *On The Edge: Political Cults Right and Left* (Armonk, NY: M.E. Sharpe, 2000)

Trotsky, Leon. *My Life: An Attempt at an Autobiography* (New York: Pathfinder Press, 1970)

— *Our Political Tasks* (London: New Park Publications, 1979 [1904])

Upham, Martin Richard, 'The History of British Trotskyism to 1949', unpublished PhD thesis, University of Hull, September 1980

Virdee, Satnam. *Racism, Class and the Racialized Outsider* (London: Macmillan/Red Globe Press, 2014)

Whelan, Dermot. *The Socialist Labour League and Irish Marxism (1959–1973): A Disastrous Legacy* (No Place of Publication: League for a Workers Republic, 1973)

Whelan, Tony. *The Credibility Gap: The Politics of the SLL* (No Place of Publication: International Marxist Group, 1970)

Wohlforth, Tim. *The Prophet's Children: Travels on the American Left* (Atlantic Highlands, NJ: Humanities Press, 1994)

Wright, Peter; Paul Greengrass. *Spycatcher: The Candid Autobiography of a Senior Intelligence Officer* (New York: Viking Press, 1987)

Notes

PREFACE

1. Tariq Ali. *Redemption* (London: Chatto & Windus, 1990), 17–18; John Patterson. 'Kate Beckinsale: "Our Phones Were Tapped by Spooks When We Were Growing Up"', *The Guardian*, 19 May 2016; Clare Cowen. *My Search for Revolution: How We Brought Down an Abusive Leader* (Kibworth Beauchamp: Matador, 2019), 2, 46, 156, 163, 225, 244; Tim Wohlforth. *The Prophet's Children: Travels on the American Left* (Atlantic Highlands, NJ: Humanities Press, 1994), 195; Andrew Hosken. *Ken: The Ups and Downs of Ken Livingstone* (London: Arcadia Books, 2008), 127; Trevor Griffiths. *The Party* (London: Faber & Faber, 1974), 34.
2. Alex Mitchell. *Come the Revolution: A Memoir* (Sydney: NewSouth Publishing/University of New South Wales Press, 2011), 202.
3. Hosken, 'Ken' (2008), 127.
4. Interview with Geoff Barr, 14 May 2023. On the other hand, Barr's wife, born in Northern Ireland, felt Healy's speeches were absolutely terrible, akin to hardline Protestant preachers she had experienced as a child.
5. Wohlforth, 'Prophet's Children' (1994), 205, 220.
6. Interview with Philip Edwards, 16 November 2022.
7. Barr calls them a cult but also admits that he would have baulked at that comparison when he was a WRP member. Barr makes the good point that calling them a cult is a limited explanation, but so also is the political argument that they should be seen as an extreme Leninist organisation. Interview with Geoff Barr, 14 May 2023. They were a multi-dimensional organisation requiring multi-dimensional analyses.
8. 'What Is To Be Done?' (1902) in James E. Connor, ed. *Lenin on Politics and Revolution: Selected Writings* (New York: Pegasus, 1968). See also: Ronald Grigor Suny. *Stalin: Passage to Revolution* (Princeton, NJ: Princeton University Press, 2020), 265.
9. Elbaum, 'Revolution in the Air' (2002), 147.
10. Marcel Liebman; Brian Pearce, Trans. *Leninism under Lenin* (London: Jonathan Cape, 1975), 26.
11. 'What is To Be Done?' in Connor, 'Lenin on Politics' (1968), 36.

12. Lenin's *State and Revolution*, completed on the eve of the 1917 Revolutions, directly argues for a withering of the state and the founding of a democratic future. See also Neil Harding. *Lenin's Political Thought: Theory and Practice in the Democratic and Socialist Revolutions* (Chicago, IL: Haymarket Press, 2009). Harding's work is part of a broader current that seeks to recover a democratic Leninism; the very fact that this has to be recovered is bound up with the fact that most examples of real existing Leninism have been *un*-democratic if not even fully *anti*-democratic.

13. Paul Le Blanc. *Lenin: Responding to Catastrophe, Forging Revolution* (London: Pluto Press, 2023), 37, 117; Lars Lih. *Lenin Rediscovered: What is to be Done? in Context* (Chicago, IL: Haymarket Books, 2008); Elbaum, 'Revolution in the Air' (2002), 152.

14. Elbaum, 'Revolution in the Air' (2002), 153. See also, Georg Lukács. *Lenin: A Study in the Unity of His Thought* (London: Verso, 1997 [1924]), which oscillates between non-democratic and democratic conceptions of Leninism.

15. Wohlforth, 'Prophet's Children' (1994), 301.

16. Quoted in John Medhurst. *No Less Than Mystic: A History of Lenin and the Russian Revolution for a 21st Century Left* (London: Repeater, 2017), 526.

17. Leon Trotsky. *My Life: An Attempt at an Autobiography* (New York: Pathfinder Press, 1970).

18. Leon Trotsky. *Our Political Tasks* (London: New Park Publications, 1979 [1904]); Isaac Deutscher. *The Prophet Armed: Trotsky, 1879–1921* (London: Verso, 2003 [1954]), 74. The great Hungarian Marxist György Lukács observed that Trotskyism was just as liable to end in an undemocratic state/society as other variants of Leninism. Georg Lukács; E. San Juan Jr, ed. *Marxism and Human Liberation* (New York: Delta Books, 1973), 68.

CHAPTER 1

1. A Tribute to Gerry Healy, *Socialist Future*, Vol. 7, No. 5 (December 1998–January 1999); Alex Mitchell. *Come the Revolution: A Memoir* (Sydney: NewSouth Publishing/University of New South Wales Press, 2011), 220. My thanks to Conor McNamara for helping me track down information on Healy's birth.

2. Corinna Lotz; Paul Feldman. *Gerry Healy: A Revolutionary Life* (London: Lupus Books, 1994) 194. Mickie Shaw's biography of her husband pulls a similar rhetorical move: 'The workers and peasants of Russia had toppled the decadent and reactionary Tsarist regime and were rapidly assimilating the art of revolution when Robert Shaw was

born on March 29, 1917.' Mickie Shaw. *Robert Shaw: Fighter for Trotskyism, 1917–1980* (London: New Park Publications, 1983), 9.

3. Conor McNamara. *War and Revolution in the West of Ireland: Galway, 1913–1922* (Dublin: Irish Academic Press, 2018); Fergus Campbell. *Land and Revolution: Nationalist Politics in the West of Ireland, 1891–1921* (Oxford: Oxford University Press, 2005).

4. David North. *Gerry Healy and his Place in the History of Fourth International* (Detroit, MI: Labor Publications, 1991), 115.

5. Michael Healy is, of course, not on the full list of Galway casualties provided in McNamara, 'War and Revolution' (2018), 221–222.

6. Lotz & Feldman, 'Gerry Healy' (1994), 195.

7. Lotz & Feldman, 'Gerry Healy' (1994), 172; Andy Blunden, a member of the WRP from 1973 until the split in 1985, sees Healy as solely a product of British politics, since all of his formative experiences were in Britain as an adult not Ireland as a child. Interview with Andy Blunden, 14 July 2022.

8. Lotz & Feldman, 'Gerry Healy' (1994), 27, 177, 195.

9. Interview with Marie Monaghan, 22 February 2022; interview with 'Elizabeth', 14 March 2022.

10. Interview with Gerry Downing, 12 March 2022.

11. Interview with Dave Bruce, 1 July 2022.

12. Mitchell, 'Come the Revolution' (2011), 289.

13. Dennis Tourish and Tim Wohlforth give the date of 1926/age 14, *On the Edge: Political Cults Right and Left* (Armonk, NY: M.E. Sharpe, 2000), 157; Lotz & Feldman, 'Gerry Healy' (1994), 48.

14. Hunter, 'Lifelong Apprenticeship' (1997), 143.

15. Lotz & Feldman, 'Gerry Healy' (1994), 195.

16. Interview with Liz Leicester, 6 June 2023.

17. Interview with Marie Monaghan, 22 February 2022.

18. 'Gerry Healy: A Chronology', *The Marxist Monthly: Theoretical Journal of the Marxist Party*, Vol. 2, No. 12 (1 February 1990), 500; Mitchell, 'Come the Revolution' (2011), 511; Satnam Virdee. *Racism, Class and the Racialized Outsider* (London: Macmillan/Red Globe Press, 2014), 87; North, 'Gerry Healy' (1991), 2. See also Peter Shipley. *Revolutionaries in Modern Britain* (London: Bodley Head, 1976), 79, which says Healy joined CPGB as a thirteen-year-old in 1928 – either the age or the year, if not both, are wrong – and left eight years later, 'disillusioned by the failure of the Communists to win mass support among the working class'.

19. John McIlroy. 'Thomas Gerard (Gerry) Healy (1913–1989): Trotskyist Leader.' In Keith Gilbert and David Howell (eds), *Dictionary of Labour Biography*, Volume 12 (Palgrave Macmillan, Basingstoke, 2005).

20. Sam Bornstein; Al Richardson. *Against the Stream: A History of the Trotskyist Movement in Britain, 1924–38* (London: Socialist Platform, 1986), 20, 23, 51; Thomas Linehan. *Communism in Britain, 1920–30: From the Cradle to the Grave* (Manchester: Manchester University Press, 2007), 3; Raphael Samuel. *The Lost World of British Communism* (London: Verso, 2006), 82.

21. James McAdams. *Vanguard of the Revolution: The Global Idea of the Communist Party* (Princeton, NJ: Princeton University Press, 2017), 4.

22. As late as 1932, British Trotskyists were still able to get their criticisms of the party printed in CPGB publications; Wisconsin Historical Society, James P. Cannon Papers, Box 20, Folder 10, *Minutes of the International Secretariat of August 32rd [sic, 23rd?], 1932*.

23. Bob Pitt. *The Rise and Fall of Gerry Healy*, 7.

24. Paul Buhle. *Marxism in the United States: A History of the American Left*, 3rd edition (London: Verso, 2013), 201.

25. John Kelly. *Contemporary Trotskyism: Parties, Sects and Social Movements in Britain* (London: Routledge, 2018), 26. A 1932 letter from British Trotskyists said they had eight members, still in the Communist Party; Wisconsin Historical Society, James P. Cannon Papers, Box 20, Folder 10 (Minutes of the International Secretariat, 1931–1933), *Minutes of the International Secretariat*, 20 July 1932.

26. Marisa McGlinchey, a scholar of 'dissident' Irish Republicanism, also infamous for its splits and fusions, has observed that 'When tactics are elevated to the position of principle… little room for compromise is present either internally or between groups.' *Unfinished Business: The Politics of 'Dissident' Irish Republicanism* (Manchester: Manchester University Press, 2019), 39, 41.

27. Alex Callinicos. *Trotskyism* (Minneapolis, MN: University of Minnesota Press, 1990), 41.

28. Bornstein & Richardson, 'Against the Stream' (1986), 275. The quote here from Jock Haston is from an interview with Al Richardson, conducted on 30 April 1978.

29. John McIlroy. 'James Ritchie (Jock) Haston (1912–86): Trotskyist Leader and Workers' Educator'. Keith Gilbert and David Howell (eds), *Dictionary of Labour Biography*, Volume 12 (Basingstoke: Palgrave Macmillan, 2005); www.marxists.org/history/etol/writers/mcilroy/jock-haston.htm.

30. Quoted in full in 'Gerry Healy: A Chronology', *The Marxist Monthly: Theoretical Journal of the Marxist Party*, Vol. 2, No. 12 (1 February 1990), p.500; Mitchell, 'Come the Revolution' (2011), 511–512; North, 'Gerry Healy' (1991), 1, 5–7. In their overly sympathetic biography of him, Corinna Lotz and Paul Feldman say that it was a shock for 'the 22-year-old Healy' to find himself at odds with his former CPGB

comrades in 1937. But by this year he was 24, so if we assume the age
is correct it would suggest he actually became a Trotskyist in 1935 or
that, at the least, some of the details he imparted to his biographers
were faulty.

31. Glasgow Caledonian University Archive Centre, GCATT/WIL/19,
Report of Trotskyists Active in London, CPGB Report, n.d.; GCATT,
The Attack Upon the Party from the So-Called 'Extreme Left', Commu-
nist Party Document, April 1964, Uncatalogued. In 1985, an article in
Morning Star, the CPGB's organ, said Healy had left the Communists
in 1936. 'Identity Crisis hits WRP', *Morning Star*, 30 October 1985.
For further information on CPGB monitoring of Healy, which lasted
into the 1950s, see: Neil Redfern. 'No Friends to the Left: The British
Communist Party's Surveillance of the Far Left, c. 1932–1980'. *Contemporary British History*, Vol. 28, No. 3 (2014), 341–360.

32. Bornstein & Richardson, 'Against the Stream' (1986), 33.

33. Cowen, 'My Search for Revolution' (2019), 216.

34. Glasgow Caledonian University Archive Centre, Bill Hunter Papers,
'Forums: The Wortley Hall Conference', *The Newsletter*, Vol. 1, No. 1,
10 May 1957; Wisconsin Historical Society, James P. Cannon Papers,
Box 23, Folders 1–2, Press Cuttings, 'Mr. Healy Supplies Labour with
Alternative Policy', *The Guardian*, ca. 1958 ['Mr Healy said that he
was expelled from the Communist party in 1936 for his opposition
to the Moscow trials.']. Stephen Frank Rayner. 'The Classification and
Dynamics of Sectarian Forms of Organisation: Grid-Group Perspec-
tives on the Far-Left in Britain', unpublished PhD thesis, University
College London, 1979, 176.

35. See the discussions in Cannon, 'History of American Trotskyism'
(1944); Reg Groves. *The Balham Group: How British Trotskyism Began*
(London: Pluto, 1974).

36. Shaw, 'Robert Shaw' (1983), 64.

37. Glasgow Caledonian University Archive Centre, Bill Hunter Papers,
Box 29, *History of the British Trotskyist Movement*, Lecture by Gerry
Healy, SLL Summer Camp, 6 August 1964.

38. Ted Grant. *History of British Trotskyism* (London: Wellred Publications, 2002), 92–93.

39. Lotz & Feldman, 'Gerry Healy' (1994), 197–199; Hunter, 'Lifelong
Apprenticeship' (1997), 69.

40. Harry Ratner. *Reluctant Revolutionary: Memoirs of a Trotskyist, 1936–
1960* (London: Socialist Platform, 1994), 19.

41. Mary and John Archer. 'Notes on Healy's Role in Early Days of
British Trotskyist Movement.' In Joseph Hansen, *et al. Healy's Big Lie:
The Slander Campaign Against Joseph Hansen, George Novack, and
the Fourth International* (New York: Socialist Workers Party, 1976).

The Archers said Healy had been in the YCL immediately prior to becoming a Trotskyist. This recollection was published in a very polemical attack on Healy, so the tone and content should be taken with caution.

42. Sam Bornstein and Al Richardson. *The War and the International: A History of the Trotskyist Movement in Britain, 1937–1949* (London: Socialist Platform, 1986), 2.

43. Bertrand M. Patenaude. 'Trotsky and Trotskyism'. Silvio Pons; Stephen A. Smith, eds. *The Cambridge History of Communism, Volume 1: World Revolution and Socialism in One Country* (Cambridge: Cambridge University Press, 2020), 205–208; Kelly, 'Contemporary Trotskyism' (2018), 27.

44. Kelly, 'Contemporary Trotskyism' (2018), 27.

45. Bill Hunter. *Lifelong Apprenticeship: The Life and Times of a Revolutionary, Vol. 1: 1920–1959* (London: Index Books/Porcupine Press, 1997), 33.

46. Lotz & Feldman, 'Gerry Healy' (1994), 199–200.

47. Shaw, 'Robert Shaw' (1983), 66–67.

48. Lotz & Feldman, 'Gerry Healy' (1994), 201.

49. Shaw, 'Robert Shaw' (1983), 39–41.

50. Lotz & Feldman, 'Gerry Healy' (1994), 202.

51. Bornstein & Richardson, 'War and the International' (1986), 10.

52. Bob Pitt. *The Rise and Fall of Gerry Healy*, 8.

53. Ciaran Crossey and James Monaghan, 'The Origins of Trotskyism in Ireland'. *Revolutionary History*, Vol. 6, Nos. 2 & 3 (1996), 11.

54. Hunter, 'Lifelong Apprenticeship' (1997), 147–149.

55. McIlroy. 'Thomas Gerard (Gerry) Healy (1913–1989): Trotskyist Leader.' In Gilbert and Howell, 'Dictionary', (2005).

56. Lotz & Feldman, 'Gerry Healy' (1994), 202.

57. Lotz & Feldman, 'Gerry Healy' (1994), 8.

58. Hunter, 'Lifelong Apprenticeship' (1997), 144, 152. In a March 1944 letter to an American comrade, Healy mentions a factory in which he worked at this time: Wisconsin Historical Society, James P. Cannon Papers, Box 22, Folder 8, Letter from G. Healy to Comrade Loris [Marc Loris?], 6 March 1944.

59. Glasgow Caledonian University Archive Centre, GCATT/WIL/19, *Report on Trotskyite Activity in Britain*, CPGB Report, May 1943 and GCATT/WIL/19, *Report of Trotskyists Active in London*, CPGB Report, n.d.

60. Shaw, 'Robert Shaw' (1983), 40. For overview of the idea of 'Revolutionary Defeatism', which all British Trotskyists espoused, see: Hull History Centre, Jock Haston Papers: UDJH/13/A/14, *Revolutionary Defeatism*, RSL Conference Resolution, n.d.

61. Bornstein & Richardson, 'War and the International' (1986), 53.
62. Bornstein & Richardson, 'War and the International' (1986), 115.
63. Buhle, 'Marxism in the United States' (2013), 200. What Buhle says of the American Trotskyist party The Workers Party would also be true of Healy's various parties: they built support that was 'a mile wide, but an inch thick'.
64. Strikes (Incitement), *Hansard*, Volume 399: debated on Friday 28 April 1944; University of Warwick Modern Records Centre, Papers of Ken Tarbuck, MSS 75/3/4/158, 'Miners Say "Ban 2 Papers"', Undated Daily Mail Press Cutting.
65. University of Warwick Modern Records Centre, Papers of Ken Tarbuck, MSS 75/7/1/2-17, 'Warning All Anti-Nazis/Information you may want to keep', Communist Party Leaflet, n.d. [ca. 1942–1944].
66. Hull History Centre, Jock Haston Papers, UDJH/13/A/12, *Report on Negotiations with the W.I.L.*, Revolutionary Socialist League Report, December 1941.
67. Hunter, 'Lifelong Apprenticeship' (1997), 129.
68. Hunter, 'Lifelong Apprenticeship' (1997), 155, 157.
69. Hull History Centre, Jock Haston Papers, UDJH/14/A/7, *Internal Bulletin: Our Most Important Task*, Draft Document by Gerry Healy, 30 August 1943.
70. Hull History Centre, Jock Haston Papers, UDJH/14/A/7, Letter from E. Grant [Ted Grant] to Gerry Healy, 21 August 1943.
71. Bob Pitt. *The Rise and Fall of Gerry Healy*, 12–15.
72. Bob Pitt. *The Rise and Fall of Gerry Healy*, 18–19. See also: University of Warwick Modern Records Centre, Papers of Ken Tarbuck, MSS 75/3/2/33, *Bolshevik Method and Revolutionary Sincerity: A Reply to Comrade Healy*, Political Bureau Document, 2 September 1943.
73. 'Appendix I: Statement of the Political Committee of the WIL on the Expulsion of Gerry Healy', 15 February 1943, in Grant, 'History of British Trotskyism' (2002), 229–231. For an original copy of this, see: University of Warwick Modern Records Centre, Papers of Ken Tarbuck, MSS 75/3/2/15A, *Statement of the P.B.* [Political Bureau] *on the Expulsion from W.I.L. of G. Healy*, 7 February 1943. The expulsion appears to have happened on 7 February, but the statement was not realised until 15 February.
74. Bornstein & Richardson, 'War and the International' (1986), 101.
75. University of Warwick Modern Records Centre, Papers of Ken Tarbuck, MSS 75/7/1/1, Assorted Press Cuttings, 28 April 1944.
76. Lotz & Feldman, 'Gerry Healy' (1994), 207.
77. National Archives of the UK, WP (44), 202, 13 April 1944, www.marxists.org/history/etol/revhist/brittrot/homeoff.html.
78. Hunter, 'Lifelong Apprenticeship' (1997), 134.

79. Hunter, 'Lifelong Apprenticeship' (1997), 162.
80. University of Warwick Modern Records Centre, Papers of Ken Tarbuck, MSS 75/7/1/2-17, Jock Haston Electoral Literature, 1945; Kelly, 'Contemporary Trotskyism' (2018), 130.
81. Evan Smith, Matthew Worley, 'The Far Left in Britain from 1956' and John Callaghan, 'Engaging with Trotsky: The Influence of Trotskyism in Britain', both in Evan Smith and Matthew Worley, eds. *Against the Grain: The British Far Left from 1956* (Manchester: Manchester University Press, 2014).
82. Bornstein & Richardson, 'War and the International' (1986), 160. See also: Martin Richard Upham. 'The History of British Trotskyism to 1949', unpublished PhD thesis, University of Hull, September 1980.
83. University of Warwick Modern Records Centre, Papers of Ken Tarbuck, MSS 75/3/4/29, G. Healy, *International Bulletin*, New Series, No.9, *On our Tasks and Perspectives*, June 1945, See also, in the same collection: MSS 75/3/4/96, G. Healy, 'Against the Politics of Stagnation', 2 July 1947, *Internal Bulletin*.
84. Wisconsin Historical Society, James P. Cannon Papers, Box 22, Folder 8, Letter from James Cannon to Gerry Healy, 12 June 1947.
85. Hunter, 'Lifelong Apprenticeship' (1997), 231.
86. Hunter, 'Lifelong Apprenticeship' (1997), 143.
87. University of Warwick Modern Records Centre, Papers of Ken Tarbuck, MSS 75/3/4/71, *Labour Party Faction Report*, n.d. [ca. 1946].
88. Bob Pitt. *The Rise and Fall of Gerry Healy*, 22.
89. John Callaghan. *British Trotskyism: Theory and Practice* (Oxford: Basil Blackwell, 1984), 75.
90. Ratner, 'Reluctant Revolutionary' (1994), 144.
91. McIlroy. 'Thomas Gerard (Gerry) Healy (1913–1989): Trotskyist Leader.' In Gilbert and Howell, 'Dictionary', (2005).
92. Gerry Healy. *Stop This War! Hands off the Arab People* (London: New Park Publications, n.d. [1956]); Gerry Healy. *Stop the Tory War: Throw Them Out!* (London: New Park Publications, n.d. [1956]).
93. Tourish & Wohlforth, 'On the Edge' (2000), 158.
94. Glasgow Caledonian University Archive Centre, GCATT, G. Healy, 'Plain Speaking on War and Peace', *Labour Review*, Vol. 1, No. 3 (September/November, 1952). See also: GCATT, G. Healy, 'The Way to Socialism in Britain', *Labour Review*, Vol. 1, No. 2, a fair-minded but still critical review of Aneurin Bevan's socialism. It is written with a tone of genuine comradeliness at odds with Healy's later style.
95. Hunter, 'Lifelong Apprenticeship' (1997), 233; University of Warwick Modern Records Centre, Papers of Ken Tarbuck, MSS 75/4/2/16, 'Declaration on the Dissolution of the Revolutionary Communist Party and the Entry of its Members into the Labour Party', *Socialist Appeal*, Special Number, July 1949.

96. Ian Birchall. *Tony Cliff: A Marxist for His Time* (No place of publication (London?): Bookmarks, 2011), 98; University of Warwick Modern Records Centre, Papers of Ken Tarbuck, MSS 75/3/4/69, G. Healy, 'Some Remarks on the Russian Question', in *RCP Conference Documents 1946*, this document outlines his criticisms of Jock Haston on the contentious issue of 'degenerated workers' state' vs 'state capitalist' perceptions of the USSR.

97. It does appear that some supporters of the Haston faction joined Healy's Club after the dissolution of the open RCP. Shipley, 'Revolutionaries' (1976), 67.

98. Tourish & Wohlforth, 'On the Edge' (2000), 158.

99. Bornstein & Richardson, 'War and the International' (1986), 230–231.

100. Shaw, 'Robert Shaw' (1983), 91.

101. The SWP appears to have provided $1,150 to aid with the purchase of printing equipment, with the expectation that The Club would repay this by buying SWP literature and by doing some printing work for them; Wisconsin Historical Society, James P. Cannon Papers, Box 25, Folders 6–8, Letter from 'Smith' to 'Burns' [Gerry Healy], 7 December 1953.

102. Bob Pitt. *The Rise and Fall of Gerry Healy*, 33.

103. Wisconsin Historical Society, James P. Cannon Papers, Box 22, Folder 8, Letter from G. Healy to Comrade Loris [Marc Loris], 6 March 1944.

104. Hunter, 'Lifelong Apprenticeship' (1997), 255, 258, 264, 309; Lotz & Feldman, 'Gerry Healy' (1994), 212–213.

105. Birchall, 'Tony Cliff' (2011), 121.

106. 'Party Action against Socialist Weekly: "Tribune" Criticism of Executive'. *Times*, 13 August 1954; 'Using the Club'. *Socialist Outlook*, No. 149 (8 October 1954).

107. Hunter, 'Lifelong Apprenticeship' (1997), 153.

108. Shaw, 'Robert Shaw' (1983), 95–96.

109. Shipley, 'Revolutionaries' (1976), 80.

110. Kelly, 'Contemporary Trotskyism' (2018), 40.

111. Kelly, 'Contemporary Trotskyism' (2018), 43.

112. Callaghan, 'British Trotskyism' (1984), 69–70.

113. Callaghan, 'British Trotskyism' (1984), 71.

114. Hunter, 'Lifelong Apprenticeship' (1997), 334.

115. Smith & Worley, 'The Far Left in Britain from 1956' in Smith & Worley, 'Against the Grain' (2014), 5.

116. North, 'Gerry Healy' (1991), 29.

117. Brian Behan. *With Breast Expanded* (London: MacGibbon & Kee, 1964), 131.

118. Cowen, 'My Search for Revolution' (2019), 268; Kelly, 'Contemporary Trotskyism' (2018), 43.

CHAPTER 2

1. Griffiths. *The Party* (1974), 57–58.
2. Correspondence with Sean Matgamna, July 2022.
3. Interview with Tariq Ali, 22 June 2022.
4. Lotz & Feldman, 'Gerry Healy' (1994), 15, 29. For summaries of Healy's philosophy, see: *Notes on the Practice of Cognition* and *Syllabus: A Course of 10 Lectures on Dialectical Materialism*, n.d., both in University of Warwick Modern Records Centre, Papers of Chris and Ann Talbot, Box 1, 1072/1/2/2.
5. Lotz & Feldman, 'Gerry Healy' (1994), 44.
6. Cowen, 'My Search for Revolution' (2019), 174, 177.
7. North, 'Gerry Healy' (1991), 87.
8. Lotz & Feldman, 'Gerry Healy' (1994), 155–156.
9. 'College of Marxist Education', Advertisement, *News Line*, 28 August 1978.
10. Markham, 'Our Time of Day' (2014), 34.
11. Wohlforth, 'Prophet's Children' (1994), 241; Lotz & Feldman, 'Gerry Healy' (1994), 50.
12. Kelly, 'Contemporary Trotskyism' (2018), 96.
13. G. Healy. 'The "Cell" of Materialist Dialectics'. *The Marxist Monthly*, Vol. 1, No. 2 (April 1988). Andy Blunden remembers Hegel as being 'a bit dyslexic' and recalls how he would regularly mispronounce 'causality', a key term in Hegelianism, as 'casuality'; Healy almost certainly wasn't dyslexic, but this certainly points to the degree to which his lectures were, as Blunden says, 'bollocks'. Blunden says Healy could occasionally be insightful in his philosophy but he 'certainly hadn't read Hegel'. And as Blunden points out, Lenin's notes on Hegel make little sense if one has not read Hegel to start with. When Blunden himself read Hegel's *Logic*, he kept it quiet because he knew the party frowned on this. Interview with Andy Blunden, 14 July 2022.
14. Michael Banda, *Whither Thornett?* (London: New Park Publications, 1975), 24–25; David North. *The Heritage We Defend: A Contribution to the History of the Fourth International*, 2nd edition (Oak Park, MI: Mehring Books, 2018), 81–82.
15. Bob Pitt. *The Rise and Fall of Gerry Healy*, 142. See also, University of Warwick Modern Records Centre, Papers of Chris and Ann Talbot, Box 1, 1072/1/1/3, CC Report, Draft Notes by GH, 27 January 1979. Amidst discussions of US foreign policy, global class conflict and the disintegration of capitalism, Healy outlines his 'philosophy': 'Thoughts expressed in word form must correspond to the *very essences of things*, that is to a real deepening of our *knowledge of the class struggle of today*… Forms of thought are incapable of embrac-

ing truth because "truth" is *infinite* (relative) whilst forms of thought are *finite* (absolute).' Even allowing for the rough format of notes for a public talk, it is clear that there is not much beneath the surface here.

16. North 'Heritage We Defend' (2018), 439.
17. Interview with Alex Steiner, 17 May 2022.
18. Letter from Alasdair MacIntyre to Gerry Healy, 10 May 1960 and Letter from Gerry Healy to Alasdair MacIntyre, 19 May 1960 in *Socialist Labor League, Internal Bulletin No.4, National Conference, June 4, 5, 6,* n.d. [1960], University of Warwick Modern Records Centre, Papers of Alan Clinton, MSS 539/1/1.
19. Wohlforth, 'Prophet's Children' (1994), 217.
20. John Bloxam Private Files, Letter from G. Healy to All Branch Secretaries, 9 February 1979.
21. Glasgow Caledonian University Archive Centre, GCATT, Uncatalogued Files, *Draft Resolution for the 13th Annual Conference of the Socialist Labour League,* 29–31 May 1971.
22. Interview with Robert Myers, 23 June 2022.
23. Wohlforth, 'Prophet's Children' (1994), 195.
24. Bob Pitt. *The Rise and Fall of Gerry Healy,* 20.
25. Bob Pitt. *The Rise and Fall of Gerry Healy,* 5.
26. www.wsws.org/en/special/library/the-icfi-defends-trotskyism-1982-1986/02.html.
27. Mike Banda, 'Morality and the Revolutionary Party', *News Line,* 2 November 1985.
28. Mike Banda, 'What is Trotskyism? Or, Will the Real Trotsky Please Stand Up', *Communist Forum,* No. 4, November 1986.
29. Lotz & Feldman, 'Gerry Healy' (1994), 294.
30. Hosken, 'Ken' (2008), 128.
31. Interview with Dave Bruce, 1 July 2022.
32. Lotz & Feldman, 'Gerry Healy' (1994), 84, 93.
33. Lotz & Feldman, 'Gerry Healy' (1994), 57.
34. Bob Pitt. *The Rise and Fall of Gerry Healy,* 51.
35. Bob Pitt. *The Rise and Fall of Gerry Healy,* 75.
36. Bob Pitt. *The Rise and Fall of Gerry Healy,* 86, 92.
37. Lotz & Feldman, 'Gerry Healy' (1994), 292–293.
38. *The Marxist Monthly,* Vol. 1, No. 5.
39. Bob Pitt. *The Rise and Fall of Gerry Healy,* 3, 72.
40. Bob Pitt. *The Rise and Fall of Gerry Healy,* 120, 121.
41. 'Election '87: Deathroes [*sic*] of Parliamantary Democracy', *Marxist Review,* Vol. 2, No. 5 (May 1987).
42. *The Marxist Monthly,* Vol. 1, No. 5.
43. Cowen, 'My Search for Revolution' (2019), 93.
44. Interview with 'Judith', 21 February 2022.

45. Bob Pitt. *The Rise and Fall of Gerry Healy*, 51.
46. Interview with Garth Frankland, 8 August 2022; interview with Liz Leicester, 6 June 2023.
47. Interview with Mike Richardson, 8 June 2023.
48. Bob Pitt. *The Rise and Fall of Gerry Healy*, 3.
49. Jack Gale. *Oppression and Revolt in Ireland* (London: Workers Revolutionary Party, 1975); interview with Gerry Downing, 12 March 2022; Gerry Downing, 'Ard Fheis: A Question of How Much Emphasis on the Electoral Campaign', *Workers Press*, 22 November 1986. From the contents of this, and the way in which he comments directly on what happened there, Downing was almost certainly present at the *Ard Fhéis*, though Danny Morrison, then a member of the Ard Comhairle (executive committee) of Sinn Féin emphatically denies that the WRP delegates would have been invited in an official capacity. Correspondence with Danny Morrison, 14 November 2022.
50. Michael McKinley, 'Of "Alien Influences": Accounting and Discounting for the International Contacts of the Provisional Irish Republican Army'. *Conflict Quarterly*, Vol. 11, No. 3 (summer 1991), 10–11.
51. Interview with Gerry Downing, 12 March 2022.
52. Interview with Dave Bruce, 1 July 2022; Brodie Nugent, Evan Smith. 'Intersectional Solidarity? The Armagh Women, the British Left and Women's Liberation'. *Contemporary British History*, Vol. 31, No. 4 (2017), 611–635.
53. Wohlforth, 'Prophet's Children' (1994), 207–208.
54. Interview with Tariq Ali, 16 June 2022; interview with Alex Steiner, 17 May 2022. For an explanation of the (often quite convoluted) reasoning behind the SLL's opposition to joining the anti-war movement, see: Cliff Slaughter. *A Balance Sheet of Revisionism* (London: A Newsletter Pamphlet, 1969).
55. Mitchell, 'Come the Revolution' (2011), 215.
56. University of Warwick Modern Records Centre, Papers of David Spencer, MSS 164/1A/1, *Political Letter, No.2*, Open Letter to SLL Members from Gerry Healy, 15 August 1962.
57. Kelly, 'Contemporary Trotskyism' (2018), 80; Karen Blick. 'Obituary: Adam Westoby'. *Revolutionary History*, Vol. 5, No. 4 (1994).
58. Chris Bailey. 'Theoretical Foundations of Healyism'. *New Interventions*, Vol. 3, No. 1 (1992).

CHAPTER 3

1. From articles like 'Will Mr. Gaitskell Resign' and 'Should MPs Carry Out Party Policy', in 'A daily bulletin presented free to delegates and visitors' at the Labour Party's annual conference, it is clear how much

the SLL was aggravating the Labour leadership. Glasgow Caledonian University Archive Centre, Bill Hunter Papers, *Newsletter*, Conference Special, No. 2, 4 October 1960.

2.   A broad overview of Healy's early political career, up to the SLL period, can be found in George Thayer. *The British Political Fringe: A Profile* (London: Anthony Blond, 1965), 126–137; See also Robert J. Alexander. *International Trotskyism, 1929–1985: A Documented Analysis of the Movement* (Durham, NC: Duke University Press, 1991), 437–481.

3.   Callaghan, 'British Trotskyism' (1984), 77.

4.   Gerry Healy. *The Future of the Labour Party* (No Place of Publication: 1960).

5.   Norman Harding. *Staying Red: Why I Remain a Socialist* (London: Index Books, 2005), 83.

6.   Hunter, Lifelong Apprenticeship' (1997), 396; G. Healy. 'Some Reflections on the Socialist Labour League'. *Forum*, March 1960.

7.   Rob Sewell. 'Postscript' in Grant, 'History of British Trotskyism' (2002), 207.

8.   University of Warwick Modern Records Centre, Papers of Bob Purdie, MSS 149/1/4/1, 'Draft Resolution on the Labour Party', April 1961.

9.   Mitchell, 'Come the Revolution' (2011), 225.

10. In a precise recap of this idea that Leninist parties always see themselves as brains removed from the proletarian body, SLL/WRP theorist Cliff Slaughter once said that Bolshevik parties 'are based on the scientific theories of Marx and Engels, developed by Lenin and Trotsky; these theories do not arise directly out of the experience of the working class, but are brought into the class struggle "from without"'. Cliff Slaughter. *The Class Nature of the "International Socialism" Group* (London: Socialist Labour League, n.d.).

11. National Archives, CAB 186/8, p.17 and annex pp. 2 and 5, quoted in Mitchell, 'Come the Revolution' (2011), 231.

12. Bornstein & Richardson, 'War and the International' (1986), 187–189.

13. Callaghan, 'British Trotskyism' (1984), 77, 80–81.

14. Hunter, 'Lifelong Apprenticeship' (1997), 50.

15. Patenaude, 'Trotsky and Trotskyism' (2020), 208. The only electorally successful Trotskyist party, the Lanka Sama Samaja Party (LSSP) in Sri Lanka had only established a formal connection to the Fourth International in 1950 but made sure to retain its autonomy. When the LSSP built ties in the early 1960s with the Sri Lanka Freedom Party (a left-of-centre party and still one of the largest parties in Sri Lanka today), the relations with the Fourth International finally cracked. Its connections to the Freedom Party were part of what allowed it to be successful, and that is also part of what broke its connections with the less flexible Fourth International. Y. Ranjith Amarasinghe. *Rev-*

olutionary Idealism and Parliamentary Politics: A Study of Trotskyism in Sri Lanka (Colombo: Social Scientists' Association, 1998), 4, 250, 262–263.

16. Document 20b, Letter from the Bureau of the IS to G. Healy, September 23, 1953, in Cliff Slaughter, ed. Trotskyism vs. Revisionism: A Documentary History, Vol. I, The Fight against Pabloism in the Fourth International (London: New Park Publications, 1974), 329–330; Document 21, Letter from G. Healy to the International Secretariat, 10 July 1957 in Cliff Slaughter, ed. Trotskyism vs. Revisionism: A Documentary History, Vol. III, The Socialist Workers Party's road back to Pabloism (London: New Park Publications, 1974), 39.

17. Wohlforth, 'Prophet's Children' (1994), 94–95.

18. Pierre Frank. The Fourth International: The Long March of the Trotskyists (London: Ink Links, 1979), 111. Pierre Frank did know Gerry Healy, having met him in London after the war; Ratner, 'Reluctant Revolutionary' (1994), 111.

19. This might be the same meeting in Toronto that Tim Wohlforth describes and which he dates to 1960. 'Prophet's Children' (1994), 94–95.

20. Ratner, 'Reluctant Revolutionary' (1994), 212.

21. Interview with Granville Williams, 4 January 2023.

22. 'Ernest Tate Beaten by Squad at SLL Meeting' in Marxism vs. Ultra-Leftism: The Record of Healy's break with Trotskyism (New York: Socialist Workers Party, 1974), 108.

23. 'The Beating of Ernie Tate', in Marxism vs. Ultra-Leftism: The Record of Healy's break with Trotskyism (New York: Socialist Workers Party, 1974), 108–121; interview with Tariq Ali, 16 June 2022; John Bloxam Private Files, Ernie Tate, Open Letter to Members and Supporters of the Socialist Labour League, 19 January 1967; University of Warwick Modern Records Centre, Papers of Alan Clinton, MSS 539/1/1, 'Open letter from Ernie Tate', 15 December 1966.

24. University of Warwick Modern Records Centre, Papers of E.A. Whelan, MSS 95/3/1/1, Statement by Editorial Board of Keep Left Concerning Alleged Threats of Violence against Delegates and Visitors to the Young Socialists' Conference, 23 April 1962.

25. Shaw, 'Robert Shaw' (1983), 113.

26. Bob Pitt. The Rise and Fall of Gerry Healy, 123–124.

27. Interview with Andy Blunden, 14 July 2022.

28. Letter from Liam Kelly to Andy Bolton, 26 April 1960 in University of Warwick Modern Records Centre, Papers of Alan Clinton, MSS 539/1/1. Socialist Labor League, Internal Bulletin No.2, National Conference, June 4, 5, 6, n.d. [1960].

29. Tourish & Wohlforth, 'On the Edge' (2000), 160.

30. Tourish & Wohlforth, 'On the Edge' (2000), 160; Émile Perreau-Saussine; Nathan J. Pinkoski, Trans. *Alasdair MacIntyre: An Intellectual Biography* (South Bend, IN: University of Notre Dame Press, 2022), 23–24; Neil Davidson. 'Alasdair MacIntyre and Trotskyism'. In Paul Blackledge and Kelvin Knight, eds. *Virtue and Politics: Alasdair MacIntyre's Revolutionary Aristotelianism* (South Bend, IN: University of Notre Dame Press, 2011), 152–176.

31. Letter from Alasdair MacIntyre to Gerry Healy, 10 May 1960, in University of Warwick Modern Records Centre, Papers of Alan Clinton, MSS 539/1/1, *Socialist Labor League, Internal Bulletin No.4, National Conference, June 4, 5, 6*, n.d. [1960], 1.

32. Peter Fryer. *The Battle for Socialism* (London: Socialist Labour League/ Plough Press, 1959).

33. Cowen, 'My Search for Revolution' (2019), 198.

34. Bob Pitt. *The Rise and Fall of Gerry Healy*, 59.

35. Wisconsin Historical Society, James P. Cannon Papers, Box 21, Folder 7 (SLL Internal Documents 1959), Peter Fryer, *An open letter to members of the Socialist Labour league and Other Marxists*, 19 September 1959.

36. Tourish & Wohlforth, 'On the Edge' (2000), 159.

37. Peter Fryer. *Staying Power: The History of Black People in Britain* (London: Pluto Press, 1984). One of Healy's most perceptive published works, *Revolution and Counter-Revolution in Hungary* (London: New Park Publications, n.d.), drew heavily on Fryer's original reporting from Budapest.

38. See also, Wisconsin Historical Society, James P. Cannon Papers, Box 2, Folder 7 (SLL Internal Documents 1959), Peter Cadogan, *The 1959 Situation in the Socialist Labour League*, which recounts unsuccessful efforts to promote reform within the SLL.

39. Ratner, 'Reluctant Revolutionary' (1994), 228.

40. Wohlforth, 'Prophet's Children' (1994), 198.

41. Interview with Andy Blunden, 14 July 2022.

42. Interview with Bridget Fowler, 15 June 2022.

43. Cowen, 'My Search for Revolution' (2019), 70–71, 73.

44. Interview with Tariq Ali, 16 June 2022.

45. Interview with Geoff Barr, 14 May 2023.

46. Tariq Ali. *Street-Fighting Years: An Autobiography of the Sixties* (London: Verso, 2005), 188.

47. Interview with Tariq Ali, 16 June 2022; see also, Ali's harsh criticisms of the SLL in *The Coming British Revolution* (London: Jonathan Cape, 1972).

48. Interview with Dave Bruce, 1 July 2022.

49. Tony Whelan says the recruiting of Young Socialists saw the SLL membership grow from about 300 to 1,000 between 1959 and 1964. Tony Whelan. *The Credibility Gap: The Politics of the SLL* (No Place of Publication: International Marxist Group, 1970).

50. Interview with Sean Matgamna, July 2022.

51. University of Warwick Modern Records Centre, Papers of E.A. Whelan, MSS 95/3/1/1, Letter from A.L. Williams, General Secretary of the Labour Party, to Constituency and local Labour Parties and Branches of the Young Socialists, 24 May 1962; University of Warwick Modern Records Centre, Papers of Bob Purdie, MSS 149/1/4/1, *Youth and the Revolutionary Party*, Draft Conference Resolution by the National Committee, 28–29 November 1964. The 10,500 circulation is cited in University of Warwick Modern Records Centre, Papers of E.A. Whelan, MSS 95/3/1/1, *Statement by Editorial Board of Keep Left Concerning Alleged Threats of Violence against Delegates and Visitors to the Young Socialists' Conference*, 23 April 1962. The circulation seems high but also is more specific than these claims usually are since this was a Labour Party publication, not just an SLL one, there is every chance this is accurate.

52. Interview with 'Judith', 21 February 2022.

53. 'The repeated crises of the CPUSA [Communist Party of USA] fulfilled Trotskyist predictions without usually leading to significant recruitment by the latter.' Buhle, 'Marxism in the United States' (2013), 200.

54. Smith & Worley, 'The Far Left in Britain from 1956' in Smith & Worley, 'Against the Grain' (2014), 5.

55. Interview with Garth Frankland, 8 August 2022.

56. Jack Saunders. *Assembling Cultures: Workplace Activism, Labour Militancy and Cultural Change in Britain's Car Factories, 1945–1982* (Manchester: Manchester University Press, 2019), 71, 197, 198.

57. Kelly, 'Contemporary Trotskyism' (2018), 44. The Communist Party estimated in 1964 that 'It is very unlikely that it has a membership of more than a few hundred.' Glasgow Caledonian University Archives Centre, GCATT, *The Attack Upon the Party from the So-Called "Extreme Left"*, Communist Party Document, April 1964, Uncatalogued.

58. Glasgow Caledonian University Archives Centre, GCATT, Uncatalogued Files, Gerry Healy, *A Political Letter to All Members: We Must Change Our Method of Work*, 10 January 1965. Years later, the journalist and one-time communist Frank Chapple claimed he had once heard a story of an SLL meeting where Healy ordered all present to admit the mistakes they had made in their political careers. 'Finally, and to everyone's utter amazement, he pointed his finger at them and said: "I'm guilty too. I have tolerated *your* mistakes for far too long. I

have been lenient with you, but never again!'" Frank Chapple, 'Gerry's Guilty Past', *Mail*, 31 October 1985. This is a bit too fun an anecdote to be believable, though it would not be totally out of character for Healy.

59. Glasgow Caledonian University Archive Centre, GCATT, Uncatalogued Files, *Draft Resolution for the 13th Annual Conference of the Socialist Labour League*, 29–31 May 1971.

60. Hunter, 'Lifelong Apprenticeship' (1997), 50.

61. Wohlforth, 'Prophet's Children' (1994), 226–227.

62. Interview with Liz Leicester, 6 June 2023.

63. Cowen, 'My Search for Revolution' (2019), 46, 53.

64. Interview with Clare Cowen, 15 May 2023.

65. Interview with Andy Blunden, 14 July 2022.

66. Joseph Hansen, ed. *Healy "Reconstructs" the Fourth International* (New York: Socialist Workers Party, 1966); Joseph Hansen, ed. *Marxism vs. Ultra-Leftism: The Record of Healy's Break with Trotskyism* (New York: Socialist Workers Party, 1974); Wohlforth, 'Prophet's Children' (1994), 135, 136–137. Healy provided a characteristically self-aggrandising defence of his actions in *Problems of the Fourth International* (No Place of Publication, n.d. [1966]).

67. Interview with Alex Steiner, 17 May 2022. Because of the Voorhis Act – the 1940 Anti-Propaganda Act, introduced by Rep. Jerry Voorhis (D-CA), requiring the registration of any US organisation acting as the agent of a foreign entity – the WL never formally joined the ICFI, but existed in sympathy with them.

68. Wohlforth, 'Prophet's Children' (1994), 219.

69. Interview with Jim Monaghan, 4 July 2022. See also the useful short history of the group: www.leftarchive.ie/article/1393/.

70. Wohlforth, 'Prophet's Children' (1994), 219.

71. Dermot Whelan. *The Socialist Labour League and Irish Marxism (1959–1973): A Disastrous Legacy* (No Place of Publication: League for a Workers Republic, 1973). The League for a Workers Vanguard, according to Whelan, primarily devoted itself to building a youth movement and Healy seems to have come to Ireland in 1970 and 1971 to lead educational work within the Irish Young Socialists. Whelan says the SLL leadership refused to see any difference between Protestant and Catholic workers in Northern Ireland, presumably because of a class determinism that left no space for 'subjective' identity. The LWV was led by David Fry, a Trinity graduate, who seems to have been hand selected by Healy for his loyalty.

72. Barry Healy, a member of the rival Australian Socialist Workers Party, says the SLL were thuggish, 'almost like a criminal gang... so prone to violence' and with a bullying internal regime. According to Barry Healy, they pushed party members to take out mortgages on

their homes and give the money to the party. If members left, they would 'terrorise' them; he remembers one SLL member in Sydney who left and joined the SWP. The SLL smashed his house's windows and damaged his car, told people in his neighbourhood he was a paedophile and called his employer to out him as a communist. It was not until he left the SWP that the SLL left him alone. They would not tolerate their members leaving for any other party; interview with Barry Healy, 14 July 2022. Healy is no relation to Gerry Healy. The Australian SWP was connected to the American SWP. For other evidence of violence in the Australian SLL, see 'Statement to the Left and Working-Class Press: SLL Violence in the Workers Movement', *Australasian Spartacist*, No. 21, July 1975; 'SLL thugs threaten, assault ex-member', *Direct Action*, 19 May 1977.

73. Interview with Tariq Ali, 16 June 2022; interview with Barry Healy, 14 July 2022.
74. 'David Mercer, 1928–1980: An Appreciation', *News Line*, 11 August 1980; interview with Liz Leicester, 6 June 2023.
75. Sheila Rowbotham. *Promise of a Dream: Remembering the Sixties* (London: Verso, 2019 [2000]), 199, 253–254. See also Celia Hughes. *Young Lives on the Left: Sixties Activism and the Liberation of the Self* (Manchester: Manchester University Press, 2015), 148–149.
76. Interview with Barry Healy, 14 July 2022.
77. 'Keeping Faith: An Interview with Stuart Hood'. *Edinburgh Review*, 78 (1988), 201–202.
78. Mitchell, 'Come the Revolution' (2011), 201–206.
79. Kika Markham. *Our Time of Day: My Life with Corin Redgrave* (London: Oberon Books, 2014), 19–20.
80. Markham, 'Our Time of Day' (2014), 21.
81. Deirdre Redgrave; Danaë Brook. *To Be a Redgrave: Surviving Amidst the Glamour* (New York: Linden Press/Simon & Schuster, 1982), 165, 195–197.
82. Bob Pitt. *The Rise and Fall of Gerry Healy*, 104.
83. Correspondence with Sean Matgamna, July 2022.
84. Mitchell, 'Come the Revolution' (2011), 263.

CHAPTER 4

1. Tourish & Wohlforth, 'On the Edge' (2000), 156.
2. Vanessa Redgrave. *Vanessa Redgrave: An Autobiography* (New York: Random House, 1994), 185; Dan Callahan. *Vanessa: The Life of Vanessa Redgrave* (New York: Pegasus, 2014), 97; Redgrave and Brook, 'To Be a Redgrave' (1982), 204–205.
3. Callahan, 'Vanessa' (2014), 97.

4. Tourish & Wohlforth, 'On the Edge' (2000), 160.
5. Mitchell, 'Come the Revolution' (2011), 366.
6. Callahan, 'Vanessa' (2014), 97.
7. Bob Pitt. *The Rise and Fall of Gerry Healy*, 104.
8. Ali, 'Redemption' (1990), 18, 21; Cowen, 'My Search for Revolution' (2019), 102.
9. Interview with Clare Cowen, 15 May 2023.
10. Callahan, 'Vanessa' (2014), 127. O'Grady wrote several articles on Ireland for the *Marxist Review*.
11. Mitchell, 'Come the Revolution' (2011), 258.
12. Wohlforth, 'Prophet's Children' (1994), 204–205; Mitchell, 'Come the Revolution' (2011), 246.
13. Dominic Sandbrook. *Seasons in the Sun: The Battle for Britain, 1974–1979* (London: Penguin Books, 2012), 303.
14. University of Warwick Modern Records Centre, Papers of Alan Clinton, MSS 539/1/5, 'Road to Workers Power': Anti-Tory Rally and Pageant of History, Programme, 11 March 1973.
15. John Patterson. 'Kate Beckinsale: "Our Phones Were Tapped by Spooks When We Were Growing Up"', *The Guardian*, 19 May 2016.
16. Liz Leicester, UCPI Evidence Hearings, Tranche 1 (Phase 3), Day 5, (13 May 2022), AM (accessible at: www.youtube.com/watch?v=LuxlfotVxro).
17. Mitchell, 'Come the Revolution' (2011), 368.
18. Wohlforth, 'Prophet's Children' (1994), 204–205, 297.
19. Wohlforth, 'Prophet's Children' (1994), 141.
20. Redgrave & Brook, 'To Be a Redgrave' (1982), 197.
21. Mitchell, 'Come the Revolution' (2011), 368.
22. Harding, 'Staying Red' (2005), 210; Mitchell, 'Come the Revolution' (2011), 366.
23. Mitchell, 'Come the Revolution' (2011), 236.
24. Cowen, 'My Search for Revolution' (2019), 102.
25. Redgrave, 'Autobiography' (1994), 192–193, 202.
26. Redgrave, 'Autobiography' (1994), 299.
27. Interview with Liz Leicester, 6 June 2023.
28. Harding, 'Staying Red' (2005), 192.
29. Tourish & Wohlforth, 'On the Edge' (2000), 163.
30. Callahan, 'Vanessa' (2014), 106–107.
31. Harding, 'Staying Red' (2005), 217–218.
32. 'Vanessa Redgrave Loses', *New York Times*, 4 May 1979; Kelly, 'Contemporary Trotskyism' (2018), 140.
33. Harding, 'Staying Red' (2005), 213–214; interview with 'Judith', 21 February 2022.
34. Callahan, 'Vanessa' (2014), 103.

35. Callahan, 'Vanessa' (2014), 104–105.
36. Callahan, 'Vanessa' (2014), 106.
37. Mitchell, 'Come the Revolution' (2011), 353–354.
38. Bob Pitt. *The Rise and Fall of Gerry Healy*, 115.
39. Interview with Clare Cowen, 15 May 2023.
40. Lotz & Feldman 'Gerry Healy' (1994), 269–270.
41. Redgrave & Brook, 'To Be a Redgrave' (1982), 232.
42. John Bloxam Private Files, Letter from M. Banda to All Branch Secretaries, 6 February 1979; '£70,000 Libel Fund was Helped on by Sunday's Gala Concert', *News Line*, 30 January 1979.
43. Harding, 'Staying Red' (2005), 206.
44. Mitchell, 'Come the Revolution' (2011), 371.
45. Shaul Magid. *Meir Kahane: The Public Life and Political Thought of an American Jewish Radical* (Princeton, NJ: Princeton University Press, 2021), 139–140.
46. Bob Pitt. *The Rise and Fall of Gerry Healy*, 125.
47. Redgrave, 'Autobiography' (1994), 282.
48. Corin Redgrave, 'A Bolshevik Until His Dying Day', *Marxist Monthly*, Vol. 2, No. 12 (February 1990).
49. Callahan, 'Vanessa' (2014), 163.
50. Lotz & Feldman, 'Gerry Healy' (1994), 17, 100, 120. On Holt and her sympathies for Healy, see her eulogy speech, 'Broad Shoulders to Lean Upon', *Marxist Monthly*, Vol. 3, No. 2 (April 1990).
51. 'Healy's Theatre of the Absurd', *Workers News*, No. 6 (December 1987).
52. Redgrave, 'Autobiography' (1994), 319.
53. Lynn Barber. 'She's Got Issues: Interview'. *The Observer*, 19 March 2006.
54. Callahan, 'Vanessa' (2014), 268.
55. Callahan, 'Vanessa' (2014), 299.
56. Redgrave & Brook, 'To Be a Redgrave' (1982), 196, 206.

CHAPTER 5

1. Hughes, 'Young Lives on the Left' (2015), 230.
2. Max Elbaum. *Revolution in the Air: Sixties Radicals Turn to Lenin, Mao and Che* (London: Verso, 2002), 16–17.
3. Kelly, 'Contemporary Trotskyism' (2018), 46, 55.
4. Hull History Centre, Papers of Tom Kemp, Box 20, *Draft Resolution: Perspectives for Building the Revolutionary Party in Britain*, Seventh Annual Conference of the Socialist Labour League, 5–7 June 1965.
5. Elbaum observes a similar problem of skewed and ultimately inaccurate perspectives in the American New Left, 'Revolution in the Air' (2002), 88.

6. Terence Renaud. *New Lefts: The Making of a Radical Tradition* (Princeton, NJ: Princeton University Press, 2021), 286–287.

7. For an example of this kind of post-68 dogmatism, see: University of Warwick Modern Records Centre, Papers of Alan Clinton, MSS 539/1/1, *Draft Resolution: Perspectives for the Transformation of the SLL into a Revolutionary Party*, Socialist Labour League Central Committee, 1 February 1973. See also, Kelly, 'Contemporary Trotskyism' (2018), 10–11.

8. Mike Richardson. *Tremors of Discontent: My Life in Print, 1970–1988*, Bristol Radical Pamphleteer #53 (Bristol: Bristol Radical History Group, 2021), 55.

9. Hughes, 'Young Lives on the Left' (2015), 228.

10. University of Warwick Modern Records Centre, Papers of E.A. Whelan, MSS 95/3/1/1, *Build the Party: Political Perspectives adopted by the Special Conference of the Workers Revolutionary Party*, 13–14 July and amended on 1 August 1974.

11. Interview with Vincent Doherty, 8 November 2022.

12. Alan Thornett. 'Gerry Healy: The Ceausescu of the British Trotskyist Movement'. *Socialist Outlook*, no. 21 (February 1990).

13. Robert Myers. 'Some Experiences of How Not to Organise and a More Useful One.' Angryworkers.org.

14. Lotz & Feldman, 'Gerry Healy' (1994), 1.

15. Lotz & Feldman, 'Gerry Healy' (1994), 261.

16. North, 'Gerry Healy' (1991), 57.

17. University of Warwick Modern Records Centre, Papers of Alan Clinton, MSS 539/1/1, 'WRP Membership Card', n.d. The same language was used in the 'Provisional Membership Card' issues to SLL members as it became the WRP: *Socialist Labour League Provisional Membership Card* in University of Warwick Modern Records Centre, Papers of Alan Clinton, MSS 539/1/5. See also the *Draft Constitution for the Party*, n.d. [1973] in University of Warwick Modern Records Centre, Papers of Alan Clinton, MSS 539/1/5.

18. Robin Black. *Stalinism in Britain* (London: New Park Publications, 1971). The book was written under a pseudonym.

19. Robin Blick, '57th Act Variety', *Solidarity: A Journal of Libertarian Socialism*, No. 11 (Spring, 1986); interview with Dave Bruce, 7 July 2022. Bruce says Blick later became 'a fucking nutter'.

20. Wohlforth, 'Prophet's Children' (1994), 229–230.

21. Lotz & Feldman, 'Gerry Healy' (1994), 262–263.

22. Bob Pitt. *The Rise and Fall of Gerry Healy* 108; Wohlforth, 'Prophet's Children' (1994), 229.

23. Dan Callahan. *Vanessa: The Life of Vanessa Redgrave* (New York: Pegasus, 2014), 106–107.

24. Redgrave & Brook, 'To Be a Redgrave' (1982), 208; Markham, 'Our Time of Day' (2014), 19–20.
25. Redgrave & Brook, 'To Be a Redgrave' (1982), 217.
26. Interview with Andy Blunden, 14 July 2022.
27. Wohlforth, 'Prophet's Children' (1994), 228.
28. Wohlforth, 'Prophet's Children' (1994), 196.
29. Interview with Andy Blunden, 14 July 2022.
30. Interview with Kevin Flynn, 29 September 2011, North East Labour History, Oral History Interviews: https://nelh.net/resources-library/oral-history/oral-history-political-organisations/oral-history-political-organisations-kevin-flynn/, accessed 3 January 2022; interview with Garth Frankland, 8 August 2022.
31. Interview with Philip Edwards, 16 November 2022.
32. Harding, 'Staying Red' (2005), 187–188.
33. Interview with 'Elizabeth', 14 March 2022.
34. Cowen, 'My Search for Revolution' (2019), 72, 158.
35. Harding, 'Staying Red' (2005), 189–191, 194; Cowen, 'My Search for Revolution' (2019), 158.
36. Cowen, 'My Search for Revolution' (2019), 279.
37. Rayner, 'Classification and Dynamics' (1979), 196; interview with Geoff Barr, 14 May 2023.
38. Witness Statement of Roy Battersby to the Undercover Police Inquiry, 11 February 2022.
39. Mitchell, 'Come the Revolution' (2011), 307.
40. Cowen, 'My Search for Revolution' (2019), 100. For the party's official view of Thornett at the time of his expulsion, as well as his responses, see: Michael Banda. *A Menshevik Unmasked: Reply to Alan Thornett* (Internal Bulletin: Members Only) (1974); *Internal Bulletin: For Members Only: The Anti-Party Nature of Thornett's Slander Campaign, A Letter from Alan Thornett and a Reply from the Political Committee*, 1974, both in UCL Senate House Library, GB 96 MS 1256; Glasgow Caledonian University Archives Centre, GCATT, Uncatalogued Files, Alan Thornett, *Correct the Wrong Positions of the Party – Return to the Transitional Programme*, Motion Submitted for First Annual Conference of the WRP, 1 November 1974. It is clear from the start that Thornett remained a quite orthodox Trotskyist, seeking reform within the WRP rather than a break from the WRP. The copy of the WRP's constitution in Thornett's papers has a mark made next to the section on democratic rights – 'While co-operating in carrying out the decisions of the majority, all minorities have the right to express dissenting opinions and organise within the party' – presumably made there by Thornett himself. University of Warwick Modern Records Centre,

Papers of Alan Thornett, MSS 391/3/73, *Workers Revolutionary Party Constitution*, n.d.

41. Interview with Garth Frankland, 8 August 2022.
42. Interview with Robert Myers, 23 June 2022. Thornett's status as a trade unionist was already dropping in this period, his militancy had made him a target for attacks by the mainstream press and he was probably out of step with most of the workers he represented, who were generally not as radical as the Trotskyists had hoped or believed, see: Saunders, 'Assembling Cultures' (2019), 220–222.
43. Mitchell, 'Come the Revolution' (2011), 286.
44. Wohlforth, 'Prophet's Children' (1994), 237–245; interview with Alex Steiner, 17 May 2022; 'Wohlforth Letter of Resignation', 29 September 1974, in *Trotskyism vs Revisionism, Vol. 7: The Fourth International and the Renegade Wohlforth* (Detroit, MI: Labor Publications, 1984).
45. Bob Pitt. *The Rise and Fall of Gerry Healy*, 109.
46. Hosken, 'Ken' (2008), 128; Wohlforth, 'Prophet's Children' (1994), 225.
47. Interview with Vincent Doherty, 8 November 2022.
48. Interview with Garth Frankland, 8 August 2022.
49. Interview with Alex Steiner, 17 May 2022; Myers confirms this accusation; interview with Robert Myers, 23 June 2022.
50. Interview with Geoff Barr, 14 May 2023.
51. Interview with Barry Healy, 14 July 2022.
52. Alex Mitchell and the American Trotskyist David North both visited Mexico as part of this 'investigation', claiming to have uncovered evidence there and in archives in Washington, DC. Mitchell, 'Come the Revolution' (2011), 303.
53. Wohlforth, 'Prophet's Children' (1994), 261–262; Joseph Hansen, *et al. Healy's Big Lie: The Slander Campaign Against Joseph Hansen, George Novack, and the Fourth International* (New York: Socialist Workers Party, 1976); 'Trots Feud Over Trotsky', *Observer*, 16 January 1977.
54. Interview with Tariq Ali, 22 June 2022; an open letter condemning Healy was signed by some of the leading figures in international Trotskyism: *inter alia*, Tariq Ali, Robin Blackburn, Nahuel Moreno, Tamara Deutscher, Dermot Whelan, Pierre Frank and Raya Dunayevskaya; 'The Verdict: "A Shameless Cover-Up"'. In Joseph Hansen *et al. Healy's Big Lie: The Slander Campaign Against Joseph Hansen, George Novack, and the Fourth International* (New York: Socialist Workers Party, 1976).
55. Tim Wohlforth, 'Introduction'. In Joseph Hansen *et al. Healy's Big Lie: The Slander Campaign Against Joseph Hansen, George Novack and the Fourth International* (New York: Socialist Workers Party, 1976).
56. Interview with Paul le Blanc, 18 February 2022.

57. Lotz & Feldman, 'Gerry Healy' (1994), 268.
58. Mitchell, 'Come the Revolution' (2011), 261.
59. Wohlforth, 'Prophet's Children' (1994), 259–260.
60. Wohlforth, 'Prophet's Children' (1994), 207.
61. Interview with Irving Hall, 3 December 2022; interview with Steve Zeltzer, 14 November 2022.
62. Cowen, 'My Search for Revolution' (2019), 164.
63. Cowen, 'My Search for Revolution' (2019), 152, 187; Harding, 'Staying Red' (2005), 204–205; interview with Robert Myers, 23 June 2022.
64. Harding, 'Staying Red' (2005), 209.
65. Interview with Tariq Ali, 22 June 2022.
66. 'Vanessa and the Red House Mystery', *The Observer*, 28 September 1975; Kelly, 'Contemporary Trotskyism' (2018), 96.
67. Interview with Dave Bruce, 7 July 2022.
68. Richardson, 'Tremors of Discontent' (2021), 77.
69. Chris McBride, a young WRP recruit in the early 1980s, recalls bringing a copy of Gaddafi's *Green Book* to the College, not realising how controversial this was within the party. Once his bag was searched and the offending book was found, he was duly sent home (even though his copy of the *Green Book* had been printed by the WRP's New Park Publications) and later expelled. Interview with Chris McBride, 25 July 2023.
70. Liz Leicester, UCPI Evidence Hearings, Tranche 1 (Phase 3), Day 5, (13 May 2022), AM (accessible at: www.youtube.com/watch?v=LuxlfotVxro).
71. Interview with Andy Blunden, 14 July 2022.
72. Interview with Geoff Barr, 14 May 2023.
73. 'Vanessa and the Red House Mystery', *The Observer*, 28 September 1975.
74. Cowen, 'My Search for Revolution' (2019), 108.
75. Mitchell, 'Come the Revolution' (2011), 280. Cowen 'My Search for Revolution' (2019), 197.
76. See the advert for the college in University of Warwick Modern Records Centre, Papers of Chris and Ann Talbot, Box 1, 1072/1/1/1, *Draft Resolution on Perspectives*, Second Annual Conference, 28–30 August 1976.
77. Liz Leicester, UCPI Evidence Hearings, Tranche 1 (Phase 3), Day 5 (13 May 2022), AM (accessible at: www.youtube.com/watch?v=LuxlfotVxro).
78. Interview with Paul Henderson, 30 October 2022.
79. 'Vanessa and the Red House Mystery', *The Observer*, 28 September 1975.

80. As discussed in Chapter 6, the WRP acquired a copy of a Special Branch report on the raid which does seem to confirm that the police and the newspaper were cooperating at some level.
81. Harding, 'Staying Red' (2005), 224–225; Redgrave & Brook, 'To Be a Redgrave' (1982), 231–232.
82. Mitchell, 'Come the Revolution' (2011), 279.
83. Mitchell, 'Come the Revolution' (2011), 281–284; Lotz & Feldman, 'Gerry Healy' (1994), 268–269.
84. Richardson, 'Tremors of Discontent' (2021), 56.
85. Liz Leicester, UCPI Evidence Hearings, Tranche 1 (Phase 3), Day 5 (13 May 2022), AM (accessible at: www.youtube.com/watch?v=LuxlfotVxro).
86. Interview with Chris McBride, 25 July 2023.
87. 'Revolution on the Rates', *Daily Mail*, 13 February 1976 and 'Indoctrination Scare After Teenagers' Trip to the Red House', *Times Educational Supplement*, 13 February 1976. Press cuttings of both are in: University of Warwick Modern Records Centre, Papers of Alan Clinton, MSS 539/1/6.
88. Redgrave, 'Autobiography' (1994), 279.
89. Mitchell, 'Come the Revolution' (2011), 290–291.
90. BFI, *The Money Programme* (BBC Television, 20 March 1983).
91. Theodore Draper. *The Roots of American Communism* (New York: Viking Books, 1957), 87.
92. Cowen, 'My Search for Revolution' (2019), 114, 116, 191; Mitchell, 'Come the Revolution' (2011), 292.
93. Interview with Andy Blunden, 14 July 2022.
94. BFI, *The Money Programme* (BBC Television, 20 March 1983).
95. Interview with David Parks, 23 November 2022. See also: *Labour Review*, Vol. 7, No. 4 (November 1983). According to an advert posted in this issue, Ken Livingstone was present at a *News Line* event, along with leading WRP members and the soccer player Chris Hughton.
96. Redgrave, 'Autobiography' (1994), 279.
97. Cowen, 'My Search for Revolution' (2019), 5. See also: Donald McRae. 'Chris Hughton: "I Have a Thirst for Knowledge. I Won't Always Be a Manager'. *The Guardian*, 28 April 2017.
98. Mitchell, 'Come the Revolution' (2011), 295.
99. Harding, 'Staying Red' (2005), 201.
100. BFI, *The Money Programme* (BBC Television, 20 March 1983).
101. University of Warwick Modern Records Centre, Papers of Chris and Ann Talbot, Box 1, 1072/1/1/4, 'News Line Finance and Sales', Document by Gerry Healy, 19 September 1980. The Banda brothers may have had personal business interests that helped pay for *News Line*; Rayner, 'Classification and Dynamics' (1979), 184.

102. John Bloxam Private Files, Form Letter from Sheila Torrance to Central Committee Members, 2 July 1976. The letter has spaces that Torrance could fill in to tell each branch member what increases they should make in membership numbers, paper sales and attendance at the Education Centre. In this case, Torrance ordered this branch to increase membership from 160 to 300, increase paper sales by 30 per cent and send 50 members to the Centre. This was all to be achieved by the end of August (i.e. within two months). For other examples of these forms and impossible-to-achieve sales and membership quotas, see: University of Warwick Modern Records Centre, Papers of Alan Clinton, MSS 539/1/6, 'Form for Paper Sales', 27 June 1974; University of Warwick Modern Records Centre, Papers of Alan Clinton, MSS 539/1/5, 'Open Letter to Party Members from Sheila Torrance', 9 November 1973.

103. Interview with Peter Money, 23 November 2022; Paul Thompson, a very active member in the mid-1970s, also sees *News Line* as the cause of a major change in the party. Interview with Paul Thompson, 22 November 2022.

104. Harding, 'Staying Red' (2005), 182–183; Wohlforth, 'Prophet's Children' (1994), 265–266.

105. Cowen, 'My Search for Revolution' (2019), 191.

106. Harding, 'Staying Red' (2005), 200.

107. Cowen, 'My Search for Revolution' (2019), 165.

108. Redgrave, 'Autobiography' (1994), 195.

109. Interview with Dave Bruce, 7 July 2022.

110. Harding, 'Staying Red' (2005), 183–184; Hosken, 'Ken' (2008), 126; Ken Livingstone. *You Can't Say That: Memoirs* (London: Faber & Faber, 2011), 217–219; BFI, *The Money Programme* (BBC Television, 20 March 1983).

111. Redgrave, 'Autobiography' (1994), 195; Mitchell, 'Come the Revolution' (2011), 244.

112. Lotz & Feldman, 'Gerry Healy' (1994), 270–273. Clare Cowen lists the names and address of five of them as follows: Paperbacks Centre, 28 Charlotte Street, London W1P 1NP; Paperbacks Centre, 10–12 Atlantic Road, Brixton, London, SW9; Paperbacks Centre, 389 Green Street, Upton Park, London, E3; Merseybooks, 34–36 Manchester Street, Liverpool, L1 GER; Hope Street Book Centre, 321 Hope Street, Glasgow, G33 3PT; 'My Search for Revolution' (2019), 251. See also Shaw, 'Robert Shaw' (1983), 190.

113. Interview with Dave Bruce, 7 July 2022.

114. Mitchell, 'Come the Revolution' (2011), 262.

115. Interview with Robert Myers, 23 June 2022.

116. 'Renegade from Trotskyism: G. Healy, 1913–1989'. *Tasks of the Fourth International: Journal of the Preparatory Committee for the Reconstruction of the Fourth International*, No. 8 (May 1990).

117. Mitchell, 'Come the Revolution' (2011), 317–318.

118. Interview with Andy Blunden, 27 July 2022.

119. Interview with Mike Richardson, 8 June 2023.

120. Interview with Paul Henderson, 30 October 2022.

121. Lotz & Feldman, 'Gerry Healy' (1994), 273–274.

122. Yezid Sayigh. *Armed Struggle and the Search for State: The Palestinian National Movement, 1949–1993* (Oxford/Washington, DC: Clarendon Press/Institute for Palestine Studies, 1997), 484, 501–502.

123. 'Anti-Imperialist Alliance: A Communiqué'. *News Line*, 10 August 1977.

124. Bob Pitt. *The Rise and Fall of Gerry Healy*, 115.

125. Harding, 'Staying Red' (2005), 206–207. This story is also recounted in Lotz & Feldman, 'Gerry Healy' (1994), 273–274.

126. Redgrave, 'Autobiography' (1994), 248.

127. 'A Balance Sheet of Revisionism: The Collapse of the Workers Revolutionary Party', *Workers News*, No. 1 (April 1987); 'The SLL and Irish Marxism (1959–1973): A Disastrous Legacy', *Workers News*, No. 19 (September 1989).

128. Lotz & Feldman, 'Gerry Healy' (1994), 275.

129. For examples of party election literature and strategy, see: *Election Communication*, Vanessa Redgrave Handbill, Moss Side By-Election, July 1978 and *Draft Resolution: Election Policy*, Workers Revolutionary Party Third Annual Conference, 19–21 June 1978, both in UCL Senate House Library, GB 96 MS 1256.

130. Mitchell, 'Come the Revolution' (2011), 379.

131. University of Warwick Modern Records Centre, Papers of Alan Clinton, MSS 539/1/5, *Election Communication: A Message from Michael van der Poorten*, General Election Leaflet, October 1974. Van der Poorten was Banda's legal name.

132. The ten candidates standing for the party: Kevin Flynn (Wallsend), Sylvester Smart (Lambeth Central), Michael van der Poorten (Hackney North & Stoke Newington); John Dillon (Toxteth); Royston Bull (Hayes & Harlington), Trevor Parsons (Pontefract & Castleford); Jim Bevan (Aberavon), Kate Blakeney (Swindon), Alan Wilkins (Coventry North-East) and Vanessa Redgrave (Newham North-East); Parsons was a miner and Flynn was a shipyard worker. University of Warwick Modern Records Centre, Papers of Alan Clinton, MSS 539/1/5, *Workers Revolutionary Party Manifesto*, general election, 10 October 1974.

133. John Davies, the WRP's candidate in Barnsley, took an oddly defeatist tone for his election: 'Our programme and socialist solution is quite different from all the others because it is *revolutionary*. For this reason, I am aware that the WRP vote will be small in comparison with the main political parties. But more important than votes are principles.' University of Warwick Modern Records Centre, Papers of Chris and Ann Talbot, Box 2, 1072/1/7/2, A Message from John Davies, Workers Revolutionary Party Candidate for Barnsley, May 1979.

134. Mitchell, 'Come the Revolution' (2011), 380.

135. Kelly, 'Contemporary Trotskyism' (2018), 140; John Kelly. *The Twilight of World Trotskyism* (London: Routledge, 2023), 49.

136. Liz Leicester, UCPI Evidence Hearings, Tranche 1 (Phase 3), Day 5 (13 May 2022), AM (accessible at: www.youtube.com/watch?v=LuxlfotVxro).

137. Bob Pitt. *The Rise and Fall of Gerry Healy*, 107.

138. 'Vanessa Redgrave Concedes Defeat', www.bbc.com/news/av/uk-politics-37032574.

139. Very few of Healy's speeches were ever recorded; Mitchell, 'Come the Revolution' (2011), 257–258. This perhaps stemmed from a similar desire to control his image and prevent embarrassment.

140. 'City Warned of "Political" Scheme', *Coventry Evening Telegraph*, 23 July 1981; 'Apology to Vanessa Redgrave for Libel', *Times*, 28 July 1981; 'Lefties Battle to Bend the Minds of Our Young', *News of the World*, 27 September 1981; University of Warwick Modern Records Centre, Papers of Chris and Ann Talbot, Box 1, 1072/1/2/2, Template Letter from Vanessa Redgrave, Chairman, Youth Training, n.d.

141. The Manchester community centre was in a once-derelict building bought for £8,500 and then renovated by party members. By 1985, it was apparently worth between £40,000 and £60,000. Glasgow Caledonian University Archive Centre, Bill Hunter Papers [Uncatalogued], *Some Questions for Tony Banda and Dave Hyland*, Manchester, 17 December 1985.

142. Interview with Peter Money, 23 November 2022.

143. Interview with Scotty Clark, 27 November 2022.

144. Harding, 'Staying Red' (2005), 236–239.

145. Mitchell, 'Come the Revolution' (2011), 437; Cowen, 'My Search for Revolution' (2019), 195; interview with Paul Henderson, 30 October 2022.

146. Mitchell, 'Come the Revolution' (2011), 438.

147. Cowen, 'My Search for Revolution' (2019), 180.

148. Bob Pitt. *The Rise and Fall of Gerry Healy*, 123.

149. Kelly, 'Contemporary Trotskyism' (2018), 166.

CHAPTER 6

1. Hull History Centre, Jock Haston Papers, UDJH/15/B/40, Paul Dixon, *The 1945 Congress of the R.C.P.: A Reply to Comrade Goffe and Healy*, 23 November 1945.
2. Søren Mau. *Mute Compulsion: A Marxist Theory of the Economic Power of Capital* (London: Verso, 2023), 165.
3. Interview with Clare Cowen, 15 May 2023.
4. University of Warwick Modern Records Centre, Papers of Alan Clinton, MSS 539/1/5, *A Message to all Housewives: Fight the Tory Prices Con Trick*, A Workers Press Leaflet, n.d. [ca. late 1972, early 1973], emphases added. See also the discussion in University of Warwick Modern Records Centre, Papers of Chris and Ann Talbot, Box 1, 1072/1/1/1, *Draft Resolution on Perspectives*, Second Annual Conference, 28–30 August 1976: 'Nationalise to take the profit out of food! Prices to be decided by committees of workers and housewives!' Again, in the WRP's view, 'workers' are a discrete and implicitly male category distinct from 'housewives'.
5. *Workers Press*, 14 March 1970; also discussed in Caroline Lund, 'Where the SLL Goes Wrong on Women's Liberation' (originally published in July 1970). In Joseph Hansen, ed. *Marxism vs. Ultraleftism: The Record of Healy's Break with Trotskyism* (New York: Socialist Workers Party, 1974).
6. Correspondence with Sheila Rowbotham, 19 July 2023.
7. Elbaum, 'Revolution in the Air' (2002), 137–138.
8. Interview with Clare Cowen, 15 May 2023.
9. University of Warwick Modern Records Centre, Papers of Alan Clinton, MSS 539/1/5, *Young Socialists Summer Fair*, Open Letter to *Keep Left* Readers, 1974; interview with Philip Edwards, 16 November 2022.
10. Interview with Liz Leicester, 6 June 2023.
11. Linehan, 'Communism in Britain' (2007), 96–97. Unsurprisingly, the CPGB rarely had a female membership that got above 20 per cent of the total membership, a ratio that was still probably better than that of the male-dominated WRP. See also: Joana Ramiro. 'Why Do Leftwing Women Disappear from Politics in Their 30s'. *Novara Media*, 20 September 2021.
12. Kelly, 'Contemporary Trotskyism' (2018), 27.
13. Kelly, 'Contemporary Trotskyism' (2018), 47.
14. Kelly, 'Contemporary Trotskyism' (2018), 100.
15. Interview with Paul Flewers, 10 November 2022.
16. Hughes, 'Young Lives on the Left' (2015), 235.

17. 'Women's Role is Praised in Iraq', *News Line*, 7 May 1979; 'Women in Front Line of Iran Revolution', *News Line*, 21 May 1979; 'Questions and Answers on Policies of the Workers Revolutionary Party', *News Line*, 24 September 1981.
18. University of Warwick Modern Records Centre, Papers of Chris and Ann Talbot, Box 1, 1072/1/1/4, 'End the War Between Iraq and Iran: Face the Main Zionist Enemy in Lebanon', Statement by the Political Committee of the Workers Revolutionary Party, 24 September 1980.
19. Glasgow Caledonian University Archive Centre, GCATT, James Baker, *Racialism: A Danger to Labour* (London: Newsletter/Socialist Labour League, n.d. [early 1960s]).
20. See, for example, 'Racist Violence and Police Brutality in Wolverhampton', *News Line*, 18 May 1978.
21. Glasgow Caledonian University Archive Centre, GCATT, Uncatalogued Files, Socialist Labour League, Resolutions, Ninth National Conference, 27–29 May 1967.
22. 'All Aboard the Anti-Nazi Bandwagon', *News Line*, 18 May 1978; University of Warwick Modern Records Centre, Papers of Chris and Ann Talbot, Box 2, 1072/1/7/3, *The Anti-Nazi League Fraud*, May 1978.
23. 'Political Crisis in the Socialist Workers Party', *News Line*, 4 August 1978.
24. 'Memoirs of a Teenage Trot', *The Guardian*, 18 February 2000.
25. Interview with Clare Cowen, 15 May 2023. The book was *Mrs Grundy: Studies in English Prudery*.
26. Interview with Robert Myers, 23 June 2022.
27. Elbaum, 'Revolution in the Air' (2002), 138.
28. 'The Wolfenden Report: A Socialist Doctor's View'. *The Newsletter*, Vol. 1, No. 19 (14 September 1957).
29. Redgrave & Brook, 'To Be a Redgrave' (1982), 167; Sue Bruley, 'Jam Tomorrow? Socialist Women and Women's Liberation, 1968–82: An Oral History Approach', in Smith & Worley, 'Against the Grain' (2014), 155–172.
30. Hughes, 'Young Lives on the Left' (2015), 227, 251.
31. North, 'Gerry Healy' (1991), 115.
32. Interview with Paul Flewers, 10 November 2022.
33. Sandbrook, *Seasons in the Sun* (2012), 303.
34. Interview with Clare Cowen, 15 May 2023.
35. Hughes, 'Young Lives on the Left' (2015), 227.
36. Interview with Granville Williams, 4 January 2023.
37. University of Warwick Modern Records Centre, Papers of Chris and Ann Talbot, Box 1, 1072/1/2/1, Stephen Wey, *The Liberation of Women and the W.R.P.*, 12 December 1985.

38. Liz Leicester, Clare Cowen. 'Healy's Sexual Abuse: Towards a Theoretical Understanding', *Workers Press*, 6 December 1986.
39. Glasgow Caledonian University Archive Centre, Bill Hunter Papers [Uncatalogued], Liz Leicester, Sarah Hannigan, Clare Cowen, Trudi Jackson, 'Resolution on Women', in *Workers Revolutionary Party: 9th Congress Discussion Documents*, August 1987.
40. Hull History Centre, Papers of Tom Kemp, Box 18, Memo on Creche Facilities, 8th Congress, 22 February 1986. Interestingly, the original draft stated: 'Standing orders committee wish to ensure that women comrades with young children are able to participate fully in the congress'. The word 'women' was then crossed out, making the obvious point that childcare should be a concern for men too!
41. Hull History Centre, Papers of Tom Kemp, Box 18, 'On Sexist Language', Workers Revolutionary Party Conference, September 23–24 [No Year Given, ca. 1989], Resolution Drafted by Leicester WRP Branch.
42. 'Aids: Social or Individual Responsibility' and 'Is "Safe-Sex" Middle Class?', both in *Workers Press*, 22 November 1986.
43. Interview with Clare Cowen, 15 May 2023; interview with Liz Leicester, 6 June 2023.

CHAPTER 7

1. The chronology here is partly taken from *Draft Chronology of 1985 WRP Crisis*, splitsandfusions.wordpress.com. See also: Glasgow Caledonian University Archive Centre, GCATT, Uncatalogued Files, *Why the Workers Revolutionary Party Expelled G. Healy*, undated draft.
2. Interview with Clare Cowen, 15 May 2023.
3. University of Warwick Modern Records Centre, Papers of Chris and Ann Talbot, Box 1, 1072/1/3, *Workers Revolutionary Party Internal Bulletin: A Contribution to a Critique of G. Healy's 'Studies in Dialectical Materialism' by David North, National Secretary of the Workers League, For Members Only* (London: New Park Publications, 1985).
4. Cowen, 'My Search for Revolution' (2019), 208.
5. Mitchell, 'Come the Revolution' (2011), 440–441.
6. Cowen, 'My Search for Revolution' (2019), 7.
7. Cowen, 'My Search for Revolution' (2019), 210; Harding, 'Staying Red' (2005), 246; interview with Clare Cowen, 15 May 2023.
8. Interview with Robert Myers, 23 June 2022.
9. Cowen, 'My Search for Revolution' (2019), 200.
10. Interview with Clare Cowen, 15 May 2023.
11. Mitchell, 'Come the Revolution' (2011), 450.

12. The letter was reprinted in full, but with the 26 women's names redacted, in: *Young Socialist*, Vol. 11, No. 40 (2 November, 1985), a paper that by this time was allied with David North. It is also reproduced in Cowen, 'My Search for Revolution' (2019), 237–238, along with a statement about Jennings regretting the homophobic content of the later paragraph.

13. Mitchell, 'Come the Revolution' (2011), 452.

14. Interview with Clare Cowen, 15 March 2023.

15. Harding, 'Staying Red' (2005), 250.

16. *Draft Chronology of 1985 WRP Crisis*; Cowen, 'My Search for Revolution' (2019), 228. Charlie Brandt also left the WRP at this point; as part of a broader attempt to regain control of the party, Healy targeted him for expulsion and unsuccessfully attempted to have him forcibly returned to Germany. Because of the expulsion and the secret nature of his work his role in the conspiracy was not revealed until six months later and was therefore little known.

17. Cowen, 'My Search for Revolution' (2019), 108.

18. Interview with Dave Bruce, 7 July 2022.

19. Interview with Clare Cowen, 15 May 2023.

20. Interview with Gerry Downing, 12 March 2022; interview with Alex Steiner, 17 May 2022.

21. Mitchell, 'Come the Revolution' (2011), 455; Cowen, 'My Search for Revolution' (2019), 248.

22. Cowen, 'My Search for Revolution' (2019), 212.

23. Cowen, 'My Search for Revolution' (2019), 156, 294.

24. Nicola Gavey. *Just Sex? The Cultural Scaffolding of Rape* (New York: Routledge, 2013), 136.

25. Cowen, 'My Search for Revolution' (2019), 108.

26. Cowen, 'My Search for Revolution' (2019), 223.

27. Harding, 'Staying Red' (2005), 254–260. The documents from the Control Commission that Norman Harding led are sealed in Glasgow Caledonian University Archive Centre and not available to researchers; interview with Clare Cowen, 15 May 2023.

28. Cowen, 'My Search for Revolution' (2019), 217.

29. Cowen, 'My Search for Revolution' (2019), 280; interview with Clare Cowen, 15 May 2023.

30. Cowen, 'My Search for Revolution' (2019), 225.

31. Cowen, 'My Search for Revolution' (2019), 298.

32. Cowen, 'My Search for Revolution' (2019), 292.

33. Interview with Tariq Ali, 22 July 2022.

34. Wohlforth, 'Prophet's Children' (1994), 265–266; Tourish & Wohlforth, 'On the Edge' (2000), 163–165; correspondence with Alan Thornett.

35. Interview with Garth Frankland, 8 August 2022.
36. Interview with Linda Neville, 5 July 2023.
37. Cowen, 'My Search for Revolution' (2019), 312.
38. David Weir, 'Spying for the Colonel'. *Time Out*, No. 910, 27 January/3 February 1988.
39. Bob Pitt. *The Rise and Fall of Gerry Healy*, 123–124; correspondence with Dave Bruce, 27 July 2022. Garth Frankland says he has no memory of the accusation that Healy was sexually interested in Thornett's wife and is sceptical that it could be true; interview with Garth Frankland, 8 August 2022.
40. Interview with 'Judith', 21 February 2022; Clare Cowen also remembers two sisters who she now believes Healy was coercing into having sex with him. These are presumably the same sisters; interview with Clare Cowen, 15 May 2023.
41. Interview with Geoff Barr, 14 May 2023.
42. Interview with Paul Henderson, 30 October 2022.
43. Interview with Gerry Downing, 12 March 2022.
44. Interview with Clare Cowen, 15 May 2023.
45. Interview with Dave Bruce, 7 July 2022.
46. Ali, 'Redemption' (1990), 18–19.
47. Bob Pitt. *The Rise and Fall of Gerry Healy*, 123–124.
48. Bob Pitt. *The Rise and Fall of Gerry Healy*, 125.
49. This was a not uncommon event. Robert Myers was also expelled but still expected to take part in party work. Myers says expelled members were still kept active because the party was so desperate for money; interview with Robert Myers, 23 June 2022. As Gary Younge was told: 'Nobody leaves this party… They either get kicked out or they die'; Gary Younge, 'Memoirs of a Teenage Trot'. *The Guardian*, 18 February 2000.
50. Interview with Andy Blunden, 14 July 2022.
51. Interview with Robert Myers, 23 June 2022.
52. Interview with Alex Steiner, 17 May 2022.
53. Cowen, 'My Search for Revolution' (2019), 237.
54. Lotz & Feldman, 'Gerry Healy' (1994), 2.
55. Hull History Centre, Papers of Tom Kemp, Box 20, *Resolutions from Manchester Area Aggregate*, 31 October 1985. This was also reported in the mainstream press: 'Gerry's Rival "Threw a Girl Downstairs"', *Mirror*, 5 November 1985. 'The reason given [for the assault] was because she had criticised the expulsion of her boyfriend, WRP central committee member Stewart Carter… Mr Banda did not apologise' and justified the attack by alleging that it was ordered by Healy.

56. *Draft Chronology of 1985 WRP Crisis*; University of Warwick Modern Records Centre, Papers of Chris and Ann Talbot, Box 1, 1072/1/2/2, *Extracts from Political Committee Minutes*.
57. Bob Pitt. *The Rise and Fall of Gerry Healy*, 125.
58. Mitchell, 'Come the Revolution' (2011), 453, 497. Clare Cowen remembers Alex Mitchell as a serial, if secret, chaser of female co-workers; 'My Search for Revolution' (2019), 124. Cowen says one party member told her to never get in a car alone with Alex Mitchell, though he wasn't anywhere near as abusive as Healy. He was a standard 1960s misogynist and generally patronising to women. Interview with Clare Cowen, 15 May 2023. Liz Leicester confirms that Mitchell was a misogynist: interview with Liz Leicester, 6 June 2023.
59. Cowen, 'My Search for Revolution' (2019), 236–237, 305, 318. Pirani confirms Redgrave saying this: Simon Pirani. 'The Break-Up of the WRP: From the Horse's Mouth'. libcom.org, 3 February 2013.
60. Harding, 'Staying Red' (2005), 252.
61. *Draft Chronology of 1985 WRP Crisis*.
62. *Draft Chronology of 1985 WRP Crisis*; University of Warwick Modern Records Centre, Papers of Chris and Ann Talbot, Box 1, 1072/1/2/1, *Correspondence between P. Penn and G. Healy*, September 1985. From this series of letters, it is not only clear that Penn had dismissive view of Healy's teaching but that Healy was unable or unwilling to answer Penn's pointed questions.
63. Bob Pitt. *The Rise and Fall of Gerry Healy*, 129.
64. *Draft Chronology of 1985 WRP Crisis*.
65. Cowen, 'My Search for Revolution' (2019), 287. 'Judith' also remembers stories of a high-ranking member whose daughter had been targeted by Healy; interview with 'Judith', 21 February 2022.
66. Mitchell, 'Come the Revolution' (2011), 465.
67. University of Warwick Modern Records Centre, Papers of Chris and Ann Talbot, Box 1, 1072/1/2/2, *Extracts from Political Committee Minutes*.
68. *Draft Chronology of 1985 WRP Crisis*.
69. *Draft Chronology of 1985 WRP Crisis*.
70. Mitchell, 'Come the Revolution' (2011), 463–464.
71. Lotz & Feldman, 'Gerry Healy' (1994), 9–13.
72. Bob Pitt. *The Rise and Fall of Gerry Healy*, 130–132.
73. Lotz & Feldman, 'Gerry Healy' (1994), 9. The flat was quickly taken over by other party workers; interview with Chris McBride, 25 July 2023.
74. Lotz & Feldman, 'Gerry Healy' (1994), 13.
75. University of Warwick Modern Records Centre, Papers of Chris and Ann Talbot, Box 4, 1072/3/1, *Discussion Bulletin III: Documents on the*

Expulsion of Healy and the Split in the W.R.P. (Detroit, MI: Labor Publications, 1985).

76. Cowen, 'My Search for Revolution' (2019), 300, 302; University of Warwick Modern Records Centre, Papers of Chris and Ann Talbot, Box 1, 1072/1/2/2, *Extracts from Political Committee Minutes*.

77. North, 'Gerry Healy' (1991), 102.

78. 'G. Healy Letter Is No Forgery', *The News Line* [Anti-Healy], 6 November 1985; Geoff Pilling, 'Nothing to Hide... or Fear', *News Line* [Anti-Healy], 6 December 1985; 'Redgraves Claim Healy Letter Forged', *The Guardian*, 5 November 1985; 'Vanessa Redgrave Denies WRP "Lies"', *Times*, 5 November 1985.

79. 'Redgrave Issues Writ Against the WRP', *The News Line* [Anti-Healy], 29 October 1985.

80. 'Trotskyites Throw Out Founder Healy', *The Guardian*, 24 October 1985; 'Workers' Party Founder is Thrown Out', *Times*, 24 October 1985; 'Reds-in-Beds Storm Hits Vanessa Party', *Express*, 31 October 1985; 'Red in the Bed: Sex Scandal of Sacked Trot Chief and 26 Women', *Mirror*, 31 October 1985; 'Reds in the Beds: Sex Storm Rocks Vanessa's Party', *Star*, 31 October 1985 and 'Girls Lured to Red Gerry's Casting Couch', *Star*, 1 November 1985; 'Star Vanessa in Row over Reds in the Beds: "Sexy Trot, 73"', *The Sun*, 31 October 1985. (That the tabloid press was obviously inviting its readers to enjoy all this is evident in the *Sun*'s leader: 'An amazing sex scandal has split actress Vanessa Redgrave's Workers' Revolutionary Party.' That women's lives had been greatly damaged is completely ignored.) 'Saucy Gifts by Red Gerry', *Star*, 2 November 1985 ('Randy Red Gerry Healy used party funds to buy frilly knickers and sexy dresses for his love slaves'); 'Presenting the Great Reds in the Bed Farce', *Daily Express*, 2 November 1985 ('No Sex Please, We're Trotskyists is the Funniest Farce to Hit Britain since Brian Rix Hung Up His Trousers'); 'Secrets of Randy Comrade Casanova', *Mirror*, 3 November 1985 ('Randy "Red in the Bed" Gerry Healy seduced a long line of women by telling them "Love me – for the sake of the Party" it was claimed yesterday'); 'Randy Red Supremo Grabbed My Wife', *News of the World*, 3 November 1985; 'Comrades! Now for the Real Story', *Sunday Times*, 3 November 1985. All collected in Glasgow Caledonian University Archive Centre GCATT, Uncatalogued Press Cuttings.

81. *News Line*, 20 November 1985. Discussed also in: Robin Blick. '57th Act Variety'. *Solidarity: A Journal of Libertarian Socialism*, No. 11 (Spring 1986).

82. 'G. Healy Expelled', *News Line* (Anti-Healy), 26 October 1985.

83. 'G. Healy's Expulsion: The Facts', *News Line* (Anti-Healy), 30 October 1985.

84. 'G. Healy Expelled: Interim Statement by the Young Socialists National Committee', 29 October 1985, in *Young Socialist*, Vol. 11, No. 40 (2 November 1985).

85. *Communist Forum*, No. 4, November 1986.

86. 'Statement of the International Committee of the Fourth International on the Expulsion of G. Healy', 25 October 1985.

87. 'Special Congress Resolution of the Workers Revolutionary Party (Healyite)', 26 October 1985.

88. '"Split Exposes Right-Wing Conspiracy Against Party": Statement of the Central Committee of the Workers Revolutionary Party (Healyite)', 30 October 1985.

89. Mike Banda, 'Morality and the Revolutionary Party', *News Line*, 2 November 1985.

90. Duncan Hallas, 'Cult Comes a Cropper', *Socialist Review*, No. 82 (December 1985).

91. 'Complete the Break from Healyism' *Socialist Viewpoint*, No. 9 (December 1985).

92. Birchall, 'Tony Cliff' (2011), 489.

93. Interview with Tariq Ali, 22 June 2022.

94. Kelly, 'Contemporary Trotskyism' (2018), 61.

95. *Draft Chronology of 1985 WRP Crisis.*

96. 'Forward to the 11th World Congress'. *Marxist Review*, Vol. 2, No. 6 (June 1987).

97. *The Marxist*, Vol. 1, No. 1 (June/July 1987).

98. Editorial, *Fourth International*, Vol. 13, No. 2 (Autumn 1986).

99. *Draft Chronology of 1985 WRP Crisis*; *News Line*, 16 November 1985.

100. Lotz & Feldman, 'Gerry Healy' (1994), 61.

101. Lotz & Feldman, 'Gerry Healy' (1994), 192.

102. Lotz & Feldman, 'Gerry Healy' (1994), 5–7.

103. Cowen, 'My Search for Revolution' (2019), 326.

104. Interview with Dave Bruce, 27 July 2022.

105. University of Warwick Modern Records Centre, Papers of Chris and Ann Talbot, Box 1, 1072/1/3, Internal Bulletin No.3, Simon Pirani, On Trosky's Death Mask, 26 December 1985.

106. *Draft Chronology of 1985 WRP Crisis*; Harding, 'Staying Red' (2005), 274.

107. *Communist Forum – The Morality of the WRP: An Open Letter to Cliff Slaughter from Dave Good* (No Place of Publication, ca. 1986).

108. Lotz & Feldman, 'Gerry Healy' (1994), 21; University of Warwick Modern Records Centre, Papers of Chris and Ann Talbot, Box 2, 1072/1/7/3, WRP Central Committee: Letter to all our supporters and readers, 16 December 1985.

109. Lotz & Feldman, 'Gerry Healy' (1994), 22.

110. Cowen, 'My Search for Revolution' (2019), 325.
111. 'Astmoor Litho – The Facts', *News Line*, 21 December 1985.
112. Mitchell, 'Come the Revolution' (2011), 376.
113. Cowen, 'My Search for Revolution' (2019), 160, 164, 199.
114. Cowen, 'My Search for Revolution' (2019), 152, 181. Cowen says she never got most of her assets back. Even though she owned half the Clapham premises, the party had also taken out loans with a Frankfurt bank using these properties as sureties and those loans had to be repaid; interview with Cowen, 15 May 2023.
115. Cowen, 'My Search for Revolution' (2019), 252.
116. Mitchell, 'Come the Revolution' (2011), 457–458.
117. Interview with Dave Bruce, 7 July 2022.
118. *Communist Forum – The Morality of the WRP: An Open Letter to Cliff Slaughter from Dave Good* (No Place of Publication, ca. 1986).
119. Lotz & Feldman, 'Gerry Healy' (1994), 121–122.
120. Lotz & Feldman, 'Gerry Healy' (1994), 123–125.
121. Cowen, 'My Search for Revolution' (2019), 250; the report is reprinted in 'The Financial Report', *Marxist Review*, Vol. 1, No. 4 (July 1986). For a contradictory account, see: 'How the WRP sold its Principles', *Workers News*, No. 8 (April 1988).
122. Cowen, 'My Search for Revolution' (2019), 285.
123. Lotz & Feldman, 'Gerry Healy' (1994), 4.

CHAPTER 8

1.   'Complete Support from the Movement He Led: Ken Livingstone, Labour MP for Brent East'. *Marxist Monthly*, Vol. 3, No. 2 (April 1990), 72. In his autobiography in 2011, Livingstone rightly called Healy 'autocratic', and while he did not repeat his accusations about MI5 here, he does say that Ted Knight, his long-time political ally who started his political career in Trotskyism, was under surveillance by MI5. 'You Can't Say That' (2011), 96, 97. Alex Mitchell also suggested that the split – he calls it a 'coup' – was the result of British intelligence machinations: 'Come the Revolution' (2011), 482.
2.   'The Workers' Revolutionary Party, MI5 and Libya'. *Lobster*, No. 20, November 1990.
3.   David Leigh. *The Wilson Plot: The Intelligence Services and the Discrediting of a Prime Minister* (London: Heinemann, 1988); Seumas Milne. *The Enemy Within: The Secret War against the Miners* (London: Verso, 1994); 'British Army "Could Stage Mutiny Under Corbyn", Says Senior Serving General', *The Independent*, 20 September 2015.

4. Daniel S. Chard. *Nixon's War at Home: The FBI, Leftist Guerrillas, and the Origins of Counterterrorism* (Chapel Hill, NC: University of North Carolina Press, 2021), 64.
5. 'The Workers' Revolutionary Party, MI5 and Libya'. *Lobster*, No. 20, November 1990.
6. Interview with Tariq Ali, 22 June 2022.
7. Interview with 'Judith', 21 February 2022
8. David Caute. *Red List: MI5 and British Intellectuals in the Twentieth Century* (London: Verso, 2022), 193, 250.
9. Leigh, 'The Wilson Plot' (1988), 209.
10. 'Developments in Undercover Policing Inquiry (UCPI) Expose Secret State Operation to Undermine Workers' Revolutionary Party (WRP)', Press Release, Hodge, Jones and Allen Law Firm, 22 February 2023; Scale of Police Spying was "Orwellian", Inquiry Hears'. *The Guardian*, 12 May 2022; See also, Special Branch letter to Box 500 highlighting withdrawal of its source from Workers Revolutionary Party and enclosing Special Branch report concerning Workers Revolutionary Party Education Centre in Derbyshire signed by CI Craft, 11 May 1976 (Ref: UCPI0000012240), www.ucpi.org.uk.
11. Liz Leicester, UCPI Evidence Hearings, Tranche 1 (Phase 3), Day 5 (13 May 2022), AM (accessible at: www.youtube.com/watch?v=LuxlfotVxro).
12. Interview with Granville Williams, 4 January 2023; interview with Scotty Clark, 27 November 2022; Geoff Barr, a member of the WRP in Exeter, said in 1986 that a member of CID, the Criminal Investigation Department of the Police, had been filming him while he sold copies of *Workers Press* on the High Street in Exeter. Geoff Barr, 'Snoop Scoop', *Workers Press*, 25 October 1986.
13. Redgrave and Brook, 'To Be a Redgrave' (1982), 169–170.
14. Wohlforth, 'Prophet's Children' (1994), 27, 138, 198.
15. Peter Wright, Paul Greengrass. *Spycatcher: The Candid Autobiography of a Senior Intelligence Officer* (New York: Viking Press, 1987), 360–361. The 'SWP' referred to here is presumably the British SWP, though that group did not come into existence until 1977, five years after this alleged event.
16. Caute, 'Red List' (2022), 8.
17. Ken Livingstone. 'Foreword' in Lotz & Feldman, 'Gerry Healy' (1994), v.
18. Lotz & Feldman, 'Gerry Healy' (1994), 300.
19. 'The Observer and the Special Branch' and 'Anatomy of a State Conspiracy', *News Line*, 11 November 1978. For a copy of the Special Branch report, see: University of Warwick Modern Records Centre, Papers of Chris and Ann Talbot, Box 1, 1072/1/2/2, Confidential

Report from Metropolitan Police Special Branch, 25 September 1975. The WRP presumably acquired a copy of this confidential report through the discovery process in the libel trial.

20. Stephen Dorril. *The Silent Conspiracy: Inside the Intelligence Services in the 1990s* (London: Heinemann, 1993), 8.

21. Behan, 'With Breast Expanded' (1964), 170–171.

22. John Bloxam Private Files, Letter from Mike Banda, General Secretary, to Party Branches, 24 July 1978, far more believably.

23. Lotz & Feldman, 'Gerry Healy' (1994), 35.

24. 'Healy: The Lies Continue', *Workers News*, No. 7 (February 1988).

25. Tom Burns, 'The Revolution Betrayed', *Solidarity: A Journal of Libertarian Socialism*, No. 16 (spring 1988).

26. David Weir, 'Spying for the Colonel'. *Time Out*, No. 910, 27 January/3 February 1988; Lotz & Feldman, 'Gerry Healy' (1994), 110–111, 285–286.

27. BFI. *The Money Programme* (BBC Television, 20 March 1983).

28. '"Time Out" Engages in Crude Slander of WRP', *News Line*, 24 August 1979.

29. 'Gaddafi Cash Aids Left-Wing Groups', *Sunday Telegraph*, 13 September 1981; 'Some More News from Libya', *News Line*, 21 September 1981.

30. 'A Conspiracy Exposed', *News Line*, 2 February 1979; 'The Iraq Revolution and Stalinism', *News Line*, 8 March 1979. See also: 'Solidarity with Iraqi Revolution', *News Line*, 1 July 1979; 'Letter and Reply: The Iraq Revolution and Stalinism', *News Line*, 8 March 1979. 'Political Report by David North to the International Committee of the Fourth International', 11 February 1984.

31. Robin Blick, '57th Act Variety', *Solidarity: A Journal of Libertarian Socialism*, No. 11 (spring 1986).

32. 'Anti-Iraq Petition Blocked', *News Line*, 14 July 1979; 'Reject Stalinist Lies on Iraq', *News Line*, 15 July 1979; 'Iraqi Students Banned', *News Line*, 21 May 1979.

33. 'Iraqi Union Sends Greeting', *News Line*, 7 July 1979.

34. 'How the Workers Revolutionary Party Betrayed Trotskyism, 1975–1985: Statement of the International Committee of the Fourth International, *Fourth International*, Vol. 13, No. 1 (summer 1986), 56–57.

35. Cowen, 'My Search for Revolution' (2019), 309–311.

36. Ilario Salucci. *A People's History of Iraq: The Iraqi Communist Party, Workers' Movements and the Left, 1924–2004* (Chicago, IL: Haymarket Books, 2005), 63–64; Tareq Y. Ismael. *The Rise and Fall of the Communist Party of Iraq* (Cambridge: Cambridge University Press, 2008), 185–188. Samir al-Khalil. *Republic of Fear: The Politics of Modern Iraq*

(Berkeley, CA: University of California Press, 1989). Saïd Aburish. *Saddam Hussein: The Politics of Revenge* (London: Bloomsbury, 2000), 124. Christine Moss Helms. *Iraq: Eastern Flank of the Arab World* (Washington, DC: Brookings Institution, 1984), 79. The violence against Iraqi Communists and Ba'athists who had run afoul of Saddam was very real – suppressing what had been perhaps *the largest* commu-nist party in the Middle East – even if it is never clear how complicit the WRP was in any of this. There is no mention of 'Talib Suwailh' in Hanna Batatu's *The Old Social Classes and the Revolutionary Move-ments of Iraq: A Study of Iraq's Old Landed and Commercial Classes and of Its Communists, Ba`thists and Free Officers*, a massive work, close to 1,300 pages, that provides an exhaustive survey of Iraqi com-munism and Ba'athism.

37. Personal correspondence with Joseph Sassoon (25 July 2021), Tareq Ismael (26 July 2021).

38. Despite the fact that the WRP only came into being in 1973, they claimed in 1980 that they had 'fought alongside the Arab Ba'ath Social-ist Party in countless anti-imperialist and anti-Zionist campaigns since the 1950s'. University of Warwick Modern Records Centre, Papers of Chris and Ann Talbot, Box 1, 1072/1/1/4, 'Stop Iran-Iraq War: Unite Against Imperialist Enemy', Statement by the Central Committee of the Workers Revolutionary Party, 27 September 1980.

39. Bob Pitt. *The Rise and Fall of Gerry Healy*, 118.

40. Wohlforth, 'Prophet's Children' (1994), 298; interview with Andy Blunden, 14 July 2022; BFI. *The Money Programme* (BBC Television, 20 March 1983); Clare Cowen says the printing facilities at Runcorn had contracts to print Gaddafi's Green Book as well as *Janamot*, which she remembers as a 'Tamil magazine' but may in fact be the Bengali newspaper of the same name. Cowen, 'My Search for Revolution' (2019), 179.

41. North, 'Gerry Healy' (1991), 72–73.

42. Ronald Bruce St John. *Qaddafi's World Design: Libyan Foreign Policy, 1969–1987* (Atlantic Highlands, NJ: Saqi Books, 1987), 38, 46.

43. Guy Arnold. *The Maverick State: Gaddafi and the New World Order* (London: Cassel, 1996), 69.

44. 'Extent of Libyan Backing for IRA "Shocked" British'. *RTÉ*, 28 December 2021.

45. John Oakes. *Libya: The History of Gaddafi's Pariah State* (Stroud, Gloucestershire: The History Press, 2011); Yehudit Ronen. *Qaddafi's Libya in World Politics* (Boulder, CO: Lynne Rienner, 2008); Jonathan Bearman's book is a more even-keeled analysis: *Qadhafi's Libya* (London: Zed Books, 1986).

46. Bob Pitt. *The Rise and Fall of Gerry Healy*, 118. See also: Ian Birchall, '"Vicarious Pleasure"? The British Far Left and the Third World, 1956–79' in Smith & Worley, 'Against the Grain' (2014), 190–208.

47. Sean Matgamna. 'Gaddafi's Foreign Legion to Knight's Rescue', *Socialist Organiser*, No. 33, 24 January 1981; 'When Vanessa Redgrave Sued Us', *Workers Liberty*, 5 March 2006; Sean Matgamna, 'Fighting Left Antisemitism in the 1980s', *Workers Liberty*, 23 June 2018. Matgamna's 1981 article was also reprinted as a leaflet for the WRP's 5th Congress, 31 January–2 February 1981; see the copy in University of Warwick Modern Records Centre, Papers of Chris and Ann Talbot, Box 1, 1072/1/1/4.

48. 'The Zionist Connection', *News Line*, Editorial, 9 April 1983; Hosken, 'Ken' (2008), 137, 138.

49. John Bloxam Private Files, 'Open Letter to Newsline, V. Redgrave, G. Healy from Sean Matgamna', n.d. [April/May 1983].

50. *Socialist Viewpoint*, No. 9 (December 1985).

51. Clare Cowen also makes this claim about photographs being taken of anti-Saddam protestors. 'My Search for Revolution' (2019), 309–311.

52. Interview with Andy Blunden, 14 July 2022; University of Warwick Modern Records Centre, Papers of Chris and Ann Talbot, Box 1, 1072/1/2/1, *Some question [sic] for Tony Banda and Dave Hyland, Manchester*, 17 December 1985. Clare Cowen remembers this as follows: the photographer, Ray Rising, had admitted he was the one who took photos at the embassy, and Cliff Slaughter wanted to call on him at an aggregate meeting, but in the meantime he had realigned to a pro-Healy faction and refused to admit it publicly. Another photographer, Maureen Bambrick, spoke up and confirmed the accusation. Cowen agrees Alex Mitchell was complicit in this; interview with Clare Cowen, 15 May 2023.

53. Hosken, 'Ken' (2008), 133.

54. For a copy of the report, see: Hull History Centre, Papers of Tom Kemp, Box 8, *Interim Report: International Committee Commission*, 16 December 1985.

55. Cowen, 'My Search for Revolution' (2019), 324.

56. David Weir, 'Spying for the Colonel'. *Time Out*, No. 910, 27 January/3 February 1988.

57. Bob Pitt. *The Rise and Fall of Gerry Healy*, 117.

58. Harding, 'Staying Red' (2005), 208.

59. North, 'Heritage' (2018), 435.

60. Lotz & Feldman, 'Gerry Healy' (1994), 237.

61. See: 'An Internationalist Fighter: Faisal Oueida, Representative in Britain of the Palestine Liberation Organization'. *Marxist Monthly*, Vol. 3, No. 2 (April 1990), 74.

62. *Marxist Monthly*, Vol. 2, No. 12 (February 1990), 520. The message is described as coming from 'Amm Jihad', which is probably mis-transliteration of Umm Jihad, Intissar al-Wazir.

63. 'A Commitment to the Palestinians'. *Marxist Monthly*, Vol. 3, No. 2 (April 1990), 65.

64. Ken Livingstone, 'Foreword' in Lotz & Feldman, 'Gerry Healy' (1994), v.

65. Clare Cowen provides confirmation of the stories of Jennings and Healy travelling to the Middle East and meeting Gaddafi, Arafat and 'Arab leaders in Syria, Lebanon, Iraq'. 'My Search for Revolution' (2019), 216.

66. Mitchell at the time regularly regaled the staff at *News Line* with stories of his visits around the Middle East; Cowen, 'My Search for Revolution' (2019), 121.

67. Mitchell, 'Come the Revolution' (2011), 325–327, 328, 387. Mitchell recognised 'Arafat's precarious financial status', ibid., 387, so it is difficult to square this with the claim that he was handing over large sums of money to Ted Knight.

68. Mitchell, 'Come the Revolution' (2011), 350–352.

69. Mitchell, 'Come the Revolution' (2011), 401.

70. Harding, 'Staying Red' (2005), 220–221.

71. Mitchell, 'Come the Revolution' (2011), 395.

72. Mitchell, 'Come the Revolution' (2011), 403.

CHAPTER 9

1. Lotz & Feldman, 'Gerry Healy' (1994), 16.

2. Mitchell, 'Come the Revolution' (2011), 488.

3. Lotz & Feldman, 'Gerry Healy' (1994), 17.

4. See: 'Emergency Resolutions Carried by North West Area Committee' and 'No More Burglaries: Resolution of the WRP 8th Congress', 16 March 1986, both in *Communist Forum*, No. 1, June 1986.

5. Bob Pitt. *The Rise and Fall of Gerry Healy*, 139–140; 'The Jailing of Phil Penn', *Workers Press*, No. 63 (21 February 1987).

6. Lotz & Feldman, 'Gerry Healy' (1994), 311.

7. Trotskyism Undefeated', *The Marxist*, Vol. 1, No. 2 (August/September 1987).

8. Tourish & Wohlforth, 'On the Edge' (2000), 170.

9. Tariq Ali. *Redemption* (London: Chatto & Windus, 1990), 84.

10. 'The Marxist Party Constitution (As amended by the Eight Congress, July 18th and 19th 1987), *The Marxist*, Vol. 1, No. 2 (August/September 1987).

11. Lotz & Feldman, 'Gerry Healy' (1994), 168, 180–181, 186–187.

12. *Irish Press*, 22 December 1989. My thanks to Gerard Madden for sharing this source with me.
13. *The Split in the Marxist Party: Statement by the Communist League* (Communist League Pamphlet, April 1991).
14. Corinna Lotz, Paul Feldman. 'The Truth About a Tragic Coup, London, November 27, 1990'.
15. Corinna Lotz. 'The Events of Sunday, November 11, 1990'.
16. Corinna Lotz, Paul Feldman. 'How the ICFI Tried to Cheat History: A Further Assessment, December 12, 1990'.
17. Early issues, when the organisation operated under the name 'The Communist League', featured a more overtly Trotskyist tone.
18. Markham, 'Our Time of Day' (2014), 58.
19. Kelly, 'Contemporary Trotskyism' (2018), 37. Kelly himself notes that 'we are driven, out of necessity, to follow the political science practice of using the self-reported membership figures of political parties, despite their known limitations and likely biases'. His membership numbers are probably all inflated. Ibid., 38.
20. Hull History Centre, Papers of Tom Kemp, Box 8, 'Notes on the Discussion with Comrade Moreno', Memo by Bill Hunter, 10 November 1986; interview with Philip Edwards, 16 November 2022.
21. Interview with David Parks, 23 November 2022.
22. Interview with Robert Myers, 23 June 2022. Workers Aid for Bosnia was, of course, condemned by David North's International Committee for the Fourth International: 'Behind the smokescreen of humanitarian pretenses and rhetorical appeals to proletarian internationalism, Slaughter has utilized Workers Aid to promote bourgeois nationalism and engage in outright provocations in the Balkans in direct collaboration with the Bosnian and Croatian governments and the imperialist powers'. *Marxism, Opportunism and the Balkan Crisis: Statement of the International Committee of the Fourth International* (Oak Park, MI: Labor Publication, 1994), 3.
23. Bob Pitt. *The Rise and Fall of Gerry Healy*, 135, 142.
24. Cliff Slaughter. *Not Without a Storm: Towards a Communist Manifesto for the Age of Globalisation* (London: Index Books, 2006). The material that Terry Brotherstone provides on how Slaughter (and his version of the WRP) become more intellectually open after 1985 is valuable. Slaughter drew on the work of István Mészáros, who he also knew personally; Terry Brotherstone, 'Cliff Slaughter, 1928–2021: A Life for Revolution and its Challenging Legacy'. *Critique*, Vol. 50, No. 1 (2022), 251–266.
25. Interview with Paul Thompson, 22 November 2022.
26. 'Resolution of the Western Area Committee of 15th May 1986' in *Communist Forum*, No. 1, June 1986.

27. Peter Jones, 'Statement of Resignation', 15 May 1986, in *Communist Forum*, No. 1, June 1986.
28. Draper, 'Roots of American Communism' (1957), 303.
29. Correspondence with Alan Thornett, 11 January 2022.
30. Interview with Gerry Downing, 12 March 2022.
31. Interview with 'Judith', 21 February 2022.
32. Interview with Gary Younge, 27 January 2022; Gary Younge, 'Memoirs of a Teenage Trot', *The Guardian*, 18 February 2000.
33. Interview with Gerry Downing, 12 March 2022.
34. Interview with Andy Blunden, 14 July 2022.
35. Interview with Andy Blunden, 14 July 2022.
36. 'Recollections', in Doria Pilling, ed. *Marxist Political Economy: Essays in Retrieval: Selected Works of Geoff Pilling* (London: Routledge, 2012), 12; interview with Dave Bruce, 7 July 2022.
37. Cowen, 'My Search for Revolution' (2019), 328–329.
38. Harding, 'Staying Red' (2005), 274, 282.
39. Interview with Andy Blunden, 14 July 2022; see, for example, Andy Blunden. *Hegel for Social Movements* (Chicago, IL: Haymarket, 2020).
40. Kelly, 'Contemporary Trotskyism' (2018), 46, 59; Kelly, 'Twilight of World Trotskyism' (2023), 24.
41. Cowen, 'My Search for Revolution' (2019), 334; interview with 'Elizabeth', 14 March 2022.
42. Interview with Dave Bruce, 7 July 2022.
43. Simon Pirani, 'Leninist Assumptions and Cult Hierarchies', *Weekly Worker*, No. 883, 28 September 2011.
44. Wohlforth, 'Prophet's Children' (1994), 165.
45. Callinicos, 'Trotskyism' (1990), 44. Paul Buhle has similarly observed that 'To my way of thinking, Marxism is as Marxism does, and the Latin American revolutionary who takes inspiration from Liberation Theology and economics from Marx and Lenin has as much claim to the mantle as Trotsky, Mao Zedong or Marx himself. Any other definition is the claim of an ideological holding-company': 'Marxism in the United States' (2013), 16.
46. See, for example, Jack Gale. *The Anti-Nazi League and Fascism* (London: News Line, 1978).
47. Tess Carter. 'Open Letter to Some Ex-Leaders of the ISO', *Socialist-Worker.org*, 11 April 2019; Fred Pelka. 'The Strange Case of Mark Curtis, Victim or Victimizer?', *On The Issues Magazine*, Spring 1991; Laurie Penny. 'What Does the SWP's Way of Dealing with Sexual Assault Allegations Tell Us About the Left?', *New Statesman*, 11 January 2013.
48. Kelly, 'Contemporary Trotskyism' (2018), 100.

49. Simon Pirani. 'The Break-Up of the WRP: From the Horse's Mouth'. libcom.org, 3 February 2013.
50. Interview with Philip Edwards, 16 November 2022.
51. Brian Behan, 'Our Revolutionary Democracy', *Worker's Voice*, Vol. 1, No. 1 (7 July 1960).
52. Elbaum, 'Revolution in the Air' (2002), 4.
53. Though it is also the case that Wohlforth had been an authoritarian leader of the Workers League and influenced by Healy in that regard, which he downplays in his memoirs. Interview with Alex Steiner, 17 May 2022.
54. Sheila Rowbotham. *Promise of a Dream: Remembering the Sixties* (London: Verso, 2019 [2000]), 90.
55. Sheila Rowbotham. *Daring to Hope: My Life in the 1970s* (London: Verso, 2021), 245.

CHAPTER 10

1. 'Lawsuit Alleges Harvard Ignored Sexual Harassment Complaints Against Prof. John Comaroff for Years', *Harvard Crimson*, 9 February 2022; 'Harvard asks Judge to Dismiss Comaroff Sexual Harassment Lawsuit', *Harvard Crimson*, 2 June 2022; 'Lawsuit Describes Alleged Pattern of Abuse by Former UChicago Professor John Comaroff', *Chicago Maroon*, 16 February 2022; 'Harvard Prof. John Comaroff Faces New Allegations of Misconduct in Amended Suit', *Harvard Crimson*, 29 June 2022.
2. 'The Concerted, Cowardly #MeToo Attack on Harvard Professor John Comaroff', *World Socialist Website*, 9 February 2022.
3. See the following WSWS articles: 'A Blow to the #MeToo Sexual Witch-Hunt: The Ignominious Collapse of the Case against Actor Kevin Spacey' (19 July 2019); 'The New York Times Attempts to Discredit Defense as Harvey Weinstein Trial Begins' (23 January 2020); 'Hollywood Producer Harvey Weinstein Sentenced to 23 Years in Prison: "Obscene" Culmination to a Travesty of a Trial' (12 March 2020); 'With Publication of Woody Allen's *Apropos of Nothing* Memoir, Venomous #MeToo Attacks Continue' (3 April 2020); 'HBO's Docuseries *Allen v. Farrow*: A Shameful, Vindictive, McCarthyite Attack on Filmmaker Woody Allen' (3 March 2021); '*Fourth of July* and the Vindictive Campaign against Comic Louis C.K.' (30 August 2022); 'The Los Angeles Trial of Former Hollywood Producer Harvey Weinstein and the Effort to Revive the #MeToo Witch Hunt' (9 November 2022).
4. Shuvu Batta, 'A Look Back to My split with the Socialist Equality Party/WSWS', https://theunionist.substack.com/p/a-look-back-to-my-split-with-the.

5. Interview with Shuvu Batta, 5 August 2022.

6. Interview with Shuvu Batta, 5 August 2022; correspondence with Peter Ross, 23 August 2022.

7. 'Socialism or Barbarism: Reflections on Global Disorder with David North', *The St. Andrews Economist*, November 2017.

8. Interview with Shuvu Batta, 5 August 2022.

9. The information on North/Green's early life is taken from: 'Open Semester Program', *Trinity Reporter*, Vol. 1, No. 6, January 1971; *Trinity Tripod*, 28 January 1969; '"I Personally Am Very, Very Dissatisfied With American Society": College Students Decry "Passivity" of the Past, Defend Today's Activism', *Trinity Alumni Magazine*, Summer 1968. www.waghalter.com; www.abc.net.au/radionational/programs/musicshow/david-waghalter-green/6877784; 'I. Waghalter, 68, Long a Conductor', *New York Times*, 8 April 1949; Waghalter, Toni [Obituary], *New York Times*, 1 December 1964; www.tagesspiegel.de/berlin/beatrice-waghalter-green-geb-1913-857929.html; information on Trinity itself is taken from Peter J. Knapp; Anne H. Knapp. *Trinity College in the Twentieth Century: A History* (Hartford, CT: Trinity College, 2000).

10. G. Healy, 'Political Lessons of the Split', *News Line*, 8 February 1986.

11. 'Students Vote Strikes, Wage Hikes, War's End', *Trinity Tripod*, 30 April 1971.

12. Interview with 'Shannon', 30 March 2023.

13. See, for example, 'Manifesto: The Case for a Labor Party', *Bulletin*, 26 June 1972, which does make a good case for a non-capitalist party, but never really offers concrete plans to build one other than saying a Congress of Labor should be called to start the process.

14. 'A Call to Action: Build a Labor Party', *Bulletin*, 4 February 1975.

15. Interview with Steve Zeltzer, 14 November 2022.

16. Interview with Irving Hall, 3 December 2022.

17. 'Interview With Abu Iyyad, Deputy Commander of Al Fatah', *Bulletin*, 20 July 1976; 'Gaddafi Pledges Struggle for Arab Unity', *Bulletin*, 16 September 1977; '10th Anniversary of Iraq's July Revolution: Fight Goes on Against Imperialism and Zionism', 25 July 1978. In October 1979, *Bulletin* published an adulatory account of a Libyan seminar dedicated to Gaddafi's *Green Book*: 'The Green Book: Born out of the Struggle Against Imperialism', 16 October 1979.

18. 'Millions Greet Khomeini', *Bulletin*, 2 February 1979 and 'Long Live the Iranian Revolution', *Bulletin*, 16 February 1979; 'Middle-Class Hatred of the Iranian Revolution', *Bulletin*, 13 April 1979.

19. '"The Trade Union Movement Must Take a Stand": PATCO Leader Says on Eve of Imprisonment', *Bulletin*, 22 April 1983.

20. Interview with Irving Hall, 3 December 2022; interview with Steve Zeltzer, 14 November 2022.
21. Interview with 'Shannon', 23 March 2023.
22. Tim Wohlforth. 'The New Nationalism and the Negro Question'. *Bulletin*, 24 February 1969. Wohlforth continued this article in the 10 March 1969 issue, accusing the American SWP of being apologists for Black antisemitism, and then in the 24 March issue, in which he goes back to Trotsky's writings on nationalism to hammer home his point. These three articles were then published as a pamphlet, *The New Nationalism and the Negro Question*, as advertised in the 21 April 1969 issue. See also Lucy St John, 'Black Caucuses are Reactionary', *Bulletin*, 21 April 1969.
23. Alex Steiner, 'The Gutter Politics of David North', 1 June 2018, permanent-revolution.org; interview with Irving Hall, 3 December 2022.
24. See, for example, their overly harsh critique of Chicago mayor, Harold Washington: 'Capitalist Politicians Peddle Race Poison', *Bulletin*, 31 March 1987.
25. Articles by both Wohlforth and Nancy Fields as well as advertisements for their published works continued to appear up to early September 1974; and then one day they simply stopped appearing. Wohlforth was expelled in August 1974. His former party did not publicly mention in their paper until February of the next year: 'An Answer to the Slanders of Robertson and Wohlforth', *Bulletin*, 21 February 1975.
26. 'Labor and the 1976 Elections', *Bulletin*, 2 April 1976. North is here described as National Secretary. This switch in leaders was handled subtly, less of a palace coup and more of a quiet changing of the guard. Interview with 'Shannon', 30 March 2023.
27. See the advertisement for his talks in Detroit, Dayton, OH and St Louis, *Bulletin*, 23 April 1973; 'Marxism: A World Scientific Outlook', *Bulletin*, 23 September 1977.
28. 'Launch $100,000 Expansion Fund', *Bulletin*, 29 May 1979. The following year, the party started a $150,000 fund: '$150,000 fund for Revolutionary Daily Paper', *Bulletin*, 22 July 1980. Issues started to be emblazoned in 1977 with a logo saying 'Forward to the Daily Revolutionary Newspaper'. On 25 August 1981, the paper featured a notice on the back cover, where updated figures for the $150,000 were posted, saying the fund was complete. By 29 September 1981, the party had started a new $50,000 fund, and the daily paper fund was not mentioned again.
29. Confidential FBI Dossier on the Workers League, Started August 1967, revised August 1974 [No Call Number], Accessed via Freedom of Information Act request [FOIPA Request No.: 1573442-000, July 2023]; *Memo from Director, FBI, to SAC [Special Agent in Charge]*,

Albany, Subject: Workers League, 2 August 1971, National Archives, FBI Central Records Center 100A-BT-9079 [Accessed under FOIA Request No. RD 77341, December 2023].

30. Interview with Irving Hall, 3 December 2022.

31. 'Ed Heisler: The FBI agent, the Socialist Workers Party and the Assassination of Tom Henehan', *News Line,* 18 July 1981; University of Warwick Modern Records Centre, Papers of Chris and Ann Talbot, Box 4, 1072/2/4, International Committee of the Fourth International, *The Murder of Tom Henehan: Martyr of the Fourth International* (New York: Labor Publications, 1978).

32. Interview with Alex Steiner, 4 July 2023.

33. 'Launch $100,000 Tom Henehan Memorial Fund: Build the Daily Revolutionary Paper', *Bulletin,* 28 October 1977.

34. 'Second Gunman Indicted', *Bulletin,* 28 November 1980. 'Two Gunmen Convicted of Tom Henehan's Murder', *Bulletin,* 24 July 1981. Torres was found guilty of second-degree murder and Sequinot was found guilty of first-degree manslaughter. Nonetheless, on 21 August 1981, *Bulletin* printed a piece entitled 'The Assassination of Tom Henehan: The Investigation Must Continue'.

35. Interview with Alex Steiner, 4 July 2023.

36. Archives of Michigan, Record Group 2003-46, Department of Commerce, Bureau of Commercial Services, Corporations Division, Annual Reports, Roll 2176, Frame 2185, Microfilm #9975, *Vernor Distributors, Inc., 1980 Michigan Annual Report.* Sheila Leburg is listed as president, Ann Porster as secretary, David N. Green as treasurer, and Fred Mazelis as Vice President. The company was incorporated on 6 March 1980 with 200 shares, valued at $5 per share, giving a modest valuation of $1,000. Leburg was a prominent WL member and ran for congressional election for them in 1976. Ann Porster only took behind-the-scenes roles; in a Statement of Ownership included in a 7 October 1977 issue of *Bulletin* she was described as the paper's business manager.

37. Glasgow Caledonian University Archive Centre, Simon Pirani Papers [Uncatalogued], *Workers Revolutionary Party Internal Bulletin*: Report by Cde David North, National Secretary of the Workers League, to WRP Special Congress, October 26th 1985.

38. Hull History Centre, Papers of Tom Kemp, Box 8, Resolution from Glasgow North East Branch of the WRP, 30 November 1985; University of Warwick Modern Records Centre, Papers of Chris and Ann Talbot, Box 1; 1072/1/2/1, Open Letter from Mike Banda, General Secretary, to all Members of the WRP, 8 November 1985.

39. Glasgow Caledonian University Archive Centre, Simon Pirani Papers [Uncatalogued], *Workers Revolutionary Party Internal Bulletin*: Report

by Cde David North, National Secretary of the Workers League, to WRP Special Congress, October 26th 1985.

40. Glasgow Caledonian University Archive Centre, GCATT, Uncatalogued Files, *Whither Banda*, Statement by W. Hunter, G. Pilling, C. Smith, n.d. [1986]. See also: Glasgow Caledonian University Archive Centre, Bill Hunter Papers [Uncatalogued], *Open Letter to Comrade North*, n.d. [ca. early 1986].

41. David North, 'In Defense of "Security and the Fourth International"', *Bulletin*, 25 February 1986; University of Warwick Modern Records Centre, Papers of Chris and Ann Talbot, Box 3, 1072/2/1-2, 'An Open Letter to Cliff Slaughter from Alan Gelfand', 22 February 1987, in *Fourth International*, Vol. 14, No. 2 (June 1987). See also, in this same issue, David North, 'A Comment on the Gelfand Letter' (March 1987) and 'Second Letter to Cliff Slaughter from Alan Gelfand' (2 May 1987). For a latter-day revising of this accusation, see: Eric London. *Agents: The FBI and GPU Infiltration of the Trotskyist Movement* (Oak Park, MI: Mehring Books, 2019).

42. *The Historical and International Foundations of the Socialist Equality Party* (Oak Park, MI: Mehring Books, 2008), 150.

43. Kelly, 'Contemporary Trotskyism' (2018), 61.

44. Kelly, 'Twilight of World Trotskyism' (2023), 62.

45. Kelly, 'Contemporary Trotskyism' (2018), 61–62.

46. Kelly, 'Twilight of World Trotskyism' (2023), 96.

47. Interview with Scott Solomon, 3 August 2022.

48. 'Northites Inc.: Toeing the Bottom Line', www.bolshevik.org/1917/no30/no30-GRPI-WSWS.html.

49. Interview with Scott Solomon, 3 August 2022.

50. Interview with Steve Fox, 19 August 2022; interview with Jacob Morrison and Adam Keller, 1 December 2022.

51. Interview with Alex Steiner, 4 July 2023.

52. Information on the ownership, founding and share value of the companies is taken from publicly filed reports and documents (https://cofs.lara.state.mi.us/SearchApi/Search/Search). Other material is taken from: 'People', *Crain's Detroit*, 2 February 1998; 'Grand River Printing, Inc.', *Crain's Detroit*, 6 September 1999; 'Business Diary', *Crain's Detroit*, 24 August 1998; 'Printing Plant Moves with Lear's Help', *Crain's Detroit*, 12 January 2004; 'Finalists: Part 1 of 2', *Crain's Detroit*, 21 June 2004; 'Business Diary', *Crain's Detroit*, 9 February 2004. North still maintains an ownership in Academic Marketing Services (which also operates under the name Aperture Content), which had initially been part of Grand River.

53. Shuvu Batta, 'A Look Back to My Split with the Socialist Equality Party/WSWS', https://theunionist.substack.com/p/a-look-back-to-my-split-with-the; interview with Shuva Batta, 5 August 2022.
54. Shuvu Batta, 'A Look Back to My Split with the Socialist Equality Party/WSWS', https://theunionist.substack.com/p/a-look-back-to-my-split-with-the; emphases in original.
55. Shuvu Batta, 'My Defense and Critique of the ICFI's Practice', 29 January 2021, https://classconscious.org/2021/04/26/my-defense-and-critique-of-the-icfis-practice-jan-29th-2021/; interview with Shuvu Batta, 5 August 2022.
56. Kelly, 'Twilight of World Trotskyism' (2023), 97–98.
57. Kelly, 'Contemporary Trotskyism' (2018), 143. Emphases in original.
58. Letter from Joseph Kishore, 2 April 2021, permanent-revolution.org.
59. Shuvu Batta, 'A Look Back to My Split with the Socialist Equality Party/WSWS', https://theunionist.substack.com/p/a-look-back-to-my-split-with-the.
60. Open letter to Peter Ross from Joseph Kishore & David North, 26 March 2021, permanent-revolution.org.
61. Correspondence with Peter Ross, 23 August 2022.
62. Tom Hall, Joseph Kishore. 'The RWDSU's Debacle at Amazon', WSWS. org, 10 April 2021; interview with Jacob Morrison and Adam Keller, 1 December 2022.
63. Interview with Shuvu Batta, 5 August 2022.
64. David Green, 'Letter to the Editor and Letter to President Berger-Sweeney', Trinity Tripod, 13 September 2020. Green/North's Trinity connection clearly matters to him. His books are regularly listed in the alumni magazine, in their 'Recent Publications' section, also under his legal name. See: Trinity Reporter, Fall 2017 and Trinity Reporter, Fall 2021.
65. 'Time Magazine and Ibram X. Kendi Promote a Race-Obsessed, Money-Hungry "Black Renaissance"', WSWS, 16 February 2021; 'Ibram X. Kendi, Keeanga-Yamahtta Taylor Awarded MacArthur Foundation "Genius Grants"', WSWS, 10 October 2021.
66. Gilbert Achcar. 'On Gutter Politics and Purported Anti-Imperialism', New Politics, 10 October 2019.

Index

Thanks to our Patreon subscriber:

Ciaran Kane

Who has shown generosity and
comradeship in support of our publishing.

Check out the other perks you get by subscribing
to our Patreon – visit patreon.com/plutopress.

Subscriptions start from £3 a month.

The Pluto Press Newsletter

Hello friend of Pluto!

Want to stay on top of the best radical books
we publish?

Then sign up to be the first to hear about our
new books, as well as special events,
podcasts and videos.

You'll also get 50% off your first order with us
when you sign up.

Come and join us!

Go to bit.ly/PlutoNewsletter